John Augustine Zahm, James Charles Carberry

Evolution and Dogma

John Augustine Zahm, James Charles Carberry

Evolution and Dogma

ISBN/EAN: 9783741190124

Manufactured in Europe, USA, Canada, Australia, Japa

Cover: Foto ©Lupo / pixelio.de

Manufactured and distributed by brebook publishing software (www.brebook.com)

John Augustine Zahm, James Charles Carberry

Evolution and Dogma

PREFATORY NOTE.

PART Second of this work covers substantially the same ground as my lectures on Evolution, delivered before the Madison and Plattsburgh Summer Schools and before the Winter School of New Orleans. Indeed, the chief difference between the subject-matter of Part Second, and that of the lectures as given at the Summer and Winter Schools, consists in the foot-notes which have been added to the text, and in a more exhaustive treatment of certain topics herein discussed than was possible in the time allotted to them in the lecture hall.

J. A. ZAHM, C. S. C.

NOTRE DAME UNIVERSITY, December 18, 1895.

TABLE OF CONTENTS.

INTRODUCTION. . . . . xiii–xxx PAGES

PART I.

EVOLUTION, PAST AND PRESENT.

CHAPTER I.
NATURE AND SCOPE OF EVOLUTION.
EARLY Speculations Regarding Nature and Man — Comprehensiveness of Evolution — Evolution Defined — Literature of Evolution — Freedom from Bias in the Discussion of Evolution. 13–22

CHAPTER II.
EARLY EVOLUTIONARY VIEWS.
FIRST Studies of Nature — Evolution Among the Greeks — Aristotle's Observations — Mediæval Writers. . . . 23–30

CHAPTER III.
FOSSILS AND GIANTS.
EARLY Notions Regarding Fossils — Italian Geologists on Fossils — Legends About Giants — True Significance of Fossils — Controversy in the French Academy. . . 31–40

CHAPTER IV.
SPONTANEOUS GENERATION AND SCIENTIFIC DISCOVERY.

EARLY Views Regarding Abiogenesis — Fathers and School-men on Abiogenesis — Redi's Experiments — Later Researches — General Advance in Science — Chemistry and Astronomy — Testimony of Biology. 41–54

CHAPTER V.
FROM LORD BACON TO CHARLES DARWIN.

FIRST Materials for the Controversy — Bacon and Kant — Linnæus and Buffon — Erasmus Darwin and Lamarck — Species and Varieties. 55–64

CHAPTER VI.
CONTROVERSY AND PROGRESS.

DARWIN'S "Origin of Species" — Herbert Spencer and Compeers — Science and Philosophy — Anticipations of Discoveries — Species and Creation — Evolutionists and Anti-Evolutionists — No Via Media Possible — The Miltonic Hypothesis — Views of Agassiz — Evolution. 65–83

CHAPTER VII.
EVIDENCES OF EVOLUTION.

SYSTEMS of Classification — Cuvier and His Successors — Points of View — Taxonomic Divisions — Plato's "Grand Ideas" — Cuvier on Species — Definition of Species — Difficulties Regarding Species — Agassiz' Views — Species in the Making — De Candolle and Baird — Evidences of Organic Evolution — A Philological Illustration — Tree-like System of Classification — The Argument from Structure and Morphology — Rudimentary Organs — Argument from Embryology — Amphioxus and Loligo — Meaning of Recapitulation — Geographical Distribution of Organisms — Facts of Geological Succession — The Demonstrative Evidence of Evolution — Generalized Types — Probability of Evolution — Special Creation and Evolution. 84-139

CHAPTER VIII.
OBJECTIONS AGAINST EVOLUTION.

DECLARATIONS of Anti-Evolutionists — Historical and Archæological Objections — Egyptian Mummies — Testimony of the Monuments — Evidence from Plants — Views of Agassiz, Barrande and Others — Misapprehension of the Nature of Evolution, and Answer to Objections — Existence and Cause of Variations — Paucity of Transitional Forms — Variations and the Formation of Fossiliferous Deposits — Romanes on Difficulties Attending Preservation of Fossils — Small Percentage of Fossil Forms — Extraordinary Intercalary Forms — Imperfection of the Geological Record — Time, Change and Equilibrium — Paleontology Compared With Egyptology and Assyriology — Sterility of Species When Crossed — Morphological and Physiological Species — True Significance of the Term "Species" — Factors of Evolution — Evolutionary Theories and Their Difficulties — The Ideal Theory. . . . 140-202

PART II.
EVOLUTION AND DOGMA.

CHAPTER I.
MISCONCEPTIONS OF THEORY, ERRORS IN DOCTRINE AND MISTAKES IN TERMINOLOGY.

EVOLUTION of the Evolution Theory — Evolution and Darwinism — Evolution, Atheism and Nihilism — Evolution and Faith — Evolution and Science — Ignorance of Terms — Materialism and Dualism — Pantheism — Dogma of Creation — The Vatican Council on Creation — Meaning of the Word "Nature"— Nature and God. 205–229

CHAPTER II.
MONISM AND EVOLUTION.

Hæckel and Monism — Hæckel as a Scientist — Hæckel's Nature-Philosophy — Five Propositions of Hæckel — God and the Soul — Organic and Inorganic Matter — The Religion of the Future — Hæckel's Limitations — Verbal Jugglery — False Analogy — Type of a Class. 230–253

CHAPTER III.
AGNOSTICISM AND EVOLUTION.

Nature and Scope of Agnosticism — Late Developments of Agnosticism — Mansel, Huxley and Romanes — Docta Ignorantia — Agnosticism as a Via Media — Origin of the Universe — Spencer's Unknowable — Max Müller on Agnosticism — Sources of Agnosticism — Infinite Time — Infinite Space — Mysteries of Nature — Christian Agnosticism — Gods of the Positivist and the Agnostic. 254–278

CHAPTER IV.
THEISM AND EVOLUTION.

Evolution and Faith — Teachings of St. Augustine — Views of the Angelic Doctor — Seminales Rationes — Creation According to Scripture — The Divine Administration — Efficient Causality of Creatures — Occasionalism — Anthropomorphism — Divine Interference — Science and Creation — Darwin's Objection — Limitations of Specialists — Evolution and Catholic Teaching — The Scholastic Doctrine of Species — Milton and Ray. . . 279–319

CHAPTER V.
THE ORIGIN AND NATURE OF LIFE.

SPONTANEOUS Generation — The Nature of Life — The Germ of Life — Abiogenesis — Artificial Production of Life — Protoplasm. 320-339

CHAPTER VI.
THE SIMIAN ORIGIN OF MAN.

THE Missing Link — The Human Soul — Creation of Man's Body — Mivart's Theory — Angelic Doctor on Creation of Adam — Views of Cardinal Gonzales — Opinions of Other Writers — Interpretation Not Revelation. . 340-368

CHAPTER VII.
TELEOLOGY, OLD AND NEW.

THE Doctrine of Final Causes — A Newer Teleology — Evolution and Teleology — Design and Purpose in Nature. 369-377

CHAPTER VIII.
RETROSPECT, REFLECTIONS AND CONCLUSION.

EVOLUTION Not a New Theory — Teachings of Greek Philosophers — Teleological Ideas of Anaxagoras and Aristotle — Influence of Aristotle — Darwinism Not Evolution — Evolution in the Future — Evolution Not Antagonistic to Religion — Objections Against New Theories — Galileo and the Copernican Theory — Conservatism in Science — Conflict of Opinions Beneficial — Evolution and Creationism — Errors in the Infancy of Science — Science Not Omnipotent — Bankruptcy of Science — Conquests of Science — Evidences of Design and Purpose — Rudimentary Organs — Evolution, Scripture and Theology — Evolution and Special Creation — Genesiac Days, Flood, Fossils and Antiquity of Man — Eminent Catholics on Evolution — Faith Has Nothing to Apprehend from Evolution — Misapprehensions Regarding Evolution — Evolution, an Ennobling Conception. 378-438

PART I.
INTRODUCTION.

"Il faut savoir douter où il faut, assurer où il faut, et se soumettre où il faut. Qui ne fait ainsi n'entend pas la force de la raison. Il y en a qui faillent contre ces trois principes ; ou en assurant tout comme démonstratif, manque de se connaitre en démonstration ; ou en doutant de tout, manque de savoir où il faut se soumettre ; ou en se soumettant en tout, manque de savoir où il faut juger." Pascal, "Pensées."

"We must know when to doubt, when to feel certain, when to submit. Who fails in this understands not the force of reason. There are those who offend against these three rules, either by accepting everything as evidence, for want of knowing what evidence is ; or by doubting everything, for want of knowing when to submit ; or by yielding in everything, for want of knowing when to use their judgment."

INTRODUCTION.

Τῷ μὲν γὰρ ἀληθεῖ πάντα συνᾴδει τὰ ὑπάρχοντα, τὰ δὲ ψευδεῖ ταχὺ διαφωνεῖ τἀληθές.—ARISTOTLE.

"For with the truth all things that exist are in harmony, but with the false the true at once disagrees."

THE present work is devoted chiefly to the discussion of three topics which, although in a measure independent one of the other, are, nevertheless, so closely allied that they may be viewed as parts of one and the same subject. The first of these topics embraces a brief sketch of the evolutionary theory from its earliest beginnings to the present time; the second takes up the *pros* and the *cons* of the theory as it now stands; while the third deals with the reciprocal and little-understood relations between Evolution and Christian faith.

It is often supposed by those who should know better, that the Evolution theory is something which is of very recent origin; something about which little or nothing was known before the publication of Charles Darwin's celebrated work, "The Origin of Species." Frequently, too, it is confounded with Darwinism, or some other modern attempt to explain the action of Evolution, or determine the factors which have been operative in the development of the higher from the lower forms of life. The purpose of the first six chapters of this book is to show that such views are unwarranted; that Evolution, far from being of recent date, is a theory whose germs are discernible in the earliest dawn of philosophic thought. In the two following chapters are given, in brief compass, some of the principal arguments which are usually adduced in favor of, or against, Evolution. These chapters, together with those which precede them, constitute Part First of the present volume; Part Second being wholly devoted to the consideration of the third topic, namely, Evolution in its relation to Catholic Dogma. For avowed Christians, to whatever creed they may belong, the subject relates to matters of grave import and abiding interest, and this import and interest, great as they are from the nature of the theme itself, have been enhanced a hundred fold by the protracted and violent controversies to which Evolution has given rise, no less than by the many misconceptions which yet prevail, and the many doubts which still remain to be dissipated.

Can a Catholic, can a Christian of any denomination, consistently with the faith he holds dear, be an evolutionist; or is there something in the theory that is so antagonistic to faith and Scripture as to render its acceptance tantamount to the denial of the fundamental tenets of religious belief? The question, as we shall learn, has been answered both affirmatively and negatively. But, as is evident, the response cannot be both yea and nay. It must be one or the other, and the query now is, which answer is to be given, the negative or the affirmative?

Whatever may be the outcome of the controversy, whatever may be the results of future research and discovery, there is absolutely no room for apprehension respecting the claims and authority of Scripture and Catholic Dogma. Science will never be able to contradict aught that God has revealed; for it is not possible that the Divine works and the Divine words should ever be in any relation to each other but one of the most perfect harmony. Doubts and difficulties may obtain for a time; the forces of error may for a while appear triumphant; the testimonies of the Lord may be tried to the uttermost; but in the long run it will always be found, as has so often been the case in the past, that the Bible and faith, like truth, will come forth unharmed and intact from any ordeal, however severe, to which they may be subjected. For error is impotent against truth; the pride of man's intellect is of no avail against the wisdom of the Almighty. False teaching and false views of nature are but the vain projections of the imaginations of men; false theories and false hypotheses are often no more than what St. Augustine aptly designates "the great absurdities of great teachers—*magna magnorum deliramenta doctorum.* How true, indeed, the words of the old distich:

    Nostra damus quum falsa damus, nam fallere nostrum est,
    Et quum falsa damus, nil nisi nostra damus.

The fictions of opinions are ephemeral, but the testimonies of the Lord are everlasting. *Opinionum commenta delet dies*, says Cicero. This utterance of the old Roman philosopher applies with singular point to all those conjectures of scientists, philosophers and exegetists, who fail to make their views a true reflex of the teachings of nature, *naturæ indiciæ*, or who promulgate theories manifestly antagonistic to the declarations of faith or of the Inspired Record.

A striking illustration of the unwisdom of committing one's self to premature notions, or unproved hypotheses, especially before all the evidence in the case is properly weighed, is afforded in the long and animated controversy respecting the authorship of the Pentateuch. Many reasons have been assigned by the higher critics why it could not have been the production of Moses, to whom it has so long been ascribed by a venerable tradition, and one of the objections urged against the Mosaic authorship was, that written language was unknown in the age during which the Jewish legislator is reputed to have lived. Now, however, the distinguished philologist and archæologist, Prof. Sayce, comes forward and proves, beyond doubt or quibble, that the contention of the higher critics respecting the authorship of the Bible is ill-founded. So sure, indeed, is he, whereof he speaks, that he does not hesitate to assert "not only that Moses *could* have written the Pentateuch, but that it would have been something like a miracle if he had not done so."

Even in Germany, the great stronghold of the Higher Criticism, we meet with the expression of similar views, and that, too, on the part of such noted Biblical scholars as Rupprecht, and Dr.

INTRODUCTION. xvii

Adolph Zahn of Stuttgart. The former, as a result of his investigations, declares positively "that the Pentateuch dates back to the Mosaic period of Divine revelation, and that its author is Moses himself, the greatest prophet in Israel." And as to the groundless assertion that writing was unknown at the time of the Hebrew law-giver, we have the deliberate statement of Sayce that "Canaan, in the Mosaic age, like the countries which surrounded it, was fully as literary as was Europe in the time of the Renaissance."[1]

Such and similar instances of premature claims for unwarranted hypotheses, should teach us the wisdom of practicing a proper reserve in respect of them, and of suspending judgment until we can yield assent which is based on unimpeachable evidence. But this does not imply that we should go to the extreme of conservatism, or display a fanatical obstinacy in the assertion of traditional views which are demonstrably untenable. There is a broad reach between ultra-conservatism and reprehensible liberalism or arrogant temerity. In this golden mean

---

[1] See *The Contemporary Review*, pp. 480–481, for October, 1895. Cf., also, by the same author, The Higher Criticism and the Verdict of the Monuments, chapter II, and Literature of the Old Testament in "The People's Bible History," mentioned later. In the last-named contribution to Biblical lore, the erudite Oxford divine affirms, and without fear of contradiction, "that one of the first and most important results of the discoveries which have been pouring in upon us during the last few years, is the proof that Canaan was a land of readers and writers long before the Israelites entered it, and that the Mosaic age was one of high literary activity. So far as the use of writing is concerned, there is now no longer any reason for doubting that the earlier books of the Bible might have been contemporaneous with the events they profess to record."

there is ample field for research and speculation, without any danger on the one side of trenching on faith, or of putting a bar to intellectual progress on the other. The Fathers of the early Church and the Schoolmen of mediæval times, show us what liberty of thought the Catholic may enjoy in the discussion of all questions outside the domain of revealed truth.

I am not unaware of the fact that Evolution has had suspicion directed against it, and odium cast upon it, because of its materialistic implications and its long anti-Christian associations. I know it has been banned and tabooed because it has received the cordial *imprimatur* of the advocates of Agnosticism, and the special commendation of the defenders of Atheism; that it has long been identified with false systems of philosophy, and made to render yeoman service in countless onslaughts against religion and the Church, against morality and free-will, against God and His providential government of the universe. But this does not prove that Evolution is ill-founded or that it is destitute of all elements of truth. Far from it. It is because Evolution contains so large an element of truth, because it explains countless facts and phenomena which are explicable on no other theory, that it has met with such universal favor, and that it has proved such a powerful agency in the dissemination of error and in giving verisimilitude to the most damnable of doctrines. Such being the case, ours is the duty to withdraw the truth from its enforced and unnatural alliance, and to show that there is a sense in which

Evolution can be understood—in which it must be understood, if it repose on a rational basis—in which, far from contributing to the propagation of false views of nature and God, it is calculated to render invaluable aid in the cause of both science and religion. From being an agency for the promulgation of Monism, Materialism and Pantheism, it should be converted into a power which makes for righteousness and the exaltation of holy faith and undying truth.

It were puerile to imagine that religion has anything to fear from the advance of science, or from Evolution receiving all the prominence which the facts in its favor will justify. Science and religion, revelation and nature, mutually supplement one another, and it would be against the best interests of both religion and science to do aught that would divorce them, or prevent their remaining the close allies which Infinite Wisdom designed them to be. "Logically regarded, the advance of science, far from having weakened religion has immeasurably strengthened it." So wrote shortly before his death one who, during the best years of his life, was an ardent Darwinian and an avowed agnostic. And the same gifted votary of science declared, that "The teleology of revelation supplements that of nature, and so, to the spiritually minded man, they logically and mutually corroborate one another."[1]

It behooves us to realize that in our age of doubt and intellectual confusion, when so many seek in the gloaming what is visible only in the effulgence of the

---
[1] "Thoughts on Religion," p. 179, by George Romanes.

midday sun, when the skeptic sees an interrogation point at the end of every proposition, and when uncertainty and mystery hover over so much we should like to know — it behooves us, I say, to realize, that we must have recourse to everything that is calculated to dispel the darkness with which we are surrounded, and to relieve the harrowing doubts with which so many of our fellow men are oppressed. But more than this. Important as it is for us to bear in mind that we live in an age of doubt and disquietude, it is none the less important for us not to lose sight of the fact that our lot is cast in an age of dissent and conflict.

Religion is assailed on all sides; principles we hold most dear are treated with contumely and scorn, and the very foundations of belief in a personal Creator, and in the immortality of the soul, are systematically attacked by the enemies of God and His Church. If, then, we would accomplish anything in the conflict which is now raging so fiercely all around us, it is imperative that we should provide ourselves with the most approved means of attack and defense, and that we should be able not only to guard the stronghold of the faith, but that we should likewise be equipped and ready to meet our enemies out in the open. In these days of Maxim guns, old worn-out blunderbusses are worse than useless. To attempt to cope with the modern spirit of error by means of antiquated and discarded weapons of offense and defense, were as foolish as to pit a Roman trireme or a mediæval galley against a modern steel cruiser or the latest type of battleship.

To pass from the language of metaphor to language simple and unadorned, our great, or more truthfully our greatest enemy, in the intellectual world to-day, is Naturalism—variously known as Agnosticism, Positivism, Empiricism — which, as Mr. Balfour well observes, " is in reality the only system which ultimately profits by any defeats which theology may sustain, or which may be counted on to flood the spaces from which the tide of religion has receded." [1]

It is Naturalism that, allying itself with Evolution, or some of the many theories of Evolution which have attracted such widespread attention during the last half century, has counted such a formidable following that the friends of religion and Scripture might well despair of final victory, did they not know the invincibility of truth, and that, however it may be obscured for a time, or however much it may apparently be weakened, it is sure to prevail and in the end issue from the contest triumphant.

In writing the present work I have ever had before my mind the words of wisdom of our Holy Father, Leo XIII, concerning the duty incumbent on all Catholics, to turn the discoveries of science into so many means of illuminating and corroborating the teachings of faith and the declarations of the Sacred Text. In public and in private, in season and out of season, in briefs, allocutions and encyclicals, he has constantly and strenuously urged a thorough study of science in all its branches. But nowhere does he insist more strongly on the profound study of

---
[1] "The Foundations of Belief," p. 6.

science, than in his two masterly encyclicals "Æterni Patris" and "Providentissimus Deus." In these noble utterances both the clergy and the laity are stimulated to take an active part in the contest which is everywhere so furious; "to repulse hostile assaults," and that, too, by "modern methods of attack," and by "turning the arms of a perverted science into weapons of defense."[1] He tells us that "a knowledge of natural science will be of very great assistance in detecting attacks on the Sacred Books and in refuting them." For "attacks of this kind," the venerable Pontiff remarks, "bearing as they do on matters of sensible experience, are peculiarly dangerous both to the masses and also to the young who are beginning their literary studies."

In reading these precious documents one would almost think that the Holy Father had in mind the manifold materialistic hypotheses, so dangerous to the faith of the uninstructed, which have grouped themselves around the much-abused theory of contemporary Evolution. For, is it not a matter of daily observation and experience, that there is an increasing number of pious but timid souls who are sorely distressed by doubts which have been occasioned by the current theories of Transformism? They imagine, because it is continually dinned into

---

[1] "Quoniam igitur tantum ii possunt religioni importare commodi, quibus cum catholicæ professionis gratia felicem indolem ingenii benignum numen impertiit; ideo in hac acerrima agitatione studiorum, quæ Scripturas quoquo modo attingunt, aptum sibi quisque eligant studii genus, in quo aliquando excellentes obiecta in illas improbæ scientiæ tela, non sine gloria, repellant." From the encyclical "Providentissimus Deus."

their ears, that there is a mortal antagonism between the principles of faith and the teachings of Evolution. They are assured, moreover, not only that such an antagonism actually exists, but also that it is based on undeniable facts, on absolute demonstration. They are told that if they wish to be consistent, if they wish to obey the certain behests of reason, they must choose between Evolution and faith, between science and superstition. The result is, too often, alas! that they make shipwreck of their faith, and plunge headlong into the dark and hopeless errors of Naturalism.

But not only have I been ever mindful of the teachings of the venerable Pontiff, Leo XIII; I have also, to the best of my ability, striven to follow the path marked out by those great masters of Catholic philosophy and theology, St. Augustine and St. Thomas of Aquin. I have always had before me their declarations respecting creation, and the manner in which we may conceive the world to have been evolved from its pristine chaotic condition to its present state of order and loveliness. And to make my task easier, I have had frequent recourse to those two modern luminaries of science and faith, the profound Jesuit, Father Harper, and the eminent Dominican, Cardinal Gonzales. To the "Metaphysics of the School," by the former, and to "La Biblia y la Ciencia," by the latter, I am specially indebted for information and points of view that it would be difficult to find elsewhere. Both of these distinguished scholars evince a rare mastery of the subjects which they discuss with such lucidity, and one may safely follow them with the utmost confidence, and with the full assurance that ample justice will always be done to the claims of both science and Dogma.

In the present work I have studiously avoided everything that could justly be construed as an exaggeration of the results achieved by science, or as a minimizing of the dogmatic teachings of the Church of God. I have endeavored to present Catholic doctrines and scientific tenets in their true light, and to exhibit the mutual relations of one to the other in the fairest possible manner. Purely *ex parte* statements and special pleadings are alien from a professedly didactic work, and hence my constant effort has been to avoid all bias, to present impartially and dispassionately both sides of controverted questions, and to favor only such conclusions as seemed to be warranted by indisputable evidence.

The Church is committed to no theory as to the origin of the world or its inhabitants. Hence, as a Catholic, I am bound to no theory of Evolution or of special creation, except in so far as there may be positive evidence in behalf of such theory. As a man of science I must estimate, as everyone else must estimate, the merits or demerits of any hypothesis respecting the genesis and development of the divers forms of life, simply and solely by the arguments which can be advanced in its support. I have no prepossessions for Evolution; nor have I any prejudice against special creation. If it can be demonstrated that Evolution is the *modus creandi* which the Almighty has been pleased to adopt, I shall rejoice that one of the greatest of the world-problems has at length received a solution. If, on the other hand, it can be shown that the traditional view of special creation is the one to which we must give our adhesion, I shall rejoice equally, for the sole desire of every student of nature, as well as the sole desire of every son of the Church, should be the truth, and the truth whole and undefiled.

I have, then, no pet theory to exploit, nothing sensational to defend, nothing to uphold that is inconsistent with the strictest orthodoxy or the most rigid Ultramontanism. My sole aim and purpose in writing this work has been, I repeat it, to remove misconceptions, to dispel confusion, to explain difficulties, to expose error, to eliminate false interpretation, to allay doubt, to quiet conscience, to benefit souls. How far I have succeeded remains for others to judge. That in the discussion of so many difficult and delicate questions, I may have made statements that could be improved, or should be somewhat modified, is quite possible. But if, in anything, I have been wanting in accuracy of expression; if I have misstated a fact of science, or misapprehended a Dogma of faith; I shall consider it a special favor to have my attention directed to what, on my part, is wholly an unintentional error.

It will not do to say, as has been said, that the discussion, whether from the platform or elsewhere, of such topics as constitute the main feature of this work, is inopportune or inexpedient. If the reasons already assigned did not suffice to justify the expediency and opportuneness of such discussions, the example given by the International Catholic Scientific Congress ought to dispel all doubts that might be still entertained on the subject. For on every occasion the Congress has yet assembled, the discussion of evolutionary topics has been given special prominence. And the interest exhibited in such discussions was not confined to laymen and specialists, but it was shared in by distinguished prelates and scholars of international reputation. They recognized the necessity of having all possible light on a question of such widespread interest; of seeking by all possible means to attain the truth respecting a subject which has been so prolific of error and has proved such an agency for evil. What these learned and zealous men deemed it wise to do, in the cultured capitals of the Old World, we certainly can and ought to do in this land of ours, where ignorance of the subject in question is more dense and where knowledge is more needed. The fact that certain propositions in this work have given rise to such misunderstandings, and have led to such misdirected controversy and such useless logomachy as have prevailed during some months past, is the best evidence that there is yet much to be learned regarding what is so often incontinently condemned without a hearing.

The great trouble now, as it has always been, is the very general ignorance of the elench on the part of those who pose as critics of Evolution and of evolutionary theories. Without a sufficient knowledge of the facts they venture to discuss, they are often led to make statements which a wider acquaintance with nature compels them to retract. Evolution, however, has not fared differently from the other grand generalizations that now constitute the foundations and pillars which support the noble and imposing edifice of science. The Copernican theory, it will be remembered, was denounced as anti-Scriptural; Newton's discovery of universal gravitation was condemned as atheistic; while the researches of geologists were decried as leading to infidelity, and as being "an awful evasion of the testimony of Revelation." That the theory of Evolution should be obliged to pass through the same ordeal as awaited other attempts at scientific progress, is not surprising to those who are familiar with the history of science; but it is not a little strange that there are yet among us those who derive such little profit from the lessons of the past, and who still persist in the futile attempt to solve by metaphysics problems which, by their very nature, can be worked out only by the methods of induction.

Dr. Whewell, the erudite author of the "History of the Inductive Sciences," was wont to declare that every great discovery in science had to pass through three stages. "First people said, 'It is absurd!' then they said, 'It is contrary to the Bible!' and finally they said, 'We always knew it was so!'" The truth of this observation of the famous Master of Trinity is well exemplified in the case of Evolution. There are some who still denounce it as contrary to reason; there are others who honestly believe that it contradicts Scripture; while there are not a few, and the number is rapidly augmenting, who are convinced that the germs of the Evolution theory are to be found in Genesis, and that its fundamental principles were recognized by Aristotle, St. Augustine and St. Thomas of Aquin. The final result of the controversy belongs to the future. If the theory which has excited such animosity, and provoked such unbridled disputes, be founded on the facts of nature, it will ultimately prevail, as truth itself will prevail in the end; if, however, it repose only on assumption and unsupported hypotheses, if it have no better foundation than a shifting reef, it is doomed, sooner or later, to the fate which awaits everything that is unwarranted by nature or is at variance with truth.

Strange as it may appear, there are still some well-meaning people who foolishly imagine, that science, when too profoundly studied, is a source of danger to faith. Such a notion is so silly as scarcely to deserve mention. Pope's well-known verse: "A little learning is a dangerous thing," has its application here, as in so many other instances. The familiar quotation from Bacon: "A little philosophy inclineth a man's mind to Atheism, but depth in philosophy bringeth men's minds about to religion," expresses a truth which holds good for science as well as for philosophy. Illustrations of the truth of the second part of this statement are found in the lives of Copernicus, Galileo, Kepler, Linnæus, Newton, Cuvier, Cauchy, Agassiz, Barrande, Leverrier and numberless others of the world's most illustrious discoverers and most profound thinkers. The great Linnæus, than whom no one ever studied nature more carefully or deeply, saw in all created things, even in what was apparently the most insignificant, evidences of the power and wisdom and goodness of God, which to him were simply overwhelming.[1] And the immortal Pasteur, whose recent death a whole world mourns, whose exhaustive study of nature has been a subject of universal comment and admiration, did not hesitate towards the end of his glorious career to declare, that careful and profound study inspires in one the deepest and the most childlike faith, a faith like unto that of a people who are proverbial for the earnestness and simplicity of their religious spirit, the faith of the pious and unspoiled inhabitants of Catholic Brittany.[2]

In one of his sublime *pensées*, Pascal, applying the method of Descartes to the demonstration of faith, and causing this instrument of science to confound all false science, declares that "we must begin by showing that religion is not contrary to reason; then that it is venerable, to give respect for it; then to make it lovable, and to make good men hope that it is true; then to show that it is true."[3] Some-

---

[1] In the introduction to his "Systema Naturæ," the Swedish botanist writes: "Deum sempiternum, immensum, omniscientem, omnipotentem, expergefactus a tergo transeuntem vidi et obstupui. Legi aliquot ejus vestigia per creata rerum, in quibus omnibus, etiam in minimis ut fere nullis, quæ vis! quanta sapientia! quam inextricabilis perfectio!"

[2] "Quand on a bien étudié," the renowned savant avers, "on revient à la foi du paysan breton. Si j'avais étudié plus encore, j'aurais la foi de la paysanne bretonne."

[3] "Il faut commencer par montrer, que la religion n'est point contraire à la raison; ensuite qu'elle est vénérable, en donner respect; la rendre ensuite aimable, faire souhaiter aux bons qu'elle fût vraie; et puis, montrer qu'elle est vraie."

thing akin to the idea contained in this beautiful passage, has been uppermost in my mind in the penning of the following pages. A kindred thought has been dominant in every topic discussed. It has given me courage to undertake, and strength to complete, a work which otherwise would never have been attempted, and which, during the whole course of its preparation, I would fain have seen intrusted to more competent hands. My sole, my ardent desire, has been to show that there is nothing in true science, nothing in any of the theories duly accredited by science and warranted by the facts of nature, nothing in Evolution, when properly understood, which is contrary to Scripture or Catholic teaching; that, on the contrary, when viewed in the light of Christian philosophy and theology, there is much in Evolution to admire, much that is ennobling and inspiring, much that illustrates and corroborates the truths of faith, much that may be made ancillary to revelation and religion, much that throws new light on the mysteries of creation, much that unifies and coördinates what were otherwise disconnected and disparate, much that exalts our ideas of creative power and wisdom and love, much, in fine, that makes the whole circle of the sciences tend, as never before, *ad majorem Dei gloriam.*

PART I.

EVOLUTION, PAST AND PRESENT.

CHAPTER I.

NATURE AND SCOPE OF EVOLUTION.

Early Speculation Regarding Nature and Man.

FROM time immemorial philosophers and students of nature have exhibited a special interest in all questions pertaining to the origin of man, of the earth on which he lives and of the universe to which he belongs. The earliest speculations of our Aryan forefathers were about the beginnings of things. Questions of cosmology, as we learn from the tablets preserved in the great library of Assurbanipal in Nineveh, received their meed of attention from the sages of ancient Assyria and Babylonia. And long before Assyria, Babylonia and Chaldea had reached the zenith of their power, and before they had attained that intellectual eminence which so distinguished them among the nations of the ancient world, the peoples of Accad and Sumer had raised and discussed questions of geogony and cosmogony. They were a philosophical race, these old Accadians and Sumerians, and, as we learn from the records which are constantly being exhumed in Mesopotamia, they had a breadth of view and an acuteness of intellect, which, considering their environment and the age in which they lived, were simply astonishing. Well have they been called "the teachers of Greece," for all the subtlety of thought and keenness of perception, all the love of science, art and letters, which were so characteristic of the Greek mind, were possessed in an eminent degree by those old pre-Babylonian masters who thought and taught and wrote many long generations before Abraham left Ur of the Chaldees, untold centuries before Thales taught and Homer sang. And the musings of the mystic Hindu along the banks of the Indus and the Ganges; the meditations of the Egyptian priest in the temples of Memphis and Heliopolis; the speculations of the wise men of Attica and Ionia, all turned more or less on the same topics which possessed such a fascination for the sages of old Chaldea, and which were discussed with such zest in the schools of Nineveh and Babylon.

Whence are we? Whither are we going? Whence this earth of ours and the plants and animals which make it their home? Whence the sun, and moon, and stars—those distant and brilliant, yet mysterious representatives of our visible universe? Did they have a beginning, or have they existed from all eternity? And if they had a beginning, are they the same now as they were when they first came into existence, or have they undergone changes, and, if so, what are the nature and the factors of such changes? Are the development and mutations of things to be referred to the direct and immediate action of an all-powerful Creator, or are they rather to be attributed to the operation of certain laws of nature—laws which admit of determination by human reason, and which, when known, serve as a norm in our investigations and experiments in the organic and inorganic worlds? Are there special interventions on the part of a Supreme Being in the government of the universe, and are we to look for frequent, if not constant, exhibitions of the miraculous in the natural world? Has God's first creation of the universe and all it contains, of the earth and all that inhabits it, been followed by other creations at divers periods, and if so, when and where has such creative power been manifested?

These are a few of the many questions about the genesis and development of things which men asked themselves in the infancy of our race. And these are questions which philosophers are still putting to themselves, and which, notwithstanding the many thousands of years during which they have been under discussion, have to-day a greater and more absorbing interest than in any former period of human history.

It is beside my present purpose to enumerate the various theories in science to which the discussion of the questions just propounded have given rise, or to dwell on the divers systems of philosophy and religion which have been the natural outgrowth of such or similar discussions. Materialism, Pantheism, Emanationism, Hylozoism, Traducianism, Atheism and other isms innumerable have always been, as they are to-day, more or less closely identified with many of the speculations regarding the origin and constitution of the visible universe. And despite the great advances which have been made in our knowledge of nature and of the laws which govern the organic and inorganic worlds, many of the questions which so agitated the minds of the philosophers of the olden time, are still as far from solution as they were when first proposed. New facts and new discoveries have placed the old problems in a new light, but have diminished none of their difficulties. On the contrary, the brilliant search-light of modern science has disclosed new difficulties which were before invisible, and proved that those which were considered before are in many respects far graver than was formerly imagined. With the advance of science, and the progress of discovery, many problems, it is true, find their solution, but others, hydra-like, arise in their place and obtrude themselves on the scientist and philosopher, and will not down until they have received due recognition.

Comprehensiveness of Evolution.

To answer some, if not all, of the questions just alluded to; to explain the phenomena of the cosmos; to solve the problems of life and mind, and throw light on the beginning and development of things, recourse is now had to a system of philosophy and science which, within the last few decades, has attained a special vogue under the name of Evolutionism, or, as its adepts prefer to call it, Evolution. Evolution, we are assured, is the magic word which explains all difficulties; the "open sesame" which admits us into the innermost arcana of nature. We are told of the Evolution of the earth, of the Evolution of the solar system, of the Evolution of the sidereal universe. Men discourse on the Evolution of life, the Evolution of the organic and inorganic worlds, the Evolution of the human race. We have similarly the Evolution of society, government, religion, language, art, science, architecture, music, literature, chemistry, physics, mathematics, and the various other branches of knowledge as well. We now talk of the Evolution of the steamboat, the locomotive, the dynamo, the machine-gun, the telescope, the yacht and the bicycle. All that ministers to comfort, luxury and fashion are objects of Evolution. Hence it is that we hear people speak of the Evolution of the modern house-furnace and the cooking-stove; the Evolution of the coach and the dog-cart; the Evolution of seal-skin sacques, high-heeled shoes and of that periodically recurrent *bête noire* of fond husbands and indulgent papas—the latest pattern of a lady's hat. Anything which has developed or improved—and what has not?—is spoken of as having come under the great law of Evolution, and, presto! all is explained, and any little enigmas which before may have existed instantly vanish.

As is evident from the foregoing, Evolution may mean a great deal, or it may mean little or nothing. It is manifestly a term of very general application and may often be very misleading. Properly understood it may be of signal service to the searcher after truth, while, on the contrary, if it is constituted an ever-ready *deus ex machina*, capable of solving all difficulties, it may lead to inextricable confusion and tend to obscure what it was designed to illumine. It is obvious, too, that we must restrict the meaning of the word Evolution, for it does not come within the scope of our work to speak of Evolution in general. We have to consider only a particular phase of it, and for this purpose it is important to have a definition of what is meant by Evolution.

Evolution Defined.

Herbert Spencer, who is regarded by his admirers as the great philosopher of Evolution, defines it to be a "change from an indefinite, incoherent homogeneity, to a definite, coherent heterogeneity; through continuous differentiations and integrations.'[1] And the operation of Evolution," continues the same authority, "is absolutely universal. Whether it be in the development of the earth, in the development of life upon its surface, in the development of society, of government, of manufactures, of commerce, of language, of literature, science, art, this same advance from the simple to the complex, through successive differentiations, holds uniformly. From the earliest traceable cosmical changes down to the latest results of civilization, we shall find that the transformation of the homogeneous into the heterogeneous, is that in which Evolution essentially consists."[2]

Spencer's definition, however, exact as it may be deemed, embraces far more than we shall have occasion to consider, for my task shall be confined

---
[1] "First Principles," p. 216.
[2] Id.—p. 148.

to the Evolution of the earth and its inhabitants, and only incidentally shall I refer to cosmic Evolution. Indeed, properly speaking, the Evolution of which I shall treat shall be limited almost entirely to organic Evolution, or the Evolution of the plants and animals which live or have lived on this earth of ours. All references, therefore, to the Evolution of the earth itself from its primeval nebulous state, and to the Evolution of organic from inorganic matter, will be mostly by way of illustration, and in order to show that there is no breach of continuity between organic Evolution, which is my theme, and inorganic or cosmic Evolution.

Literature of Evolution.

The subject is a vast one, and to treat it adequately would require far more space than I have at my disposal. It has indeed a literature and a bibliography of its own—a literature whose proportions are already stupendous, and are daily, and with amazing rapidity, becoming more collossal. For the past third of a century, since the publication of Darwin's "Origin of Species," it has been uppermost in the minds of everyone given to thinking on serious subjects. Everybody talks about Evolution, and more write about it than about any other one subject.

More than five thousand distinct works, relating to Goethe, who died in 1832, have, it is estimated, already been printed, and additions are continually being made to this enormous number. Peignot, who wrote in 1822, declared that up to his day more than eighty thousand distinct works had appeared on the history of France. The number of volumes that have been written on our Civil War can soon be enumerated by myriads, and still other works on the same subject are being published in rapid succession. Startling, however, as these figures may appear, they are insignificant in comparison with those relating to the subject of Evolution. In every language of the civilized world, books, brochures, and magazine articles innumerable, have been written on Evolution, and the number of publications of various kinds specially treating of this topic is now almost beyond computation.

Such being the case, it will evidently be impossible for me to do more than give a brief sketch of the history of Evolution, and of its status to-day in the world of thought, religious, scientific and philosophic. It is something that one cannot develop *dans un mot*, as a certain French lady expected of a noted savant, when asking him to explain his system of philosophy. For a similar reason, also, I can discuss but briefly the bearings of Evolution on religion and Catholic dogma. I shall, therefore, have to limit myself to a few general propositions, and refer those who desire a more exhaustive treatment of the subjects discussed, to the many elaborate and learned works that have been given to the world during the past few decades.

Freedom From Bias in the Discussion of Evolution.

I may here be permitted, before going further, to remind the reader that it is of prime importance, in the discussion of the subject of Evolution, especially in its relation to religion and dogma, for one to weigh fairly and dispassionately the arguments and objections of evolutionists, and to divest one's self of all bias that may proceed from prejudice or early education, to consider the question on its merits, and not to let one's mind be swayed by preconceived, or it may be, by erroneous notions. Let the value of the evidence adduced be estimated by the rules of logic and in the light of reason. This is essential. In the discussion of the subject during the past thirty and odd years much has been said in the heat of controversy, and on both sides, that had no foundation in fact. There have been much exaggeration and misrepresentation, which have given rise to difficulties and complications that might easily have been avoided if the disputants on both sides had always been governed by a love of truth, and the strict rules of dialectics, rather than by passion and the spirit of party. Misguided zeal and ignorance of the true teachings of the Church, always betray one into making statements which have no foundation in fact, but, in the discussions to which the subject of Evolution has given rise, there has often been exhibited, by both the defendants and the opponents of the theory, a lack of fairness and a bitterness of feeling that are certainly not characteristic of those whose sole desire is the attainment of truth. Such polemics have injured both parties, and have delayed a mutual understanding that should have, and would have, been reached years ago if the ordinary rules of honest controversy had always been inviolably observed.

Now that the smoke of battle is beginning to vanish, and that the participants in the contest have time to reckon results and to look back to the causes which precipitated the struggle, it is found, and I think generally conceded, that certain of the representatives of science were the ones who brought on an imbroglio for which there was not the slightest justification. But it is the old story over again—hatred of religion concealed behind some new discovery of science or enveloped in some theory that, for the nonce, was raised to the dignity of an indisputable dogma. It was not, it is true, so much the chief representatives of science who were to blame as some of their ill-advised *assecla*, who saw in the new teachings an opportunity of achieving notoriety, and, at the same time, of venting their spleen against the Church and casting obloquy on religion and Scripture.

CHAPTER II.

EARLY EVOLUTIONARY VIEWS.

First Studies of Nature.

EVOLUTION, as we now know it, is a product of the latter half of the present century. It would, however, be a mistake to imagine that Minerva-like it came forth from the brain of Darwin or Spencer, or that of anyone else, as the fully-developed theory which has caused so great a stir in the intellectual world. No; Evolution, as a theory, is not the work of one man, nor the result of the work of any body of men that could be designated by name. Neither is it the product of any one generation or epoch. On the contrary, it has been the joint achievement, if such it can be called, of countless thinkers and observers and experimenters of many climes and of many centuries. It is the focus towards which many and divers lines of thought have converged from the earliest periods of speculation and scientific research down to our own. The sages of India and Babylonia; the priests of Egypt and Assyria; the philosophers of Greece and Rome; the Fathers of the early Church and the Schoolmen of the Middle Ages, as well as the scholars and discoverers of subsequent ages, contributed toward the establishment of the theory on the basis on which it now reposes.

This being the case, it will help us to a more intelligent appreciation of the theory to take a brief retrospect of the work accomplished by the earlier workers in the field, and to review some of the more important observations and discoveries which led up to the promulgation of Evolution as a theory of the universal application which is now claimed for it. Such a review will likewise serve another purpose. We are often disposed to imagine that all the great discoveries and generalizations in science are entirely the result of modern thought and investigation. We forget that the way has been prepared for us by those who questioned nature thousands of years ago, but who, not having the advantages or appliances of modern research, were unable to possess themselves of her secrets. We underrate and disparage the work of the earlier students and speculators, because we are oblivious of the fact that they planted the germ which we see developed into the full-grown tree, because we do not realize that we are reaping what others have sown. All great movements in the world of thought are, we should remember, simply the integration of infinitesimals; the summation of an almost infinite series of factors which are ordinarily ignored or disregarded. The successful generalizer and the framer of legitimate scientific theories are, as a rule, those who avail themselves of the data and patient indications of others, who accumulate and correlate disjointed and independent observations which, separately considered, have little or no value, and which tell us little or nothing of the operations of nature and nature's laws. Thus

Kepler's laws were based on the observations of Tycho Brahe; Newton's great discovery of the law of universal gravitation was founded on Abbé Picard's measurement of the earth's meridian; and Leverrier's discovery of the planet Neptune was suggested by the perturbations which various astronomers had observed in the motion of Uranus. So, too, is it, but to a greater extent, in respect of the theory of Evolution. It is the result not only of the observations of the immediate predecessors of those who are now regarded as the founders of the theory, but of data which have been amassed and of reflections which philosophers have been making since our Aryan forefathers first began to interrogate nature and seek a rational explanation of the various mutations which were observed to characterize the earth's surface and its inhabitants.

Evolution Among the Greeks.

Thales, who was one of the first philosophers that attempted a natural explanation of the universe, in lieu of the myths which had so long obtained, taught that all life had its origin in water. Anaximander, who flourished six centuries B.C., seems to forestall certain evolutionary theories which were taught twenty-five hundred years later. "The first animals," τὰ πρῶτα ζῶα, he tells us, "were begotten in moisture and earth." Man, according to the same philosopher, "must have been born from animals of a different form, ἐξ ἀλλοειδῶν ζωων, for, whereas other animals easily get their food by themselves, man alone requires long rearing. Hence, had man been originally such as he is now, he could never have survived." He first propounded the theory of "fish-men," which, in a modified form, was adopted by Oken. Anaximenes, a pupil of Anaximander, made air the cause of all things, while Diogenes of Appolonia held that all forms of animal and plant life originated from primordial slime — the prototype of Oken's famous *Urschleim*. Anaxagoras sought the beginnings of animated nature in germs which preëxisted in nature, and were distributed throughout the air and ether. In Empedocles, who is sometimes spoken of as the father of the Evolution idea, we find the germ of what Darwin calls "natural selection,"[1] and what Spencer denominates "the survival of the fittest." With the representatives of the Ionian schools, he was a believer in spontaneous generation, or abiogenesis, but he approximated more closely to the teachings of modern Evolution than did any of his predecessors or contemporaries. He recognized the gradual development of the higher from the lower forms of life, and taught that plants made their appearance before animals.

Aristotle's Observations.

But the greatest of the Greek naturalists, as he was also the greatest of Greek philosophers, was

---

[1] In his "Physics," II, cap. VIII, Aristotle refers to natural selection and the survival of the fittest, as taught by Empedocles and others, as follows: " For when the very same combinations happened to be produced which the law of final causes would have called into being, those combinations which proved to be advantageous to the organism were preserved; while those which were not advantageous perished, and still perish, like the minotaurs and sphinxes of Empedocles."

Aristotle. Unlike Plato, who laid special stress on *a priori* reasoning as the source of true knowledge, even in the natural and physical sciences, he insisted on observation and experiment. "We must not," he tells us in his "History of Animals," "accept a general principle from logic only, but must prove its application to each fact. For it is in facts that we must seek general principles, and these must always accord with facts. Experience furnishes the particular facts from which deduction is the pathway to general laws."

When we consider how happy the Stagirite was in his generalizations from the meager facts at his command, how remarkable was his prevision of some of the most important results of modern investigation, how he had not only a true conception of the modern ideas of Evolution, but had likewise a clear perception of the principle of adaptation, when we remember that he was cognizant of the analogies, and probably also of the homologies between the different parts of an organism, that he was aware of the phenomena of atavism and reversion and heredity, and that he foreshadowed the theory of epigenesis in embryonic development, as taught by Harvey long ages afterwards, when we call to mind all these things, we are forced, I repeat, to conclude that the immortal Greek not only fully understood the value of induction as an instrument of research, but also that he was quite as successful in its use, considering his limited appliances for work, as was any one of his successors who lived and labored in more favored times.

He, then, and not Empedocles, should be regarded as the father of the Evolution theory. The poet-naturalist of Agrigentum made, indeed, some observations in embryology, the first recorded, and may thus have been led to some of his fortunate guesses at the truth of Evolution; but there is reason to believe that most, if not all of his theories, were based on *a priori* speculation rather than on experiment. He had by no means the wide acquaintance with nature which so distinguished Aristotle; neither did he possess the logical acumen, nor the skill in inductive reasoning we so much admire in the Samian philosopher. So far as was possible in his time, the Stagirite based his evolutionary views on observation and experiment, rather than on metaphysical ratiocination, and this is more than can be said of any of his predecessors, whether of the Ionian, Pythagorean or Eleatic schools, or of those immediately subsequent.[1]

Mediæval Writers.

The foregoing views of the Greek philosophers found acceptance at a later date with the philosophers of Rome, and prevailed, with but slight modifications, during the entire period of the Middle Ages. They were commented on by a number of Arabian writers, notably Avicenna, Avempace, Abu-

---

[1] For an exhaustive exposition of the views of the Greeks, on the subjects discussed in the foregoing paragraphs, consult Zeller's "Philosophy of the Greeks." See also Ueberweg's "History of Philosophy."

bacer,¹ and Omar "the learned," as well as by many of the Schoolmen, especially Albertus Magnus. The last-named scholar was remarkable for his extended knowledge of nature. Besides discussing the theories which had been framed by his predecessors, he was a keen observer and skillful experimenter, and it is not too much to say that he contributed more towards the advance of science than anyone who had lived since the time of Aristotle.

The illustrious pupil of Albertus Magnus, St. Thomas Aquinas, deserves a special mention here for his teachings respecting organic Evolution. Accepting the views of Aristotle, St. Gregory of Nyssa and St. Augustine, regarding the origin and development of animal and plant life, he laid down principles concerning derivative or secondary creations, which

---

¹In a curious philosophical romance Abubacer writes as follows on the birth of what he designates the " nature-man : " "There happens to be," he says, " under the equator an island, where man comes into the world without father or mother. By spontaneous generation he arises directly, in the form of a boy, from the earth, while the spirit, which, like sunshine, emanates from God, unites with the body, growing out of a soft, unformed mass. Without any intelligent surroundings, and without education, this 'nature-man,' through simple observation of the outer world, and through the combination of various appearances, rises to the knowledge of the world and of the Godhead. First, he perceives the individual, and then he recognizes the various species as independent forms, but as he compares the varieties and species with each other, he comes to the conclusion that they are all sprung from a single animal spirit, and, at the same time that the entire animal race forms a single whole. He makes the same discovery among the plants, and finally he sees the animal and plant forms in their unity, and discovers that among all their differences they have sensitiveness and feeling in common; from which he concludes that animals and plants are only one and the same thing." How like unto many modern speculations this fancy of the old Arab philosopher !

scientists and theologians now recognize to be of inestimable value. As we shall have occasion, in the sequel, to examine at length the teachings of the Angelic Doctor on this topic, it will suffice for the present simply to advert to them, and to signalize in advance their transcendent importance.

CHAPTER III.

FOSSILS AND GIANTS.

Early Notions Regarding Fossils.

IN the beginning of the sixteenth century geological phenomena began to attract more attention than they had hitherto received. Special interest was centered in fossils, which were so universally distributed over the earth's surface, and their study contributed materially towards placing the theory of Evolution on a firmer basis than it ever before possessed. Aristotle and other Greek writers had, indeed, made mention of them, but did not, as it appears, devote to them any particular study.

Theophrastus, a pupil of Aristotle, supposed them to be due to "a certain plastic virtue" of the earth, which possessed the power of fashioning inorganic matter into organic forms.

The distinguished painter, Leonardo da Vinci, one of the most gifted men that ever lived, was among the first to dispute the absurd theories which were currently accepted regarding the nature and origin of fossils. "They tell us," he says, "that these shells were formed in the hills by the influence of the stars; but I ask, where in the hills are the stars now forming shells of distinct ages and species? And how can the stars explain the origin of gravel, occurring at different heights and composed of pebbles rounded as by the motion of running water; or in what manner can such a cause account for the petrification in the same places of various leaves, sea-weeds and marine crabs?"

Fracostoro, a contemporary of Da Vinci, followed in the footsteps of the illustrious artist, and taught that fossils were the exuviæ of animals that formerly lived where their remains are now found. He showed the futility of the opinion then prevalent which attributed fossils to the action of the Noachian Deluge, which, according to the ideas then entertained, not only strewed the earth's surface with the remains of the animals which were destroyed, but also buried them at great depths on the highest mountains.

Clear and cogent arguments like those adduced by Da Vinci and Fracostoro should have sufficed to end all controversy regarding the true nature of fossils, but unfortunately for the cause of science the dispute was destined to last nearly three centuries longer. All sorts of imaginary causes were feigned to account for the petrified organic forms everywhere abundant, and no theory was too fantastical to attract supporters, provided only it was not antagonistic to the notions of geogony and cosmogony then popularly received.

Thus, according to Agricola, fossils were the product of a certain *materia pinguis*, or fatty matter, set in fermentation by heat; porous bodies, like bones and shells, according to Mattioli, were petrified by what he designated a "lapidifying juice," while according to Fallopio, of Padua, petrified shells were produced by the "tumultuous movements of the terrestrial exhalations." Olivi, of Cremona, considered fossils as mere *lusus naturæ*, or "sports of nature," while others regarded them as mere stones which "had assumed their peculiar configuration by the action of some occult 'internal principle' from the influence of the heavenly bodies;" and others still maintained that they were bodies formed by nature "for no other end than to play the mimic in the mineral kingdom."

That such fanciful notions regarding the nature of fossils could ever have been seriously entertained by men of sound judgment now seems almost inexplicable. But if we reflect a moment we shall see that almost equally ridiculous views of nature are held by even eminent men of science at the present day. As for the students of nature who lived some centuries ago, it may be pleaded in extenuation of the errors into which they lapsed, that some of the theories which they deemed to be beyond question appeared to give color to their beliefs.

Among these was the theory of spontaneous generation, or the theory that certain living plants and animals are produced spontaneously from inorganic matter, or spring from organic matter in a state of decomposition. And then, too, they were confirmed in their views by observing the peculiar forms assumed by stalactites and stalagmites which grew under their very eyes; by the strange figures found in agates, notably the moss agate, and the still stranger figures which often characterize what is known as landscape marble, in which trees, castles, mountains and other objects are frequently depicted with striking fidelity.

But in spite of the yoke of authority, especially of Aristotle, which bore heavily upon the students of science, and notwithstanding the generally received teaching, often based on the Bible, to oppose which required considerable courage, new views were slowly but surely supplanting the old. And strange as it may seem, it was not some philosopher who was the first to proclaim the truth, but the celebrated potter, Bernard Palissy. "He was the first," says Fontenelle, "who dared assert in Paris that fossil remains of testacea and fish had belonged to marine animals."

Italian Geologists on Fossils.

A century after Palissy's time, in 1669, Nicholas Steno, a Danish Catholic priest, showed the identity of the teeth and bones of sharks then living in the Mediterranean with those of fossil remains found in Tuscany. "He also compared the shells discovered in the Italian strata with living species; pointed out their resemblance and traced the various gradations from shells which had only lost their animal gluten, to those petrifactions in which there was a perfect substitution of stony matter."

And yet, notwithstanding the observations of such men as Steno, Palissy, and others, the old notions, according to which fossils were the products of a certain plastic virtue latent in nature, or were deposited *in situ* by Noah's flood, still found favor with the majority of geologists. This was especially the case with the physico-theological writers of England, who, in spite of the discoveries of the Italian geologists, still persisted in accommodating all geological phenomena to their fanciful interpretations of the Scriptural accounts of the Creation and the Deluge. Thus Woodward taught that "the whole terrestrial globe was taken to pieces and dissolved by the Flood," and that subsequently the strata " settled down from this promiscuous mass as any earthy sediment from a flood."

Such views were in marked contrast with those held by the learned Carmelite friar, Generelli, who strongly argued against the unreasonableness of calling "the Deity capriciously upon the stage, to make Him work miracles for the sake of confirming our preconceived hypotheses." He insisted on it that natural causes were competent to explain geological phenomena, and to account for the occurrence of fossil remains on hills and mountains. In referring to the formation of mountains and their denudation by the action of the elements, he forestalls the teachings of modern geologists when he declares "that the same cause which, in the beginning of time, raised mountains from the abyss, has down to the present day continued to produce others, in order to restore from time to time the losses of all such as sink down in different places, or are rent asunder, or in other ways suffer disintegration."[1]

---

[1] See Lyell's "Principles of Geology," vol. I, p. 54.

Legends About Giants.

As illustrating the difficulties which students of science had to contend with, I may here refer to another curious but deeply-rooted notion that long prevailed regarding certain fossils. Accepting as certain the ordinary interpretation of the Hebrew word *nephilim*, נְפִילִים, in Genesis, vi, 4, as meaning giants, or persons of extraordinary stature, and taking as literal the mythical or exaggerated accounts of giants who were reputed to have lived in the early ages of the world, the discoverers of large fossil bones had no hesitation in pronouncing them the remains of some one or other great giant of legendary lore.

Greek and Roman authors, no less than German, French and English writers at a much later period, give us very detailed descriptions of the remains of giants discovered in various quarters of the earth. The bones found in one place, were, it was asserted, those of Antæus or Orestes, those in another, of the giant Og, King of Bashan, while those of still another locality were identified as the skeleton of the famous Teutobocchus, king of the Teutons and Cimbri, who was defeated by the Roman general, Marius. According to the accounts which have come down to us, the teeth of these giants each weighed several pounds and were in some instances as much as a foot long, while the estimated stature of others of the giants whose remains are described was no less than sixty cubits. Later investigators, however, had no difficulty in showing that the supposed teeth of giants were nothing other than the molars of some extinct elephant or mammoth; that what were regarded as the vertebræ and femurs of Titans and giants belonged in reality to certain monstrous pachyderms long since extinct, and that what was exhibited as the hand of one of the huge representatives of the human family proved, on examination, to be the bones of the fore-fin of a whale. And, as science advanced, it was finally discovered that there had never been any material difference in the stature of men, that the races of antiquity were no taller than those now existing, and that there is no evidence whatever that there were ever, at any period of the world's history, men of greater stature than those occasionally seen in our own day.[1]

But notwithstanding the progress of discovery, people were loath to give up their belief in giants, as they were unwilling to change their opinions respecting the plastic power of the earth and the universally exterminating effects of the Flood. Men who believed in the existence of griffons and flying dragons, and who regarded the horns of fossil rhinoceroses, so numerous in parts of Europe and Asia, as the claws of griffons and as certain proofs of the existence of these fabled creatures, could not be blamed if they gave more or less credence to the countless traditionary tales respecting Titans and giants.

True Significance of Fossils.

The true significance of fossils, however, was not understood until the time of Cuvier, the illustrious

---

[1] See Howorth's "Mammoth and the Flood," chaps. I and II, and Wood's "Giants and Dwarfs."

founder of paleontology. Many had asserted, as we have seen, that fossil remains were the exuviæ of what were once living animals, but no one before Cuvier had a true conception of their relation to the existing fauna of the globe. At the close of the last century this profound naturalist commenced an exhaustive study of the rich fossiliferous rocks of the Paris basin, and was soon able to announce to an astonished world that the fossils there discovered were not only the remains of animals long since extinct, but that they belonged to species and genera entirely different from any now existing. To the amazement of men of science he proved the existence of a tropical fauna in the latitude of Paris, and exhibited animal forms totally unlike anything now living. His discoveries carried men's minds back to times far anterior to the Deluge of Noah; back to epochs whose remoteness from our own is to be estimated by hundreds of thousands and millions of years. The theory that the fossiliferous strata of the earth were deposited by Noah's Flood was proven to be untenable and absurd, and it was therefore relegated definitively to the limbo of fanciful speculations and exploded hypotheses. Thinking men were compelled to recognize the fact that the world is much older than had been imagined; that far from having been created only a few thousand years ago, it had been in existence for many millions of years; and that many strange forms of life had inhabited the earth long before the advent of man on our planet. Further investigations carried on by Brongniart, Cuvier's collaborator, by D'Orbigny, Sedgwick, Murchison, Smith, Lyell and others, showed that there was a gradual development from the forms of life which characterize the earlier geological ages to those which appeared at later epochs. From the simple, primitive forms of the lower Silurian Age there was a steady progression towards the higher and more specialized types of the Quaternary.

Did this succession betoken genetic connection? Were the higher and later forms genealogically descended from the simpler antecedent types? Was there here, in a word, evidence of organic Evolution?

Controversy in the French Academy.

Such questions had been suggested before but they were now asked in all seriousness, and by those most competent to interpret the facts of paleontology. A storm was brewing in the scientific world, and when, in 1830, it burst in the French Academy, in the celebrated contest between Cuvier and Étienne Geoffroy Saint-Hilaire, it created an unprecedented sensation in the whole of Europe, notwithstanding the great political excitement of the time.

An anecdote, told of Goethe, shows in what light the great poet-philosopher viewed the dispute which was to have such an important bearing on the question of the origin of species. The news of the outbreak of the French Revolution of July had just reached Weimar, and the whole town was in a state of excitement. "In the course of the afternoon," says Soret, "I went around to Goethe's. 'Now,' exclaimed he to me, as I entered, 'what do you think of this great event? The volcano has come to an eruption; everything is in flames, and we have no longer a transaction with closed doors!' 'Terrible affairs,' said I, 'but what could be expected under such outrageous circumstances, and with such a ministry, otherwise than that the whole would end with the expulsion of the royal family?' 'My good friend,' gravely returned Goethe, 'we seem not to understand each other. I am not speaking of those creatures there, but of something quite different. I am speaking of the contest, so important for science, between Cuvier and Geoffroy Saint-Hilaire, which has just come to an open rupture in the French Academy!'" This individual contest between two giants was the signal for a general outbreak. The first gun was fired and a war ensued, which has continued with almost unabated vigor until the present time. The scientific world was divided into two camps, those who sympathized with the views of Geoffroy regarding Evolution, and those who sided with Cuvier, the advocate of the traditional doctrine of special creations.

Much, however, remained to be accomplished before the views of Saint-Hilaire could be considered as anything more than a provisional hypothesis. The evidence of all the sciences had to be weighed, a thorough survey of the vast field of animate nature had to be made, before the new school could reasonably expect its views to meet with general acceptance. Special and systematic investigations were accordingly inaugurated, in all parts of the world, in which representatives of every department of science took an active and interested part.

CHAPTER IV.

SPONTANEOUS GENERATION AND SCIENTIFIC DISCOVERY.

Early Views Regarding Abiogenesis.

BEFORE recounting the results of these investigations, it may not, perhaps, be out of place, briefly to summarize a chapter in the history of biology which has always had a peculiar interest for students of nature, and which, even to-day, notwithstanding many long and animated controversies on the subject, has probably a greater interest for a certain school of evolutionists than almost any other one topic. I refer to the subject of spontaneous generation, or abiogenesis,[1] to which reference has already been made *en passant*.

The discussion of this question has played such an important part in the history of science, that any treatment of the theory of Evolution which should contain no reference to the subject of spontaneous generation, would ignore one of the most essential factors in a great and long-continued controversy. In good sooth, some knowledge of the more salient facts of abiogenesis are absolutely indispensable to a proper appreciation of certain of the most interesting problems connected with the theory of Evolution

---

[1] Generatio æquivoca, heterogenesis, and autogenesis, are sometimes employed as synonyms of spontaneous generation.

as now understood. In many respects, indeed, Evolution and abiogenesis go hand in hand and what throws light on the one at the same time illuminates the other, diminishing, *pari passu*, the difficulties of both, or bringing, it may be, such difficulties into bolder relief.

The doctrine that certain animals and plants arise from the fortuitous concourse of atoms of inorganic matter, or originate from decaying animal or vegetable matter, that nature is capable of bringing forth living bodies,

"Qui rupto robore nati,
Compositive luto, nullos habuere parentes."

is one of those errors in science that can be traced back to the earliest period of scientific speculation. It received the *imprimatur* of Aristotle, who was a firm believer in spontaneous generation, and, like many other errors indorsed by the famous Stagirite, it was almost universally accepted as incontestable truth until a few decades ago. How much this belief, by engendering false notions regarding the unity and relationship of the animal world, may have retarded the progress of science, it is unnecessary here to inquire. Suffice it to say that the discussions to which the subject gave rise from time to time had no slight influence in predisposing many minds in favor of the theory of Evolution, and of throwing a certain light on the subject of organic development that could come from no other source.

According to Aristotle many of the lower forms of animal life originate spontaneously, sometimes from decomposing animal or vegetable matter, sometimes from the slime of the earth. Many insects, he tells us, spring from putrid matter; certain fish have their origin in mud and sand, while eels, we are assured, are spontaneously produced in marshy ponds.[1] Aristotle's views were shared by his countrymen as well as by the Romans—by poets and philosophers as well as by naturalists. Pliny and Varro speak of spontaneous generation as do also Virgil and Lucretius and Ovid. All readers of Ovid are familiar with the interesting account given in the "Metamorphoses" of the origin of bees, hornets and scorpions from putrid flesh, of frogs from slime, and of serpents from human marrow.[2]

Entertaining such notions regarding the origin of living things, we can understand why Rome's poet-philosopher declares "It remains, therefore, to believe that the earth must justly have obtained the name of mother, since from the earth all living

---

[1] See his "History of Animals," book V, chap. I, and book VI, chaps. xiv and xv.

[2] "Si qua fides rebus tamen est addenda probatis,
Nonne vides, quæcumque mora fluidove calore
Corpora tabuerint, in parva animalia verti?
I quoque, delectos mactatos obrue tauros;
Cognita res usu, de putri viscere passim
Florrilegæ nascuntur apes . . .
Pressus humo bellator equus crabronis origo est.
Concava littoreo si demas brachia cancro;
Cetera supponas terrae; de parte sepulta
Scorpius exibit . . .
* * * * * * * *
Semina limus habet viridea generantia ranas.
* * * * * * * * *
Sunt qui, cum clauso putrefacta est spina sepulchro,
Mutari credant humanas angue medullas."
Ovid, "Metamorphoses," Lib. XV., vv. 361, et seq.

creatures were born. And even now many animals spring forth from the earth, which are generated by means of moisture and the quickening heat of the sun."[1]

Fathers and Schoolmen on Abiogenesis.

The views of Aristotle and his successors were accepted and taught by the Fathers and the Schoolmen of the Middle Ages. St. Augustine, in discussing the question whether certain small animals were created on the fifth or sixth day, or whether they arose from putrid matter, says: "Many small animals originate from unhealthy vapors, from evaporations from the earth, or from corpses; some also from decayed woods, herbs and fruits. But God is the creator of all things. It may, therefore, be said that those animals which sprang from the bodies, and especially the corpses, of other living beings, were only created with them *potentialiter* and *materialiter*. But of those which spring from the earth, or water, we may unhesitatingly say that they were created on the fifth and sixth days." St. Thomas Aquinas acquiesces in this opinion of the great bishop of Hippo, although he declined to accept Avicenna's theory that all animals could originate spontaneously.

I direct special attention to the teachings of the Fathers and Schoolmen regarding abiogenesis, as

---

[1] "Linquitur, ut merito maternum nomen adepta
Terra sit, e terra quoniam sunt cuncta creata,
Multaque nunc etiam existant animalia terris
Imbribus, et calido solis concreta vapore."
Lucretius, "De Rerum Natura," Lib. V. 793-796.

they have a profound significance in the discussion of certain questions which shall be referred to in the sequel. The principles which they admitted have an importance that is far-reaching, and should be more generally known than they are. For the application of these principles—broad and deep they are—will enable us to refute many objections that would otherwise be unanswerable, and enable us to escape from many difficulties which frequently give both scientists and theologians no inconsiderable trouble.

For centuries after the time of St. Thomas, the theory of spontaneous generation was universally held and taught in all the schools of Europe.

And more than this. Learned men of science and grave theologians did not hesitate to give instructions as to how certain animals might be brought into existence by the mysterious power of abiogenesis. As late as the seventeenth century, the famous Jesuit scholar, Athanasius Kircher, confidently indicated the following method of producing serpents by spontaneous generation: "Take as many serpents as you like, dry them, cut them into small pieces, bury these in damp earth, water them freely with rain water, and leave the rest to the spring sun. After eight days the whole will turn into little worms, which, fed with milk and earth, will at length become perfect serpents, and by procreation will multiply *ad infinitum.*" Van Helmont gave a recipe for making fleas, while there were others who gave equally explicit directions for the production of mice from cheese, or fish by the fermentation of suitable material.

Even so late as the last century, there were learned men who did not hesitate to declare that mussels and shell-fish are generated from mud and sand, and that eels are produced from dew.

Redi's Experiments.

The first one effectively to controvert the doctrine of abiogenesis was Francesco Redi, of the celebrated *Academia del Cimento*, of Florence. In his remarkable work entitled "Esperienze intorno alla Generazione degl' Insetti," published in 1668, he distinctly enunciates the doctrine that there is no life without antecedent life—*omne vivum ex vivo*—that all living organisms have sprung originally from preëxisting germs, and that the apparent production of organized beings from putrefied animal matter, or vegetable infusions, is due to the existence or introduction of germs into the matter from which such beings seem to originate.

The experiments by which Redi proved his assertion were as simple as they at the time were conclusive.

He placed some meat in a jar and then tied fine gauze over the top of the jar. The meat underwent putrefaction but no maggots appeared. Redi hence inferred that maggots are not generated by decomposing meat, but by something which is excluded from the jar by the gauze. He soon discovered that this something which had eluded all previous observers, was the eggs of a blow-fly, which, when deposited on meat, or dead animals, invariably gave rise to the maggots that had hitherto been regarded as spontaneously generated. By a series of similar experiments he showed that in all cases the apparent production of living from dead matter was due to the introduction, from without, of living germs into the matter from which life seemed to originate.

So deeply rooted, however, was the doctrine of spontaneous generation in the minds of men, that Redi's conclusions were far from meeting with ready acceptance. All kinds of objections were urged against his experiments and the inferences which he drew from them. Some of his opponents even went so far as to assert that his conclusions were contrary to the teachings of Scripture, which, they contended, manifestly implied, if it did not expressly affirm, the doctrine of abiogenesis. In proof of their view they referred to the generation of bees from the lion which had been slain by Samson, and which suggested the riddle that so puzzled the Philistines:—"Out of the eater came forth meat, and out of the strong came forth sweetness."[1]

From our present way of viewing the question such an objection seems very strange, to say the least, but stranger still does it appear when we reflect that it was urged in the name of theology and Scripture. The spell of antiquity and authority was still hanging over the students of nature, and it re-

---

[1] Judges, chap. xiv, 5-14.—Redi refers to the objections of his adversaries in the following passage from his "Esperienze:" "Molti e molti altri ancora vi potrei annoverare, se non fossi chiamato a rispondere alle rampogne di alcuni che bruscamente mi rammentano ciò che si legge nel capitolo quattordicesimo del sacrosanto Libro de' Giudici." p. 45.

quired an intrepid investigator like Redi, strong in his sense of right and certain in his interpretations of the teachings of experiment, to assert his intellectual freedom, and to cope with those who imagined that Aristotle could not err, and that certain metaphysical dicta, which were universally quoted, were, in natural science, to be accounted as so many canons of truth.

But, notwithstanding the opposition which he excited, Redi was triumphant, and for a long time the theory of spontaneous generation was very generally looked upon as something that had fallen into disrepute.

Later Researches.

But the victory was but temporary. The invention of the microscope, and the discovery of the world of infusorial animalculæ, which before had been invisible, resurrected the old theory of abiogenesis, and many eminent naturalists now defended it as strenuously as had any one of its supporters before the experiments of Redi had called it in question.

Among the most eminent champions of the theory of the spontaneous generation of infusory animalcules, were the English naturalist, Needham, and the distinguished French savant, Buffon. As the result of numerous experiments both these observers came to the conclusion that, whatever views might be entertained regarding the origin of the higher forms of animal life, there could be no doubt about the spontaneous production of certain of the lower animalculæ, from suitably prepared infusions of animal or vegetable matter.

This apparent victory was, however, but ephemeral. The experiments in question were taken up by a distinguished Italian ecclesiastic, the Abbate Spallanzani, who subjected them to a rigid and exhaustive examination. The result of his labors issued in proving incontestably that the experiments of Needham were defective, and that his conclusions, therefore, were unwarranted. Spallanzani demonstrated that when the necessary precautions are taken against the admission of germs into the infusions employed, no animalcules whatever are developed, and that the theories and conclusions of Buffon and Needham were not sustained by the facts in the case.

But, notwithstanding the investigations of Redi and his successors, Leeuwenhoek, Swammerdam, Reaumur and Vallisneri, and despite the researches of Spallanzani, Schultze and Schwann, Van Siebold, Leuckart, and Van Beneden, there were not wanting men who still pinned their faith to the theory of abiogenesis. Foremost among these were the celebrated chemists Berzelius and Liebig. "Was it certain," they asked, "that in the experiments which had hitherto been conducted, that the properties of the air, or oxygen of the air, or of the menstrua themselves, had not been essentially changed, and thus had rendered them incompetent to give rise to the phenomena which they would exhibit in their natural and chemically unchanged condition?"

These questions were taken up and answered in the epoch-making researches of that prince of investigators, the universally revered and world-renowned Pasteur. He demonstrated that in every instance life originates from antecedent life — *omne vivum ex vivo* — that the various forms of fermentation, putrefaction and disease are not only caused by the presence and action of certain microbes, but that these microbes, as well as organisms of a superior organization, are invariably produced by beings like themselves; that, in all cases, like proceeds from like, and that, consequently, spontaneous generation is, to use his own characterization of it, a "chimera."

Is the discussion finally closed? Has the theory of abiogenesis received its *coup de grâce?* At the present moment Pasteur and his school are undoubtedly lords of the ascendant. Will they always remain so? Time alone can answer this question. In the opinion of such men as Pouchet and Bastian, two of Pasteur's ablest antagonists, the question, so far as experiment goes, is at best settled only provisionally, and the same old controversy may break out any day, as it has so often broken out since the time of Redi, when it was declared to be definitively closed.

But, whatever be the last word of science respecting abiogenesis, the discussion of the subject has led to the discovery of many new facts of inestimable importance, and has vastly extended our view of the domain of animated nature. It has disclosed to our vision a world before unknown, the world of microbian life—a world which has been aptly described as "the world of the infinitely little."

General Advance in Science.

The general progress of science, however, points towards some process of Evolution far more unmistakably than does anything disclosed during the long controversy regarding spontaneous generation.

Geology and physical geography have taught us that our earth is subject to mutations and fluctuations innumerable; paleontology has revealed a world whose existence was not only not suspected, a few generations ago, but a world whose existence would have been unhesitatingly denied as contrary to both science and Scripture, if anyone had been bold enough to proclaim its reality. Far from being only six thousand years old, as was so long imagined, our globe, as the abode of life, must now, as is shown by the study of the multifold extinct forms entombed in its crust, reckon its age by millions, if not by tens of millions of years.

By the naturalists of the last century the number of known species of plants and animals was estimated at a few thousands, or a few tens of thousands at most. But now, owing to the impetus which has been given to the study of zoölogy and botany, especially during the past few decades, the latest census of organic beings places the number of species at a million or more. Yet formidable as this number is, the list is far from being complete. Fresh additions are being made to it every day. The researches of naturalists in the many unexplored fields of the earth; the investigations of microscopists in the boundless domain of microbian life; the dredging of the ocean depths in various parts of the globe by a constantly increasing corps of trained votaries of science, show that we are yet very far from having anything approaching a complete census of the rich and varied fauna and flora which adorn our planet.

But great as is the number of species actually existing, it is but a small fraction of those which are known to have lived and died since the dawn of life on the globe. A hundred million species or more, it has been computed, have appeared and died out since the time the *Eozoön Canadense* began its humble existence. And as our knowledge of the past history of the earth becomes more thorough, there is every reason to believe that we shall find this estimate, extravagant as it may appear to some, below, rather than above, the reality.

Synchronously with this advance in the knowledge of nature, the impression—which had all along been entertained by a greater or lesser number of philosophers and students of nature—has become stronger that all the changes and developments which the earth has witnessed; all the prodigality of form and size and color, which a bounteous nature has lavished upon a fauna and flora whose species are past numbering, is the result not of so many separate creative acts, but rather of a single creation and of a subsequent uniform process of Evolution, according to certain definite and immutable laws.

Chemistry and Astronomy.

The indications of paleontology and biology respecting Evolution have been corroborated by the revelations of chemistry, astronomy and stellar physics. Everything seems to point conclusively to a development from the simple to the complex, and to disclose "a change from the homogenous to the heterogenous through continuous differentiations and integrations."

It is simple elements that go toward building up organic and inorganic compounds. And while it is now generally believed that there are some three score and odd substances which are to be classed as elementary, there are, nevertheless, not wanting reasons for thinking that all the so-called elements are but so many modifications, so many allotropic forms, of one and the same primal kind of matter. The telescope discloses to us in the nebulæ which fleck the heavens, the primitive matter, the *Urstoff*, from which the sidereal universe was formed: "the gaseous raw material of future stars and solar systems." The spectroscope, in spite of Comte's dogmatic declaration, that we should never know anything about the chemical constitution of the stars, has not only given us positive knowledge regarding the composition of the heavenly bodies, but, thanks to the labors of Secchi, Huggins, Lockyer and others, has also furnished information concerning their relative ages, their directions of motion, and their velocities in space.

As the astronomer, the chemist, and the physicist view the material universe, it is constituted throughout of the same material, a kind of cosmic dust, similar to, if not identical with, that which composes the existing nebulæ. No form of matter has yet been discovered in any of the heavenly bodies which is not found on the earth, and there is every reason to believe that in chemical constitution the visible universe is everywhere identical. And should it eventually be demonstrated that all the known chemical elements are only modifications of one primal form of matter, and this is far from impossible, or even improbable, then will be vindicated the old Greek theory of a primordial matter, πρώτη ὕλη, a theory ardently championed by St. Gregory of Nyssa and his school, and defended in some form or other by many of the Schoolmen. And then, too, will the theory of Evolution be furnished with a stronger argument than any other single one that has yet been advanced in its support.

Testimony of Biology.

But great as was the influence of discoveries in geology, paleontology, microscopy, chemistry, astronomy and stellar physics, in preparing the minds of scientific men for the acceptance of the theory of organic Evolution, the arguments which had the greatest weight, which finally enlisted in favor of Evolution those who, like Lyell, still hesitated about giving in their adhesion to the doctrine of derivation, were those which were based on data furnished by the sciences of botany, zoölogy, physiology, and by those newer sciences, embryology and comparative osteology.

CHAPTER V.

FROM LORD BACON TO CHARLES DARWIN.

First Materials for the Controversy.

I HAVE spoken of the celebrated dispute between Cuvier and Geoffroy Saint-Hilaire, in which Goethe was so much interested. Materials for this controversy had been rapidly accumulating during the half century preceding the date when it finally broke out in the French Academy. Indeed, it would be truer to say that materials had been accumulating during two centuries prior to the historic debate between Cuvier and Geoffroy Saint-Hilaire. From the time of Bacon, Descartes and Leibnitz, more, far more, had been done towards the development of the Evolution idea than had been effected during all the centuries which had elapsed between the earliest speculations of the Ionian school and the publication of the " Novum Organum."

We have already learned what geology and paleontology contributed towards the establishment of the theory of Evolution. We have seen how the study of fossils and the careful and long-continued examination of the much-vexed question of spontaneous generation shed a flood of light on numerous problems which were before obscure and mysterious in the extreme. But while Da Vinci, Fracostoro, Palissy, Steno, Generelli, Redi, Malpighi, Leeuwenhoek, Schwammerdam and their compeers, were carrying on their investigations regarding fossils and infusoria, students in other departments of science were not idle. Gesner, Vesalius, Fallopius, Fabricius and Harvey were then conducting their famous researches in zoölogy, anatomy, and embryology, while Cesalpinus, Ray, Tournefort and Linnæus were laying the secure foundations of systematic botany and vegetable anatomy. It was to this period, indeed, that, as has been truthfully observed: " We owe the foundation of microscopic anatomy, enriched and joined to physiology; comparative anatomy studied with care; classification placed on a rational and systematic basis."

Bacon and Kant.

Lord Bacon was not only a firm believer in organic Evolution but was one of the first to suggest that the transmutation of species might be the result of an accumulation of variations. Descartes, too, inclined to Evolution rather than to special creation, and was the first philosopher, after St. Augustine, who specially insisted that the sum of all things is governed by natural laws, and that the physical universe is not the scene of constant miracles and Divine interventions. Leibnitz, like Bacon and Descartes, accepted the doctrine of the mutability of species, and showed in many passages in his works, that no system of cosmic philosophy could be considered complete which was not based on the demonstrated truths of organic Evolution. "All advances by degrees in nature," he tells us, " and nothing by leaps, and this law, as applied to each, is part of my doctrine of continuity."

Immanuel Kant, in common with his illustrious contemporary, Buffon, accepted the ideas that specific mutability results from selection, environment, adaptation and inheritance. Like the great French naturalist, too, he derived all the higher forms of life from lower and simpler forms. He recognized also the law of degeneration from original types, and the principle of the survival of the fittest, which were subsequently to play such important roles in all theories of organic Evolution. Indeed, I do not think Kant has received due recognition for his contributions towards the philosophy of the cosmos. Like Aristotle, he had a faculty for correct generalization which sometimes gave his views almost the semblance of prophecy. Taking up the nebular hypothesis, as it was left by St. Gregory of Nyssa, he adapted it to the science of his time, and in many respects forestalled the conclusions of Laplace and Herschel. Similarly he took up the principles of Evolution as they had been laid down by St. Augustine and the Angel of the Schools, and, by giving them a new dress, he anticipated much of the evolutionary teaching of subsequent investigators. Considering the time in which he wrote, nothing is more remarkable than the following comprehensive *résumé* of his views on Evolution :—

"It is desirable to examine the great domain of organized beings by means of a methodical, comparative anatomy, in order to discover whether we may not find in them something resembling a system, and that, too, in connection with their mode of generation, so that we may not be compelled to stop short with a mere consideration of forms that are, which gives us no insight into their generation, and need not despair of gaining a full insight into this department of nature. The agreement of so many kinds of animals in a certain common plan of structure, which seems to be visible not only in their skeletons, but also in the arrangement of the other parts—so that a wonderfully simple typical form, by the shortening and lengthening of some parts, and by the suppression and development of others, might be able to produce an immense variety of species—gives us a ray of hope, though feeble, that here, perhaps, some results may be obtained by the application of the principle of the mechanism of nature, without which, in fact, no science can exist. This analogy of forms—in so far as they seem to have been produced in accordance with a common prototype, notwithstanding their great variety—strengthens the supposition that they have an actual blood relationship, due to derivation from a common parent; a supposition which is arrived at by observation of the graduated approximation of one class of animals to another, beginning with the one in which the principle of purposiveness seems to be most conspicuous, namely man, and extending down to polyps, and from these even down to mosses and lichens, and arriving finally at raw matter, the lowest stage of nature observable by us. From this raw matter and its forces, the whole apparatus of nature seems to have been derived according to mechanical laws, such as those which resulted in the production of crystals, yet, this apparatus, as seen in organic beings, is so incomprehensible to us, that we conceive for it a different principle. But it would seem that the archæologist of nature, that is, the paleontologist, is at liberty to regard the great family of creatures—for a family we must conceive it, if the above-mentioned continuous and connected relationship has a real foundation—as having sprung from the immediate results of her earliest revolutions, judging from all the laws of their mechanisms known to, or conjectured by him."[1]

Passing over such speculative evolutionists as De Maillet, Maupertuis, Bonnet, Robinet and Oken, who did little more than revamp the crude notions of the old Ionian speculators, we may scan in hasty review the principal contributions made to the evolutionary movement by the great naturalists who flourished between the time of Linnæus and Cuvier.

Linnæus and Buffon.

Linnæus, who adopted the well-known aphorism of Leibnitz, *natura non facit saltum*, was as much of a special creationist and, consequently, as much opposed to Evolution as was the illustrious Cuvier. But although in the earlier part of his career he contended that there were no such things as new species—*nullæ species novæ*—still, at a later period, he was willing to admit that "all species of one genus constituted at first, that is, at creation, one species"—*ab initio unam constituerint speciem*—but maintained that "they were subsequently multiplied

---

[1] Quoted in Osborne's useful little work "From the Greeks to Darwin," pp. 101, 102,

by hybrid generation, that is, by intercrossing with other species."[1]

The first one to formulate a working hypothesis respecting the mutation of species was the eminent French naturalist, Buffon. According to Lanessan, he "anticipated not only Lamarck in his conception of the action of environment, but Darwin in the struggle for existence and the survival of the fittest." The questions of heredity, geographical distribution, the extinction of old and the apparition of new species he discussed with rare perspicacity and suggestiveness. He was undoubtedly a believer in the unity of type, and the community of origin of all animal forms, although the diverse views he entertained on these subjects at different periods of his life have led some to minimize the importance of his contributions to the theory of Evolution.[2]

---

[1] "Suspicio est," he says, "quam diu fovi neque jam pro veritate indubia venditare audeo, sed per modum hypotheseos propono ; quod scilicet omnes species ejusdem generis ab initio unam constituerint speciem, sed postea per generationes hybridas propagatæ sint. . . . Num vero hæ species per manum Omnipotentis Creatoris immediate sint exortæ in primordio, an vero per naturam, Creatoris executricem, propagatæ in tempore, non adeo facile demonstrabitur." "Amœnitates Academicæ." Vol. VI., p. 296.

It is interesting to observe that this view found favor with the celebrated Scriptural commentator, Dom Calmet. Only on the supposition that all the species of each genus originally formed but one species, was he able to explain how all the animals could find a place in the ark of Noah.

[2] Speaking of the factors of evolutionary changes he writes : " What cannot nature effect with such means at her disposal ? She can do all except either create matter or destroy it. These two extremes of power, the Deity has reserved for Himself alone; creation and destruction are the attributes of His Omnipotence. To alter and undo, to develop and renew—these are powers which He has handed over to the charge of nature."

Buffon, also, was the first to formulate the law of uniformitarianism which was subsequently developed with such care by Lyell and his school. In his "Théorie da la Terre" he tells us that "in order to understand what had taken place in the past, or what will happen in the future, we have but to observe what is going on at present.[1]

Erasmus Darwin and Lamarck.

Erasmus Darwin, a contemporary of Buffon's and the grandfather of the famous naturalist, did much to popularize the idea of Evolution. In his "Zoönomia," "Botanic Garden," and above all in his posthumous "Temple of Nature," he embodies not only the leading evolutionary views of the old Greek philosophers, as well as those of Leibnitz and Buffon, but he likewise introduces and developes new ideas of his own. He is truly a poet of Evolution and in his "Temple of Nature" we find selections of verse that for beauty and force of expression compare favorably with the finest lines of the "De Rerum Natura" of the old Roman evolutionist, Lucretius.

As the founder of the complete modern theory of descent, "Lamarck," justly observes Osgood, " is the most prominent figure between Aristotle and Darwin." He was an accomplished biologist, and a prolific writer on botanical and zoölogical subjects. He laid special stress on the effects of environment, and of use and disuse in the modification of species. He assumed that acquired characters are inherited,

---

[1] "Pour juger de ce qui est arrivé et même de ce qui arrivera, nous n'avons qu'à examiner ce qui arrive."

but never attempted to demonstrate a postulate which since his time has provoked such widespread discussion.[1]

Among the contemporaries of Lamarck, who did much to develop and corroborate the theory of Evolution, must be mentioned Goethe, who has justly been called the greatest poet of Evolution, and Treviranus. As a morphologist and osteologist, Goethe exhibited talent of the highest order, and, had he devoted his life to science instead of literature, he would have ranked with the most eminent naturalists of modern times. In referring to his essays on comparative anatomy, Cuvier declares that "One finds in them, with astonishment, nearly all the propositions which have been separately advanced in recent times." As to Treviranus, Huxley places him alongside Lamarck as one of the chief founders of the theory of Evolution, although there are many who dissent from this opinion of the great English biologist. The truth is he was rather an

---

[1] The nature and chief factors of Evolution according to Lamarck, are expressed in the following four laws :—

Première Loi.—La vie, par ses propres forces, tend continuellement à accroître le volume de tout corps qui la possède, et à étendre les dimensions de ses parties, jusqu' à un terme qu' elle amène elle-même.

Deuxième Loi.—La production d'un nouvel organe dans un corps animal résulte d' un nouveau besoin survenu qui continue de se faire sentir, et d' un nouveau mouvement que ce besoin fait naître et entretient.

Troisième Loi.—Le développement des organes et leur force d'action sont constamment en raison de l'emploi de ces organes.

Quatrième Loi.—Tout ce qui a été acquis, tracé ou changé dans l'organisation des individus pendant le cours de leur vie, est conservé par la génération et transmis aux nouveaux individus qui proviennent de ceux qui ont éprouvé ces changements. Cf. "Histoire Naturelle," and "Philosophie Zoölogique."

exponent of the views of others than an originator of any theory of his own.

Species and Varieties.

The difficulty of distinguishing species from varieties—a difficulty with which all botanists and zoölogists are familiar, and one which augments with the progress of knowledge of the fauna and flora of the world—and the almost perfect gradations characterizing the forms of certain groups of animals and plants, contributed more than anything else towards impelling naturalists from the time of Lamarck to accept the doctrine that species are derived from one another by a process of development.

Observations similar to those made by Lamarck and other naturalists, led the Rev. W. Herbert, of England, to declare, in 1837, that "Horticultural experiments have established, beyond the possibility of refutation, that botanical species are only a higher and more permanent class of varieties." He entertained the same view regarding animals, and believed "that single species of each genus were created in an originally highly plastic condition, and that these by intercrossing and by variation have produced all our existing species."

In 1844 appeared the famous "Vestiges of Creation," an anonymous work by Robert Chambers. This work created a profound sensation at the time, and although lacking in scientific accuracy in many points, and advocating theories that have long since been demolished, it passed through many editions and commanded a wide circle of readers. In Great

Britain the opposition to the views expressed in the work was violent in the extreme, although it seems that most of the adverse criticism was ill-founded. The main proposition of the author, determined on as he himself declares "after much consideration," is, "that the several series of animated beings, from the simplest and oldest up to the highest and most recent, are, under the providence of God, the results, first, of an impulse which has been imparted to the forms of life, advancing them in definite times, by generation, through grades of organization terminating in the highest dicotyledons and vertebrata, these grades being few in number, and generally marked by intervals of organic character which we find to be a practical difficulty in ascertaining affinities; second, of another impulse connected with the vital forces, tending in the course of generations to modify organic structures in accordance with external circumstances, as food, the nature of the habitat and the meteoric agencies, these being the adaptations of the natural theologian."

Prior to this time the distinguished Belgian geologist, D' Omalius d' Halloy, had expressed the opinion that new species are but modified forms of other species from which they are descended. And a short time subsequently the eminent French botanist, M. Charles Naudin, promulgated similar views, and taught that species as well as varieties are but the result of natural and artificial selection. He did not, it is true, employ these words—words which were given such vogue a short time afterwards by Darwin—but his theory implied all they express.

CHAPTER VI.

CONTROVERSY AND PROGRESS.

Darwin's "Origin of Species."

THE culmination of all the tentative efforts which had hitherto been made, towards giving a rational explanation of the mode of production of the divers species of our existing fauna and flora, was in the publication of Darwin's now famous work, "The Origin of Species," which was given to the world in 1859. Simultaneously and independently another naturalist, Mr. Alfred Wallace, who was then far away in the Malay Archipelago, had come to the same conclusions as Darwin. For this reason he is justly called the co-discoverer of the theory which has made Darwin so famous.

The publication of "The Origin of Species" was the signal for a revolution in science such as the world had never before witnessed. The work was violently denounced or ridiculed by the majority of its readers, although it counted from the beginning such staunch defenders as Huxley, Spencer, Lyell, Hooker, Wallace, and Asa Gray. Professor Louis Agassiz, probably the ablest naturalist then living, in his criticism of the book declared: "The arguments presented by Darwin, in favor of a universal derivation from one primary form of all the peculiarities existing now among living beings, have not made the slightest impression on my mind. Until the facts of nature are shown to have been mistaken by those who have collected them, and that they have a different meaning from that now generally assigned to them, I shall therefore consider the transmutation theory as a scientific mistake, untrue in its facts, unscientific in its method, and mischievous in its tendency."[1]

But in spite of the storm of criticism which the work provoked, it was not long until the great majority of naturalists had executed a complete volte-face in their attitude towards Darwinism. If they were not willing to go to the same lengths as the author of "The Origin of Species," or hesitated about conceding the importance which he attached to natural selection as an explanation of organic Evolution, they were, at least, willing to admit that he had supplied them with the working hypothesis which they were seeking.

Upon these, says Huxley, it had the effect "of the flash of light, which to a man who has lost himself in a dark night, suddenly reveals a road, which, whether it take him straight home or not, certainly goes his way." What naturalists were then looking for "was a hypothesis respecting the origin of known organic forms which assumed the operation of no causes but such as could be proved to be actually at work." "The facts of variability," continues Huxley, "of the struggle for existence, of adaptation to conditions, were notorious enough; but

---

[1] Quoted by Huxley in the "Life and Letters of Charles Darwin," by his son, vol. I., p. 538.

none of us had suspected that the road to the heart of the species problem lay through them, until Darwin and Wallace dispelled the darkness, and the beacon-fire of the 'Origin' guided the benighted."[1]

Herbert Spencer and Compeers.

With Darwin came Herbert Spencer, "the philosopher of Evolution," according to whom the entire cosmos, the universe of mind as well as the universe of matter, is governed by Evolution,[2] Evolution being a "cosmical process," which, as Grant

---

[1] Op. cit., p. 551.

[2] It is but just to remark that an essay published by Spencer in the *Leader*, in 1852, constitutes what has been called "the high-water mark of Evolution" prior to Darwin. In this essay he writes as follows: "Even could the supporters of the development hypothesis merely show that the production of species by the process of modification is conceivable, they would be in a better position than their opponents. But they can do much more than this; they can show that the process of modification has effected, and is effecting, great changes in all organisms subject to modifying influences. . . . They can show that any existing species, animal or vegetable, when placed under conditions different from its previous ones, immediately begins to undergo certain changes of structure fitting it for the new conditions. They can show that in successive generations these changes continue until ultimately the new conditions become the natural ones. They can show that in cultivated plants and domesticated animals, and in the several races of men, these changes have uniformly taken place. They can show that the degrees of difference so produced are often, as in dogs, greater than those on which distinction of species are, in other cases, founded. They can show that it is a matter of dispute whether some of these modified forms *are* varieties or modified species. And thus they can show that throughout all organic nature there is at work a modifying influence of the kind they assign as the cause of these specific differences; an influence which, though slow in its action, does in time, if the circumstances demand it, produce marked changes; an influence which, to all appearance, would produce in the millions of years, and under the great varieties of condition which geological records imply, any amount of change."

Allen phrases it, is one and continuous " from nebula to man, from star to soul, from atom to society."

Since its publication, the theory advocated by Darwin has undergone many modifications. Much has been added to it, and much has been eliminated from it. Among those who have discussed it most critically, and suggested amendments and improvements are Moritz Wagner, Nägeli, Huxley, Mivart, Wallace, Spencer, Weismann, Cope, Hyatt and Brooks, not to mention scores of others who have distinguished themselves by their contributions to Darwinian literature. But whatever may now be the views entertained regarding natural selection as a factor of organic Evolution, the theory of Evolution itself, far from being impaired, has been gaining strength from day to day, and is, we are assured by its advocates, finding new arguments in its favor in every new discovery in biology and physical science. Such being the case, it is, we are told, only a question of time, and a very short time at that, until every man who is competent to weigh evidence, shall be compelled to announce his formal acceptance of the doctrine of Evolution, however much he may now be opposed to it, and however much it may seem counter to his preconceived notions, or to traditions which he has long regarded as sacred and inviolable.

Science and Philosophy.

Evolution, it is pertinent here to observe, may be considered from two points of view, a fact which it is of prime importance always to bear in mind. It may be regarded as a *scientific theory*, devised to explain the origination of the higher from the lower, the more complex and differentiated from the simple and undifferentiated, in inorganic and organic bodies, or it may be viewed as a *philosophical system*, designed to explain the manifold phenomena of matter and life by the operation of secondary causes alone, to the exclusion of a personal Creator. In the restricted sense in which we are considering it, it is a scientific hypothesis intended to explain the origin and transmutation of species in the animal and vegetable worlds, by laws and processes disclosed by the study of nature.

Important as it is, however, it is not always an easy matter to keep the scientific theory separated from the philosophical system. Hence, naturalists and philosophers are continually intruding on each other's territory. The naturalist philosophizes, and the philosopher, if I may give a new meaning to an old word, naturalizes. For naturalists and physicists, as all are aware, are very much given to making excursions into the domain of metaphysics and to substituting speculations for rigid inductions from observed facts.

And metaphysicians sin in a similar manner by attempting to explain, by methods of their own, the various phenomena of the material world, and in seeking by simple *a priori* reasons to evolve from their inner consciousness a logical system of the physical universe. The result is inextricable confusion and errors without number. It is neither science nor philosophy, but a *mixtum compositum*, which not only gives false views of nature but still falser views of the Author of nature, if indeed it does not positively ignore Him and relegate Him to the region of the unknowable.

Such a philosophy, if philosophy it can be called, is that of Herbert Spencer, which is now so much the vogue; a philosophy which attempts to explain the origin and constitution of the cosmos by the sole operation of natural causes, and which recognizes only force and matter as the efficient cause of the countless manifestations of nature and mind which constitute the province of science and psychology.

I would not, however, have it inferred that I regard science — and by this I mean natural and physical science — and metaphysics as opposed to each other. Far from it. They mutually assist and supplement one another, and a true philosophy of the cosmos is possible only when there is a perfect synthesis between the inductions of science on the one hand and the deductions of metaphysics on the other.

Anticipations of Discoveries.

It is indeed remarkable, even in the subject under discussion, how frequently philosophers, like poets, seem to have proleptic views of nature that are not disclosed to men of science until long afterwards. All who are familiar with the history of science and philosophy will be able, without difficulty, to call to mind some of the marvelous scientific intuitions of Pythagoras, Aristotle, St. Gregory of Nyssa, St. Augustine, and St. Thomas Aquinas.

The teachings of St. Gregory of Nyssa and of St. Augustine were in this respect specially remarkable. I have elsewhere[1] shown that the views of St. Gregory respecting the origin of the visible universe, were far more precise and comprehensive than were those of the Ionian schools, and that he it was who in very truth first laid the foundations of the nebular hypothesis, elaborated and rounded out long centuries afterwards by Laplace, Herschel, and Faye. It was the great bishop of Hippo who first laid down the principles of theistic Evolution essentially as they are held to-day.[2] He taught that God created the various forms of animal and vegetable life, not actually but potentially; that He created them derivatively and by the operation of natural causes. And the teaching of St. Augustine respecting potential creation was that which was approved and followed by that great light of the Middle Ages, St. Thomas Aquinas.

In modern times Hobbes spoke of the principle of struggle—*bellum omnium contra omnes*—suggested by Heraclitus and insisted on so strongly by contemporary evolutionists. In discussing the scholastic doctrine of real specific essences, Locke developes the idea of the continuity of species, the central idea of Darwinism and of the theory of organic Evolution. He also speaks of the adaptation of organic arrangements to "the neighborhood of the bodies that surround us," and thus indicates a factor on which modern evolutionists lay much stress when

---

[1] "Bible, Science and Faith," part I, chaps. III and IV.
[2] Ibid.

they discourse on "the circumstances of the environment," the conditions of life, or the *monde ambiant*, of Geoffroy Saint-Hilaire. Leibnitz in his "Protogæa" expresses similar views on the continuity of species, that is, of a graduated series of living forms "that in each remove differ very little from one another." Distinct evolutionary views had likewise been propounded by Spinoza, Herder and Schelling, but it is unnecessary to dwell on them here.

In its growth, then, the modern theory of Evolution may aptly be compared with that of the century plant. For long generations it had been gathering material and strength, but at last, suddenly and almost unexpectedly, it blossomed forth into a working hypothesis of colossal proportions and universal application. Philosophy anticipated many, if not all its leading tenets, but it was inductive science which placed it on the foundation on which it now rests and which gave it the popularity that it now enjoys.

Species and Creation.

The pervading idea of Evolution, as we have seen, is one of change, the idea of integration and differentiation. As applied to plants and animals it is the development, by the action of natural causes, of the higher from the lower forms.

The various forms of animal and plant life according to this view are genetically related to one another. Species are therefore not immutable as is generally imagined, but mutable. What we call species are the results of descent with modification, and instead of there having been as many species of living beings in the beginning as there are now, as Linnæus believed, there was at first, as Darwin taught, only one primordial form, and from this one form, all that infinitude of forms of vegetable and animal life, which we now behold, is descended.

The question raised, therefore, is manifestly one that appeals to us for a solution. I again ask, are all the species of animals and plants, which have existed on the earth since the dawn of life, the results of separate and successive creations by an almighty Power, as has so long been believed, or are they rather the product of Evolution, acting through long ages and in accordance with certain fixed natural laws and processes?

Until the celebrated controversy, already mentioned, between Cuvier and Geoffroy, there were, as we have seen, comparatively few who were not firm believers in the doctrine of special creations, at least of all the higher forms of life. Subsequent to this event, the number, especially among naturalists, of those who favored the development hypothesis began gradually to increase. After the publication of Darwin's famous "Origin of Species," the advocates of Evolution rallied their forces in a remarkable manner, and before many years had elapsed a large majority of the working naturalists of the world were professed evolutionists.

Evolutionists and Anti-Evolutionists.

Of course there were many, even among the ablest scientists of the age, who still withheld their assent. The most distinguished of these, as we have already learned, was Professor Louis Agassiz, who remained a strenuous opponent of the new doctrine until the day of his death. Indeed, in the last course of lectures he ever gave, we find a strong arraignment of the development hypothesis, a hypothesis which was fascinating indeed, but one, so Agassiz declared, that was negatived by the facts of nature and misleading and mischievous in its tendencies. Even to-day the illustrious naturalist has sympathizers and followers and that, too, among the ablest and most conspicuous representatives of modern science. Among anti-evolutionists, living or recently deceased, I need instance only such recognized savants as the noted geologists, Sir J. W. Dawson, Barrande, Davidson, Grand Eury, Carruthers, and that veteran biologist—the rival of Pasteur on the importance and brilliance of his researches on the lower forms of life—the late Professor P. J. van Beneden, of the great Catholic university of Louvain.[1] In referring to the subject the distinguished Belgian professor asserts: "It is evi-

---

[1] The distinguished French savant, the Marquis de Nadaillac, is often spoken of as an anti-evolutionist, but this is an error. So far he is neither an evolutionist nor an anti-evolutionist; he merely suspends judgment. Before the anthropological section of the International Catholic Scientific Congress, assembled last year at Brussels, he expressed himself on the subject as follows: " Pour ma part, si je ne suis guère disposé à admettre les conclusions de l'école évolutioniste, je ne puis non plus les rejeter absolument. Le jury en Écosse, outre la réponse habituelle, a le droit, sans se prononcer sur le fait en lui-même, de répondre *not proven* — cela n'est pas prouvé. Telle est la disposition de mon esprit; telle est aujourd'hui ma conclusion; et je crois qu'elle sera celle de tous ceux qui aborderont cette étude sans parti pris et avec l'unique désir d'arriver

dent to all those who place facts above hypotheses and prejudices, that spontaneous generation, as well as the transformation of species, does not exist, at least if we only consider the present epoch. We are leaving the domain of science if we take our arms from anterior epochs. We cannot accept anything as a fact which is not capable of proof."[1]

At the present day, among men of science, evolutionists outnumber creationists fully as much as the latter outnumbered the former a half century ago. It is only rarely that we meet a scientist who does not profess Evolution of some form or other, or who does not at least think that the older views regarding creation and the origin of species must be materially modified in order to harmonize with the latest conclusions of science.

No Via Media Possible.

All the lines of thought which we have been following converge, then, as has already been observed, towards one point—the origin, or rather the genesis, of species, and their succession and distribution in space and time. Between the two theories, that of creation and that of Evolution, the lines are drawn tautly, and one or the other theory must be accepted by all who make any pretensions intelligently to discuss the subject. No compromise, no *via media*, is possible. We must needs be either creationists or evolutionists. We cannot be both.

à la verité." "Compte Rendu," Section d' Anthropologie, p. 305. Cf. also "Problème de la Vie," pp. 175–178, by the Marquis de Nadaillac.

[1] Van Beneden's "Animal Parasites and Messmates," p. 106.

The theory of emanation is not here considered, it being contrary to the principles of sound philosophy as well as to the teachings of true science. How shall we, then, regard the problem of the origin of species, and what views, expressed not in general terms but carefully formulated, have been entertained by the great thinkers of the world on this all-important, and, at present, all-absorbing topic?

Dr. Whewell, the learned historian of the "Inductive Sciences," in referring to the forms of life of geological times says: "Either we must accept the doctrine of the transmutation of species, and must suppose that the organized species of one geological epoch were transmuted into those of another, by some long-continued agency of natural causes, or else we must believe in many successive acts of creation and extinction of species, out of the common course of nature; acts which therefore we may properly call miraculous."[1]

Whewell, in common with the majority of his contemporaries—he wrote his masterly work over fifty years ago—and in common with the large body of non-scientific people still living, unhesitatingly accepted the doctrine of "many successive acts of creation," as against the theory of the transmutation of species, which he regards as negatived by "an indisputable preponderance" of evidence against it.

The Miltonic Hypothesis.

But even accepting the creational hypothesis, how are we to picture to ourselves the appearance

[1] "History of the Inductive Sciences," vol. II, p. 564.

of new species? "Are these new species," asks the erudite Master of Trinity, "gradually evolved from some embryo substance? Or do they suddenly start from the ground, as in the creation of the poet?"

"Perfect forms
Limbed and full grown: out of the ground up rose,
As from his lair, the wild beast where he wons
In forest wild, in thicket, brake, or den; . . .
The grassy clods now calved; now half appear'd
The tawny lion, pawing to get free
His hinder parts, then springs as broke from bonds,
And rampant shakes his brinded mane; the ounce,
The libbard, and the tiger, as the mole
Rising, the crumbled earth above them threw
In hillocks; the swift stag from underground
Bore up his branching head; scarce from his mould
Behemoth, biggest born of earth, upheaved
His vastness: fleeced the flocks and bleating rose,
As plants; ambiguous between sea and land
The river-horse and scaly crocodile.
At once come forth whatever creeps the ground,
Insect or worm."[1]

We have here what Huxley calls the "Miltonic hypothesis" fully developed even in its minutest details. But this view of special creation, it is but just to state, may be offset by another passage, less frequently quoted it is true, from the great bard, which as clearly tells of creation by Evolution. In both instances the archangel Raphael appears as the

---
[1] "Paradise Lost," Book VII.

speaker. And if, in the verses just quoted, the poet is in accord with the literal interpreters of the Genesiac account of creation, in the following lines he reflects the ideas of creation entertained by St. Augustine and St. Thomas Aquinas. Having spoken of "one first matter," and its subsequent progressive development, the poet continues:—

"So from the root
Springs lighter the green stalk, from thence the leaves
More airy, last the bright consummate flower
Spirit odorous breathes: flowers and their fruit,
Man's nourishment, by gradual scale sublimed,
To vital spirits aspire, to animal,
To intellectual; give both life and sense,
Fancy and understanding; whence the soul
Reason receives, and reason is her being,
Discursive or intuitive; discourse
Is oftest yours, the latter most is ours,
Differing but in degree, of kind the same."

Book V.

Again, were these new species created by single or multiple pairs; and, if by multiple pairs, was there one, or were there many centers of distribution for the individual species?

Views of Agassiz.

According to Linnæus, the great Swedish naturalist, who voiced not only the opinion of his time, but of nearly all creationists since his time, species were created by single pairs, and the present number is equal to that which was created in the beginning.¹ According to Schouw, whose views were shared by the eminent botanist, Alphonse de Candolle, in the earlier portion of his career, there was "a double or multiple origin of species, at least of some species." Professor L. Agassiz, however, went much farther. He asserted not only the multiplicity of species, but also denied that there was "any necessary genetic connection among individuals of the same species, or of any original localization more restricted than the area now occupied by the species." According to this eminent student of nature, all animals and plants have occupied, from the beginning, those natural boundaries within which they stand to one another in such harmonious relations. Pines originate in forests, heaths in heaths, grasses in prairies, bees in hives, herrings in shoals, and men in nations. He asserts that "all animals originated in vast numbers—indeed, in the average number characteristic of their species—over the whole of their geographical area, whether its surface be continuous, or disconnected by sea, lakes, rivers, or by differences of level above the sea, etc."² Elsewhere he declares: "There are in animals peculiar adaptations which are characteristic of their species, and which cannot be supposed to have arisen from subordinate influences. Those which live in shoals cannot be supposed to have been created in single pairs. Those which are made to be the food of others cannot have been created in the same proportions as

---
¹ "Species tot numeramus quot diversæ formæ in principio sunt creatæ." "Philosophia Botanica," No. 157.

² "An Essay on Classification," p. 59.

those which live upon them. Those which are everywhere found in innumerable specimens, must have been introduced in numbers capable of maintaining their normal proportions to those which live isolated, and are comparatively and constantly fewer. For we know that this harmony in the numerical proportions between animals is one of the great laws of nature. The circumstance that species occur within definite limits, where no obstacles prevent their wider distribution, leads to the further inference that these limits were assigned to them from the beginning; and so we should come to the final conclusion that the order which prevails throughout nature is intentional, and that it is regulated by the limits marked out the first day of creation, and that it has been maintained unchanged through ages, with no other modifications than those which the higher intellectual powers of man enable him to impose on some few animals more closely connected with him."[1]

According to Agassiz, therefore, not only is the origin of species supernatural, but their general geographical distribution is also supernatural. And more than this. Not only are all the phenomena of origin, distribution and extinction of animal and vegetable life, to be directly referred to the Divine will, but also, he will have it, "Every adaptation of species to climate, and of species to species, is as aboriginal, and, therefore, as inexplicable, as are the organic forms themselves." "The facts of geology,"

---

[1] "Lake Superior," p. 337.

he tells us, "exhibit the simultaneous creation, and the simultaneous destruction of entire fauna, and a coincidence between these changes in the organic world and the great physical changes our earth has undergone." "The origin of the great variety of types of animals and plants, can never," he declares, "be attributed to the limited influence of monotonous physical causes which always act in the same way." On the contrary, it necessarily displays "the intervention of a Creator" in the most striking manner, in every stage of the history of the world.

Agassiz returns to these points time and again, and illustrates his argument in ways that are always interesting, if not always conclusive. As a résumé of his teaching respecting the origin, distribution and extinction of animals and plants, and as an indication of his spirit of reverence and piety, nothing can be more explicit or edifying than the following paragraphs taken from his profound "Essay on Classification," so frequently quoted:

"The products of what are commonly called physical agents are everywhere the same, that is, upon the whole surface of the globe; and have always been the same, that is, during all geological periods; while organized beings are everywhere different, and have differed in all ages. Between two such series of phenomena there can be no causal or genetic connection.

"The combination in time and space of all these thoughtful conceptions, exhibits not only thought; it shows also premeditation, power, wisdom, greatness, prescience, omniscience, providence. In one word, all these facts, in their natural connection, proclaim aloud the one God, whom we may know, adore and love; and natural history must, in good time, become the analysis of the thoughts of the Creator of the universe, as manifested in the animal and vegetable kingdoms, as well as in the inorganic world."[1]

Evolution.

As against the doctrine of separate and successive creations, we have, as already stated, the theory of the origin of species by derivation. But as in the creational doctrine there are different views respecting the manner in which species appeared, so, likewise are there, according to Evolution, different hypotheses regarding the origin and devolopment of the divers forms of organized beings.

In the first edition of his "Origin of Species" Darwin expresses the belief that all "animals have descended from at most only four or five progenitors, and plants from an equal or lesser number." In the second edition of his work he arrives at quite a different conclusion and infers that "probably all organic beings which have ever lived on the earth have descended from some one primordial form, into which life was first breathed by the Creator."

The majority of evolutionists, who admit the existence of a personal God, accept the Darwinian view that all the forms of life at present existing in the world are derived, by the agency of natural forces and the influence of environment, from

---

[1] P. 205; cf., also, chaps. x and xvi, of Agassiz' "Methods of Study in Natural History."

one primordial created form. Evolutionists of the atheistic school, however, of which Ernst Hæckel is the chief representative, contend not only that all species of animals and plants are descended from a speck of protoplasm, a simple, structureless primitive moneron, but also that this primordial speck of protoplasm was not the work of the Deity, but was the result solely of the operation of some one of the physical forces on brute matter.

But excluding the philosophical theories which have been built on Evolution, and the religious discussions to which it has given rise, let us proceed to examine the evidences for and against it as a scientific theory. Let us inquire what are the grounds for the almost universal acceptance of this theory by contemporary scientists, and see whether the arguments advanced in its support are in accord with the canons of sound logic and the principles of true philosophy. The question is entirely one of natural science, not of metaphysics, and hence one of evidence which is more or less tangible. What, then, are the evidences of organic Evolution to which modern scientists usually appeal? This is the question to which all that precedes is but little more than a preamble, and a question, too, that well deserves our closest and most serious consideration. I shall endeavor to give the answer succinctly, but fairly, in the following chapter.

CHAPTER VII.

EVIDENCES OF EVOLUTION.

Systems of Classification.

BEFORE discussing the evidences of Evolution, or examining the arguments advanced in its support, it is advisable to have some idea of the different systems of classification which have obtained in various periods of the history of science, and to learn on what such systems were based. Have naturalists in all ages employed essentially the same systems of classification, or have their systems been widely different, if not contradictory? Are scientific classifications expressions of natural arrangements existing in animated nature, or are they but artificial devices for coördinating our knowledge of nature and facilitating our investigations? Have species, genera, families, orders, classes and branches, a real or an ideal existence? Are they manifestly disclosed in the plan of creation or are they but arbitrary categories hit upon by naturalists as convenient aids in arrangement and research? These are a few of the many questions which present themselves for an answer as we approach the subject of organic Evolution. Others there are also which might be discussed but we have not space for them now.

EVIDENCES OF EVOLUTION. 85

The system of classification of Aristotle, and of the naturalists of antiquity generally, was of the most primitive character. It recognized but two groups, γένος and εἶδος, genus and species. These terms, as a rule, had only a very vague meaning, and were frequently made to embrace groups of animals that we should now refer to orders and classes.[1] This system, however, incomplete and misleading as it was, prevailed for upwards of two thousand years, and no serious attempt was made to improve on it until the time of the great naturalist, Linnæus. He introduced new divisions and distinctions, gave to the study of zoölogy an impetus which it had never received before, and stimulated research in a manner that was simply marvelous. He was the first to introduce classes and orders into the system of zoölogy, in addition to the vague genera and species of the ancient philosophers.[2] Until the appearance of the "Règne Animal" of Cuvier, in the beginning of the present century, the "Systema Naturæ" of Linnæus, first published in 1735, was the only system of classification which received any recognition. All other attempts at classification were only

---

[1] In the sixth chapter of the first book of his "History of Animals" Aristotle distinguishes between γένη μέγιστα, γένη μεγάλα and γένος simply. This chapter will well repay perusal as illustrating the diversity of meanings given to a word which in modern zoölogy has such a definite and restricted signification. Although εἶδος had sometimes a wider meaning than we now give to this term, it must, nevertheless, in justice to the illustrious Stagirite, be said that he usually employed it in the same sense as naturalists now use the word species.

[2] Linnæus called the class, *genus summum;* the order, *genus intermedium;* the genus, *genus proximum.*

modifications of the system introduced by the Swedish naturalist. But when Cuvier—"the greatest zoölogist of all time," as Agassiz denominates him—began his epoch-making investigations, all was changed. The divisions of Linnæus were based on external resemblances. Cuvier, as the result of an extensive survey of the whole animal kingdom, and more especially in consequence of his marvelous investigations in the domain of comparative anatomy, a science of which he was the founder, demonstrated that classification should be based, not on external resemblance, but on internal structure. He was indeed the first to introduce order into chaos, and to place the science of zoölogy on something like a firm foundation.

Cuvier and His Successors.

Before Cuvier's time no attempt had been made to bring the various groups of animals under a more comprehensive division than that which exhibited the whole animal kingdom as composed of vertebrates and invertebrates; a division which was not materially different from that of Aristotle, who classed all animals as *sanguineous*, ζῶα ἔναιμα, and *asanguineous*, ζῶα ἄναιμα. But, in his memorable communication to the French Academy in 1812, Cuvier declared that his researches had led him to believe "that all animals are constructed upon four different plans, or as it were, cast in four different moulds."[1]

---

[1] The words of the French naturalist on this subject are: "Si l'on considére le règne animal d'après les principes que nous venons de poser, en se débarassant des préjugés établis sur les divisions anciennement admises, en n'ayant égard qu'à l'or-

The names given to the groups—*embranchemens*, or branches, Cuvier calls them—constructed on these four plans are vertebrates, mollusks, articulates and radiates. It will thus be seen that Cuvier introduces divisions above the classes of Linnæus. In addition to this he also interpolates families between orders and genera. And then, again, the various divisions of Cuvier admit of numerous secondary divisions, such as sections, tribes, sub-genera and others besides.

Important as was the "Systema Naturæ" in stimulating research, its influence was almost insignificant in comparison with Cuvier's masterly "Leçons sur l'Anatomie Comparée," and his no less remarkable "Règne Animal," and "Ossemens Fossiles." The publication of these *chefs-d'œuvre* not only gave to the study of natural history a stimulus it had never felt before, but it was likewise the occasion of numerous new systems of zoölogical classification of various degrees of merit.

Naturalists now vied with one another in establishing new divisions, in introducing new classes, orders, genera and species into their systems, and in claiming, each for his own system, some special value or point of superiority not possessed by the others. First came the system of Lamarck, then those of

---

ganisation et à la nature des animaux, et non pas à leur grandeur, à leur utilité, au plus ou moins de connaissance que nous en avons, ou à toutes les autres circonstances accessoires, on trouvera qu'il existe quatre formes principales, quatre plans généraux, si l'on peut s'exprimer ainsi, d'après lesquels tous les animaux semblent avoir été modelés et dont les divisions ultérieures, de quelque titre que les naturalistes les aient décorés, ne sont que des modifications assez légères, fondées sur le développement ou l' addition de quelques parties qui ne changent rien à l'essence du plan."

De Blainville, Ehrenberg, Burmeister, Von Siebold and Stannius, Leuckart, Milne-Edwards, Kölliker, Vogt, Van Beneden, Owen, Von Baer, Agassiz, Huxley, Hæckel and Ray Lankester, not to mention scores of others of lesser importance.

Points of View.

But what is more striking than the number of zoölogical systems which our century has produced, are the diverse points of view which systematists have chosen in elaborating their systems. The pre-Cuvierian taxonomists, as we have seen, based their schemes of classification on external characteristics. Cuvier insisted that taxonomy should be based on internal structure, and that the structure of the entire animal should be considered. Certain later systematists deemed this unnecessary, and attempted to build systems of classification on the variations of a single organ, or on the structure of the egg alone.

Again, according to Cuvier's classification, the four branches of the animal kingdom are distinguished by four distinct plans of structure. According to Ehrenberg "the type of development of animals is one and the same from man to the monad." According to Cuvier and his school, the four types of structure proceed along four parallel lines. According to the evolutionary school, however, the entire animal kingdom is to be conceived as a genealogical tree, *Stammbaum*, the various branches and twigs, twiglets and leaves of which, are to be regarded as the classes, orders, genera and species of which zoölogists speak.

At first classification was based on only superficial characteristics. Now we must take into account, not only external form and internal structure, not only anatomical and histological characteristics, but we must also incorporate in our classifications the teachings of embryology and cytology. We must study not only bone and muscle, but investigate the nature and structure of the cell, and study the embryo from its earliest to its latest state of development. We can now call no one master, for the days of *magister dixit* have passed. Neither Aristotle, nor Linnæus, nor Cuvier nor any other one person is to be our sole guide, but we must perforce elaborate a system from the combined observations and generalizations of not only the great masters above-mentioned, but also from those of Schwann and Von Baer, Johann and Fritz Müller, Kowalewsky and Darwin. We must discard much, once accepted as true, which more exact research has disproved, and combine into one systematic whole the gleanings of truth which are afforded by the investigations of so many students in the various departments of natural knowledge.

Taxonomic Divisions.

Our brief reference to some of the chief systems of classification conducts us naturally to a more important topic, the nature of the various categories which we have been considering.

Have branches, classes, orders, families, genera and species a real existence in nature, or are they merely more or less successful devices of scientific men to arrange and correlate the facts and phenomena of nature? Are the divisions which naturalists have introduced into their systems artificial and arbitrary, or have they rather been instituted by the Divine Intelligence as the categories of His mode of thinking? Are they but the inventions of the human mind or have "the relations and proportions which exist throughout the animal and vegetable worlds an intellectual and ideal connection in the mind of the Creator?" "Have we, perhaps," asks the eloquent Agassiz, "thus far been only the unconscious interpreters of a Divine conception, in our attempts to expound nature? And when in the pride of our philosophy we thought that we were inventing systems of science, and classifying creation by the force of our own reason, have we followed only and reproduced in our imperfect expressions, the plan whose foundations were laid in the dawn of creation, and the development of which we are laboriously studying, thinking, as we put together and arrange our fragmentary knowledge, that we are introducing order into chaos anew? Is this order the result of the exertions of human skill and ingenuity; or is it inherent in the objects themselves, so that the intelligent student of natural history is led unconsciously, by the study of the animal kingdom itself, to these conclusions, the great divisions under which he arranges animals being indeed but the headings to the chapter of the great book which he is reading."[1]

---
[1] "Essay on Classification," pp. 8, 9.

On a correct answer to this last all-important question depends, in great measure, the truth or falsity of the theory of organic Evolution. It is a shibboleth which cannot be evaded, a crux which must be explained before an intelligent discussion of the evidences of Evolution is even possible.

Plato's "Grand Ideas."

According to Plato, "the world of particular things is somehow determined by preëxisting universal ideas." Species and genera, therefore, are but expressions of the ideas of the Creator; and classifications of animals and plants, according to types, are but translations of the thoughts of God; expressions of grand ideas which from all eternity have been before the Divine mind. Types, then, are but the copy; the Divine ideas, the pattern or archetype. Species, as Plato conceived them, were immutable, and organic Evolution, as now understood, was, accordingly, impossible.

During the Middle Ages, Plato's doctrine of types was accepted without question, and species were looked upon as being as immutable as the rules of dialectics, as unchangeable as truth itself. Thus the great Scotus Erigena, probably the profoundest philosopher of his time, declares that "that art which divides genera into species, and resolves species into genera, which is called dialectics, is not the product of human ingenuity, but has its origin in the nature of things and is due to the Author of all arts which are true arts, and has been simply discovered by the wise."[1] But this classification, this division into species and genera, which, according to Erigena, is something not artificial and conventional, but something that is real and Divine, applied, in the estimation of most philosophers prior to the time of Darwin, not only to logic and metaphysics but also to the natural sciences as well.

Linnæus held similar views. He tells us explicitly that "the number of species is equal to the number of divers forms which the Infinite Being created in the beginning; which forms, according to the prescribed laws of generation, produced others, but always like unto themselves."[2]

Cuvier on Species.

But the strongest and most eminent advocate of the creation and fixity of species was Cuvier. In the introduction to his "Règne Animal" he asserts that "there is no proof that all the differences which now distinguish organized beings are such as may have been produced by circumstances. All that has been advanced upon this subject is hypothetical; experience seems to show, on the contrary, that, in the actual state of things, varieties are confined within

---

[1] "Intelligitur quod ars illa, quæ dividet genera in species et species in genera resolvit, quæ διαλεκτική dicitur, non ab humanis machinationibus sit facta, sed in natura rerum ab Auctore omnium artium, quæ veræ artes sunt, condita et a sapientibus inventa." "De Divisione Naturæ," IV, 4.

[2] "Species tot sunt, quot diversas formas ab initio produxit Infinitum Ens; quæ formæ, secundum generationis inditas leges, produxere plures, at sibi semper similes." "Philosophia Botanica," 99, 157.

rather narrow limits, and, so far as we can retrace antiquity, we perceive that these limits were the same as at the present. We are thus obliged to admit of certain forms which, since the origin of things, have been perpetuated, without exceeding these limits; and all the beings appertaining to one of these forms constitute what is termed a *species*. Generation being the only means of ascertaining the limits to which varieties may extend, species should be defined as the reunion of individuals descended from one another, or from common parents, or from such as resemble them as closely as they resemble each other; but although this definition is rigorous, it will be seen that its application to particular individuals may be very different when the necessary experiments have been made."

But not only, according to Cuvier, are existing species fixed and the result of special creative action; the same views must also be held regarding the countless geological species which have so long disappeared from the face of the earth. The great naturalist was a firm believer in the doctrine of successive creations and destructions, of a series of depopulatings and repeoplings of the world. As is well known, he was the author of the celebrated Period or Concordistic theory, which attempts to reconcile the statements of the Mosaic narrative of creation with the declarations of geology and paleontology — a theory which has had a great vogue, and which, after the lapse of three-quarters of a century, has even now not a few advocates.

Definition of Species.

We come now to the definition of the term species, the critical point in the controversy between creationists and evolutionists. Aristotle's conception of species was, as we have seen, far from being precise. With his followers, for more than two thousand years, the idea of a physiological species was vague and nebulous in the extreme. It was usually nothing more than a metaphysical concept, and was of little or no value to the working naturalist. Indeed, strange as it may seem, no definition of the term species, as it is now used, was given until the latter part of the seventeenth century. One of the first definitions found is in the "Historia Plantarum" of the noted English botanist Ray, although Yung, of Hamburg, and Tournefort, the distinguished French botanist, contemporaries of Ray, appear to have anticipated the English naturalist in arriving at a true conception of physiological species. According to Ray, "specific characters rested not only on close and constant resemblance in outward form, but also on the likeness of offspring to parent, a considerable measure of variability being, however, recognized." Ray's definition of species and Linnæus' binomial system of nomenclature, which so greatly facilitated classification, contributed immensely towards establishing order where chaos had so long reigned supreme.

It would be a mistake, however, to suppose that, after the labors of Ray, Linnæus, Cuvier, and their collaborators, there was perfect unanimity respecting the nature and signification of species. On the contrary, the divergence of views was rendered greater in proportion to the progress of research and discovery, so that it soon became difficult to find any two persons who could agree on a definition of the term "species."

Everyone who wrote on zoölogy, as we have learned, had his own system of classification. In like manner, everyone who had occasion to treat of questions of natural history found himself compelled to define the little word "species," and the definition given usually differed in important respects from those of previous investigators. Indeed, if we compare the definitions of species which have been given since the time of Ray, we shall find that there has been as great a change of opinion respecting its nature, as there has been displayed in the various systems of classification that have been elaborated since the period of Linnæus. Everywhere there is uncertainty, doubt, nebulosity.

The learned anthropologist, De Quatrefages, in his interesting work, "Darwin et ses Précurseurs Français," gives, besides his own definition of the term, no fewer than twenty definitions of species— he might have given many more—as proposed by as many eminent naturalists.[1] Some, like Ray and Flourens, base their definition on genealogical connection; others like Tournefort and De Candolle regard likeness among individuals as the essential thing in a true definition of species, while others still, and these for

[1] Pp. 186, 187.

the nonce are in the majority, aver that both filiation and resemblance must be taken into account in any true definition of the term.

Thus, the illustrious botanist Antoine Laurent de Jussieu, the founder of the "natural system" of botany, which superseded the artificial or sexual system of Linnæus, defines species as "a succession of individuals entirely alike, which are perpetuated by generation."[1] Similar definitions have been given by Lamarck, Cuvier, Johann Müller, Isidore Geoffroy Saint-Hilaire and others. According to De Quatrefages a "species is a collection of individuals, more or less resembling each other, which may be regarded as having descended from a single primitive pair by an uninterrupted and natural succession of families."[2] Agassiz, however, who, as we have seen, contended that individuals of the same species existing in disconnected geographical areas had independent origins, insisted that we are forced "to remove from the philosophic definition of species the idea of a community of origin, and consequently, also, the idea of a necessary genealogical connection."[3]

To the foregoing I may add the declarations of our eminent American botanist, Professor Asa Gray, who declares: "We still hold that genealogical connection, rather than mutual resemblance, is the fun-

---

[1] In his great work, "Genera Plantarum," Jussieu says of species: "Nunc rectius definitur perennis individuorum similium successio continuata generatione renascentium."

[2] "The Human Species," p. 36.

[3] "Essay on Classification," p. 256.

damental thing—first on the ground of fact, and then from the philosophy of the case. Practically, no botanist can say what amount of dissimilarity is compatible with the unity of species; in wild plants it is sometimes very great, in cultivated races often enormous."[1] What the learned professor here affirms of plants, may likewise, with equal truth, be predicated of animals both wild and domestic.

Difficulties Regarding Species.

What, then, is species? Is it something real, as some have averred, or is it, as others maintain, something which is only ideal? And if it have an existence, real or ideal, how may it be recognized? The definitions given do not, as we have seen, throw much light on the subject. On the contrary, they are all more or less defective, and often quite contradictory.

It is only, however, when we come to consider the practical applications of these or similar definitions, that we find how illusory and unsatisfactory they are. We have but to compare the classifications of different botanists and zoölogists when treating of the same floræ and faunæ, to realize how utterly inadequate are even the best definitions of species as guides in the classificatory work of practical naturalists. No two naturalists, it may safely be asserted, have ever yet agreed on the same classification as to species, even for the animals and plants of restricted geographical areas. Some aug-

---

[1] "Darwiniana," p. 203.

E.—7

ment the number of species; others diminish it. Some make species out of what others regard as only races or varieties; whilst others again combine in one what still others contend are demonstrably two or more distinct species.

Thus, we have it on the authority of Gray that "In a flora so small as the British, one hundred and eighty-two plants, generally reckoned as varieties, have been ranked by some botanists as species. Selecting the British genera which include the most polymorphous forms, it appears that Babbington's flora gives them two hundred and fifty-one species, Bentham's only one hundred and twelve; a difference of one hundred and thirty-nine doubtful forms. These are nearly the extreme views, but they are the views of two most capable and most experienced judges in respect to one of the best-known floras of the world. The fact is suggestive, that the best-known countries furnish the greatest known number of such doubtful cases."[1]

The relativity and variability of species are still more strikingly illustrated in the case of the hawk-weed, *hieracium*, of Germany. One author describes no fewer than three hundred species of this plant, another makes the number one hundred and six, a third reduces it to fifty-two, while a fourth is equally positive that there are but twenty species all told![2]

---

[1] "Darwiniana," p. 35. Cf. "The Origin of Species," chap. II.

[2] It was such difficulties of classification that led the naturalist, Deslonchamps, to declare: "Plus on voit d'échantillons, moins on fait d'espèces." For a similar reason Darwin exclaims: "How painfully true it is that no one has a right to

Hæckel's well-known monograph on the calcareous sponges shows, even in a more remarkable manner, to what an extent classification depends on the personal equation of the systematist, or "on his predilection for lumping and splitting." In this monograph the Jena professor, considering the same set of forms from different points of view, offers no fewer than twelve different arrangements, "among which the two most nearly conventional propose respectively twenty-one genera and one hundred and eleven species, and thirty-nine genera and two hundred and eighty-nine species."

Similar, although less marked instances of specific indefiniteness are exhibited regarding the oak, willow, beech, birch, chestnut, and other well-known trees. It is, however, in the lowest forms of life that it is most difficult to draw the line of demarcation between one species and another, and where, as all admit, the grouping of species into genera is at best a matter of conjecture. The countless and complete series of transitional forms brought up from the ocean depths by the dredge and trawl are cases in point.

But more puzzling still to the systematist, are those extraordinary microbian forms of life called *schizomycetes*, which embrace the numerous microscopic organisms known as microbes, bacteria,

---

examine the question of species who has not minutely described many. . . . After determining a set of forms as a distinct species, tearing them up and making them separate, and then making them one again (which has happened to me), I have gnashed my teeth, cursed species, and asked what sin I had committed to be so treated."

microphytes, and their congeners. Here classification is at best provisional and arbitrary, and depends entirely on the point of view from which they are studied. In such lowly forms of life, not only is the certain discrimination of species impossible, but it is impossible even to draw a hard and fast line between what is incontestably animal life on the one hand, and vegetable life on the other.

Such being the case, what, it may be asked, becomes of species? What of classification? What of the various systems which have been proposed? Have species any real existence, the question is again asked, or are they but mere figments of the imagination, *ignes fatui*, which have ever eluded the grasp of the investigator, and which are now even farther away from it than they ever were before? Are they but varying, metaphysical entities, airy nothings, convenient only for purposes of speculation and for a classification which, from the very nature of the case, must at best be but provisional and arbitrary?

In reply to these questions it may be stated that there are still those, and their number is far from being small, who yet cling to the old idea of species as something real, immutable, and always recognizable. The instances I have just alluded to may not indeed, it is conceded, exhibit all the specific definiteness of the Venus' flytrap, or the pearly nautilus, but nevertheless, it is contended, the species exist, despite the difficulties which obscure their definition, or which, for the time being, make their recognition impossible.

Agassiz' Views.

Yet even in the face of the difficulties which have been referred to, Agassiz persisted, as others still persist, in maintaining that species are entities, real or ideal, which continue to exist from generation to generation. But he went further than this, further even than most of his predecessors had been willing to go. For not only, according to his views, are species unchangeable units, but genera, orders, classes, and the other groups as well, "are founded in nature, and ought not to be considered as artificial devices, invented by man to facilitate his studies." "To me," says Agassiz, "it appears indisputable, that the order and arrangement of our studies are based on the natural, primitive relations of animal life—those systems to which we have given the names of the great leaders of our science who first proposed them, being, in truth, but translations into human language of the thoughts of the Creator." In the opinion of the illustrious Swiss savant, "man has not invented, but only traced, the systematic arrangement of nature." "The relations and proportions which exist throughout the animal and vegetable world, have an intellectual, an ideal connection in the mind of the Creator. The plan of creation, which so commends itself to our highest wisdom, has not grown out of the necessary action of physical laws, but was the free conception of the Almighty intellect, matured in His thought before it was manifested in tangible, external forms." "In a word, species, genera, families, etc., exist as thoughts; individuals as facts."[1]

Species in the Making.

But while some of the old school who are not naturalists, still subscribe to these or similar views, and while a few, possibly even among naturalists, may yet be found who entertain like notions, the great majority of working naturalists have entirely discarded the traditional idea of species, as something fixed and unchangeable, and substituted in its stead the idea of a species which is variable and transmutable. For evolutionists, all such variable and doubtful forms as those I have indicated are but "species in the making," which become definite in proportion as certain varieties become especially adapted to their environment, and become isolated by the dying out of the intermediate forms. From the evolutionary standpoint both species and classification have a significance which is not only excluded from the creationist's view, but which is absolutely incompatible with it. By the aid of the Evolution hypothesis, too, mysteries are solved which

---

[1] Cf. "Essay on Classification," chap. 1, sec. 1, and "American Journal of Science," July, 1860, p. 143. Very few naturalists, even among Agassiz' predecessors, among those, namely, who like himself, were from conviction special creationists, would, I think, subscribe to this statement. The majority of them, I am disposed to believe, regarded all divisions above species as purely conventional. For, even in pre-Darwinian days, as Romanes well observes, "the scientifically orthodox doctrine was, that although species were to be regarded as fixed units, bearing the stamp of a special creation, all the higher taxonomic divisions were to be considered as what may be termed the artificial creation of naturalists themselves."—"Darwin and After Darwin," vol. I, p. 20.

had long baffled the efforts of the keenest investigators of the old school, and a simple explanation is afforded of difficulties and apparent anomalies which, without this hypothesis, are simply inexplicable. A few simple examples will illustrate my meaning, and at the same time indicate the nature of one of the arguments adduced in favor of organic Evolution.

De Candolle and Baird.

The eminent Swiss botanist, M. Alphonse de Candolle, as the result of an exhaustive study under particularly favorable circumstances, of the oak, especially the oak of the Old World, comes to the conclusion that current notions regarding this important genus must be materially modified; that far from having the large number of species usually attributed to it, the number is in reality very small; that what are so frequently considered as species, are at best but varieties and races; that there is every reason to believe, if indeed there is not positive proof, that all the multitudinous gradations observed among oaks are originally derived from but a few forms, or that all of them may be traced back to the same primeval ancestor. His investigations regarding the oak, demonstrate beyond question what other naturalists had observed and suspected, viz: that what appears to be a distinct species, when only a few specimens from a limited area are examined, proves on the examination of a larger number of specimens, from a wider geographical area, to be, at most, but a race or a variety.

Considering the relations to each other of only existing species, De Candolle felt obliged to curtail greatly the number of species of the genus *quercus*, but when the genealogy of the oak is studied in the light of geology and paleontology, it is found that it originated far back in the Cretaceous Period, and that this ancient geologic form is undoubtedly the common ancestor of all the species and varieties now existing. For we have it on the testimony of such a competent witness as Lesquereux, that not only the oak but all "the essential types of our actual flora are marked in the Cretaceous Period, and have come to us, after passing without notable changes through the Tertiary formations of our continent."

Baird's researches upon the birds of North America, admirably corroborate De Candolle's induction, to wit: "That when a large number of specimens from a sufficiently extensive territory are examined and compared, it is found that what are ordinarily regarded as quite distinct species are often no more than races and varieties, or what evolutionists would denominate incipient species. For along the bordering lines of the habitats of such species, it is observed that the specific characters of the divers forms are so blended that it is often difficult, if not impossible, to distinguish one species from another. Indeed, whether the birds observed in such cases belong to the same or to different species will depend, mainly or entirely, either on the naturalist's point of view, or on the number of intermediate forms which he may be able to collect and compare."

Evidence of Organic Evolution.

After this long preamble respecting classification and species—a preamble which the nature and scope of the topic now under discussion have rendered necessary—we are at length prepared for an intelligent appreciation of the arguments commonly adduced in support of the theory of organic Evolution. If species are not the immutable units they have so long been considered; if, far from being easy of recognition, as is so often fancied, they are with difficulty recognizable, if at all; if, far from being permanent and unchangeable, they are, on the contrary, variable and mutable; we have legitimate *a priori* reasons for believing in the possibility of Evolution, if not in its probability. The actuality, however, of Evolution, is a question of evidence; not indeed of evidence based on metaphysical assumptions, but of evidence derived from observation and a trustworthy interpretation of the facts of nature. To the discussion of this evidence, which I shall make as brief as is consistent with clearness and the nature of the argument involved, I shall now direct the reader's attention.

The evidence usually advanced in support of organic Evolution is fourfold, and is based: First, on the classification of animals and plants; second, on their morphology; third, on their embryology; and fourth, on their distribution in space and time. This, especially the evidence derived from paleontology, is what Huxley designates as "the demonstrative evidence of Evolution," and is well worthy of our most serious consideration.

Of course it will be understood that I can give only the baldest outline of the arguments advanced in favor of the theory of Evolution as applied to plants and animals. Space precludes my doing more than this; besides it is unnecessary, as countless treatises by specialists have been written, in which the various arguments in favor of Evolution are given *in extenso*, and to these is referred the reader who is desirous of more detailed information.

The argument from classification has been incidentally touched upon in what precedes. We have noted the differences of views entertained by divers naturalists respecting the classification of certain plants and animals, and how difficulties of classification increase as we descend from higher to lower types of animated nature. On the theory that all the manifold forms of animal and vegetable life are descended from one primitive form, these difficulties, which on the special creation theory are simply inexplicable, find a ready and simple explanation. Assuming that all forms of life are originally derived from simple monera or undifferentiated particles of protoplasm, and that all are but more or less modified descendants of the same humble ancestor, we can understand why there are such striking resemblances in some instances, and such wide divergencies in others.

A Philological Illustration.

An illustration taken from philology will make this statement clearer. In the Romance languages, for instance, we observe many marked similarities of form and structure, but no one would think of asserting that all these different tongues are directly due to Divine intervention, or that Spanish is derived from Italian, or Italian from French. And yet, they are genetically related to one another, because we know that they are all derived from an older speech —the Latin. In like manner we are able to trace relationships between the numerous members of the great Aryan family of languages—between, for example, such widely dissimilar tongues as Sanscrit, Latin, Greek, Slavic, Zend, Gothic, German, Irish. We cannot, of course, arrange them in a linear series, but it can be shown that all of them are descended from the same mother-tongue and that they all, therefore, belong to the same family tree.

Tree-Like System of Classification.

As in philology, so also in botany and zoölogy, we must look upon the whole of animated nature as constituting but a single genealogical tree. The trunk of this tree represents those lower forms of life which cannot be said with certainty to be either animal or vegetable. It first bifurcates into two minor trunks, or large branches, which are known as the vegetable and animal kingdoms. Each of these trunks or branches bears other branches which denote classes, and these, in turn, ramify in such wise as to produce boughs, twigs, twiglets, and leaves, representing families, orders, genera, and species.

This tree-like system of classification of animals and plants obtained long before the time of Darwin, but he gave it a significance it never before possessed. He showed that it was in reality the only natural system, and the only one which was competent to explain the varied and complicated facts of the organic world. He demonstrated more clearly than had any of his predecessors the impossibility of attempting, as had Lamarck and others, to arrange animals and plants in a series of linear groups. By classifying animals in lineally ascending groups, Lamarck had placed snails and oysters above such marvelously organized creatures as bees and butterflies. The same system of classification would place the humble duck-bill, because it is a mammal, above the eagle and the condor, the lowly amphioxus above the crab, and the degraded lepidosiren above the salmon.

Again, the tree-like system of classification eludes such blunders and shows that differences of structure, and not complexity of organization, are to be considered in every rational attempt to ascertain the true position of any organism in the animal kingdom. Unlike all popular classifications, it is not based on mere external resemblances, but on resemblances which are deeper and more fundamental. Thus, for instance, a whale is often regarded as a fish, because, forsooth, it bears some likeness to a fish in form and habits. A closer examination, however, reveals the fact that it is more like a dog or an ox than a fish. The same may be said of other cases that might be cited, wherein the true position of an organism in the scale of life can be determined, not by superficial resemblances, but by likenesses which are revealed only by dissection—likenesses which can be fully appreciated only by the trained anatomist.

The more closely, then, one examines the divers forms of life, the stronger grows the conviction that they are genetically related in the manner indicated by a *Stammbaum*, or genealogical tree. No other system is competent to explain the facts observed; neither is there any other system which can explain the "progressive shading off of characters common to larger groups into more and more specialized characters distinctive only of smaller and smaller groups." It is just such a system as we should expect to find if the theory of descent be true; just such a system as would obtain if the law of parsimony be admitted, the law, to-wit, that "forbids us to assume the operation of higher causes when lower ones are found sufficient to explain the observed effects." Indeed, so powerful does the argument from classification appear to some minds, that it alone is regarded as decisive in favor of Evolution. Referring to this matter Mr. Fiske declares: "In my own case the facts presented in Agassiz' 'Essay on Classification' went far toward producing conviction before the publication of Mr. Darwin's work on the 'Origin of Species,' where the significance of such facts is clearly pointed out and strongly insisted upon."[1]

The Argument from Structure and Morphology.

We now pass to the argument from structure and morphology. To confine ourselves to the ver-

---
[1] "Cosmic Philosophy," vol. I, p. 454.

tebrates, which are more familiar to the general reader, we observe that all the members of this extensive group are constructed on the same general type. They belong, as it were, to the same style of architecture, and we can trace the variations of structure of similar parts with ease and precision. They are all descendants of but one archetypal form, of one primal vertebrate, from which all others are derived by adaptive modification. This is beautifully illustrated in the homologies of the vertebrate skeleton.

And here it is necessary to remark that analogous organs are by no means homologous organs. Analogous organs are those which are similar in form and function, but of different origin. Homologous organs, on the contrary, are those which, however different their form and functions, can be shown to have community of origin. Thus, the wings of birds and butterflies are analogous, but not homologous. They have the same general form and function, but they have not the same origin; that is, they have not been produced by modification from the same organ or part. On the other hand, the arms of men and apes, the fore-legs and fore-paws of mammals and reptiles, the wings of bats and birds, and the paddles of cetacea and the breast-fins of fishes are homologous, because, however diverse their forms and functions, they can all be demonstrated to have a common origin. They have essentially the same structure and are composed of the same pieces, although in view of their diverse functions they are so modified that the superficial resemblance has entirely disappeared. But although the modifications are so great, they are, nevertheless, just such modifications as would have originated from the fore-limb of some archetypal form, if this limb had been called upon to perform entirely different functions from those for which it was first adapted, or if the archetypal ancestor had been introduced to an entirely different environment from the one in which it was originally placed. Analogy, then, is but a superficial resemblance, whereas, homology is an essential and fundamental one which, in many cases, can be detected only by experts in comparative anatomy.

Now, it is precisely the fact of homology of structure, which finds its sole explanation in community of origin, that constitutes one of the strongest proofs of the theory of Evolution.

According to the evolutionary theory of natural selection, it is inferred that hereditary characters undergo a change whenever a change will better adapt an organism to changed conditions of life. The whale is again a case in point. From the best evidence obtainable, it is concluded that the ancestors of whales were land quadrupeds, which became aquatic in their habits. But such a change in their mode of life would necessitate a corresponding change in the functions of various parts and organs. The hind-legs would not be required for purposes of locomotion, and hence they would disappear. The fore-legs would be adapted for swimming, and would, therefore, be transformed into fins or paddles. There would also be important changes in the skin, teeth, muscles and form of the organism, rendering it more fish-like in shape, and better adapted for moving in the water.

But even with all these modifications, necessitated by changes of environment and consequent mode of life, the anatomist would experience no difficulty in demonstrating that the whale is not a fish, but a mammal, and in exhibiting the various homologies existing between the divers parts of this monster of the deep, as we now know it, and parts of its hypothetical terrestrial progenitor. Thus, the paddles, as we have seen, correspond to the arms of man, the fore-legs of quadrupeds, the flippers of turtles, and the wings of birds. The hind-legs are not visible, externally, it is true, but they exist internally in a rudimentary state. The same may be said of the teeth. The fully-developed baleen whale, for instance, has no teeth, for it has no need of them, but in its embryotic condition it possesses a complete rudimentary set of teeth, which are never cut, but are absorbed during the embryonic life of the organism. Similarly, the bones of the head of the whale are exactly homologous with those of the mammal, although the better to adapt it for aquatic locomotion, the shape of the head more closely resembles the head of a fish. But great and numerous as are the modifications observed, they have all been effected with the least possible divergence from the ancestral type which is compatible with the changed conditions of life. In form and in the functions of certain of its parts, the whale is a fish; in type and structure it is a mammal—a lineal descendant, according to the Evolution theory, of some mammoth terrestrial quadruped of which no trace has as yet been discovered.

Rudimentary Organs.

It were easy to multiply indefinitely examples of such rudimentary organs as those exhibited by the *cetacea*. We see them in the tails of birds, in the gill-arches of reptiles, in the dew-claws of a dog's foot, in the splint-bones of the horse, and in the wings of the ostrich and apteryx. Indeed, there is not a single representative of the higher forms of animal life, which does not exhibit one or more parts in an atrophied or rudimentary condition.

But what is the significance of such aborted and useless organs? What is their origin, and can any reason be assigned for the existence of such functionless parts? The only natural explanation which can be offered, the only rational solution of the difficulty which science can give, is that suggested by the theory of Evolution. According to the theory of descent with adaptive modification, rudimentary organs are remnants of "some generalized primal form," in which they were useful, and had a definite function to perform. By reason of changed conditions of life of the individual, and corresponding disuse of certain parts, great modifications in size and form and function ensued, and thus what was useful and necessary in the ancestral form ceased to be of value in its successor.

"Rudimentary organs," then, to quote from Darwin, "by whatever steps they may have been degraded into their present useless condition, are the record of a former state of things and have been retained solely through the power of inheritance. They may be compared with the letters in a word still retained in the spelling, but become useless in pronunciation, but which serve as a clue for its derivation. On the view of descent with modification, we may conclude that the existence of organs in a rudimentary, imperfect and useless condition, or quite aborted, far from presenting a strange difficulty, as they assuredly do on the old doctrine of creation, might even have been anticipated in accordance with the views here explained."[1]

Considering, then, these wonderful homologies, of which but brief mention has been made, and pondering over the problems raised by the existence of rudimentary or vestigial organs, in such a large portion of the animal kingdom, what inference are we to draw from the point of view of science? "What now," demands Spencer, " can be the meaning of this community of structure among these hundreds of thousands of species filling the air, burrowing in the earth, swimming in the water, creeping among the sea-weed, and having such enormous differences of size, outline and substance, that no community would be suspected between them? Why, under the down-covered body of the moth, and under the hard wing-cases of the beetle, should there be discovered the same number of divisions as in the calcare-

---

[1] "The Origin of Species," vol. II, p. 263.

ous framework of the lobster?"[1] But two answers have been given or can be given — the answer of the special creationist,[2] that all forms of life were created as we find them, and the answer of the evolutionist, who contends that community of structure betokens community of origin.

Argument from Embryology.

The argument from embryology is next in order, but it is of such a character that its full import can be appreciated only by experts in the science on which it is based. The most remarkable characteristic of the argument is that we find in the life-history of the individual, ontogeny, an epitome of its ancestral history, phylogeny. And this characteristic is not only in complete accordance with the theory of organic Evolution, but is, moreover, just what we should expect if the theory be true.

The great embryologist, Von Baer, was the first to call attention to the remarkable agreement

---

[1] "Principles of Biology," vol. I, p. 381.

[2] Replying to the argument that rudimentary organs were specially created by God in order to complete the symmetry and harmony of the organism, Dr. Maisonneuve observes: "Il me semble étrange que l'on soit obligé d'en venir à prêter à Dieu l'idée de faire des trompe-l'œil — passez-moi l'expression—et de supposer que l'Auteur de toutes choses a si mal pris ses mesures, qu'il a été obligé d'en venir à procéder comme un architecte, dont les plans mal conçus ne lui permettent plus de ne placer des fenêtres ou des lucarnes que seulment là où leur existence se trouve justifiée à tous points de vue. Car, vous reconnaitrez sans peine, j'imagine, que l'idéal pour l'architecte, c'est d'arriver à ce que chaque détail du palais qu'il construit présente à la fois toutes les qualités, utilité, agrément et beauté." "Compte Rendu du Congrès Scientifique International des Catholiques," tenu a Paris, 1891, Section d'Anthropologie, p. 59.

between the development of the individual and the development of the ancestral line to which the individual belongs. He showed that in every organism, as well as in its component parts, there is a gradual progress from the simple to the complex, from the general to the special. As Hæckel puts it, "ontogeny is a recapitulation of phylogeny, or, somewhat more explicitly, the series of forms through which the individual organism passes during its progress from the egg-cell to its fully developed state, is a brief compressed reproduction of the long series of forms through which the animal ancestors of that organism, or the ancestral forms of its species, have passed from the earliest period of so-called organic creation down to the present time."[1]

Thus, observation shows, as the theory of Evolution demands, that the germs of all animals are, at the outset, exactly like each other; but in the process of development each germ acquires, first, the differential characteristics of the sub-kingdom to which it belongs; then, successively, the characteristics of its class, order, family, genus, species and race. For example, the highest mammal, man, begins his corporeal existence as a simple germ-cell, in form and appearance like unto an adult amœba, and utterly indistinguishable from the germ-cell of other vertebrates. As development progresses the embryo gradually becomes more and more differentiated. In its earlier stages it may be recognized as the embryo of a vertebrate, but it is impossible to tell to which class of vertebrates it belongs. So far

---

[1] "The Evolution of Man," vol. I, pp. 7–8.

as appearances go, it may be that of a fish, a reptile, a bird, or a mammal. Subsequently it exhibits the characteristics of a bird or a mammal, but the order to which it pertains is disclosed only at a yet later period. At a still later stage, after manifesting the characteristics of the family, genus, and species of which it is a member, it acquires the distinguishing attributes of its race.

Amphioxus and Loligo.

A more striking instance of recapitulation is exhibited in the life-history of the amphioxus, or lancelet, interesting, among other things, for being the lowest known form of vertebrate. Here, as in the case of all other animals, the first stage of development is a simple germ-cell. This soon subdivides, but the subdivisions, instead of separating, as occurs in many of the lower forms of life, remain together and constitute what is known as the *morula* stage, because of the resemblance in shape of the group of cells to a mulberry or blackberry. They subsequently assume a tubular form, in which condition the cells are disposed around a central tube-like cavity, open at each end. This is succeeded by the *blastula* stage, in which the cells are grouped together in the form of a hollow ball, the outer cells being provided with cilia, thus enabling the embryonic amphioxus to move freely in the water. This condition is followed by a series of other changes, until, finally, the animal, after numerous and instructive transformations, acquires the adult form.

Now, the interesting fact in connection with the development of this curious animal is, that the various stages through which it passes can be paralleled by organisms which remain permanently in the conditions in which the amphioxus rests but temporarily.

The simple unicellular monad illustrates the incipient condition or first stage of the amphioxus. The second stage is paralleled by the *pandorina*, which is but a group of cells, each similar to the monad, living together in a common capsule. The third stage is represented by the remarkable *salinella*, which is a tubular structure composed of a single layer of simple, monad-like cells. The fourth condition is found in a common fresh-water *volvox*, which, like the blastula stage, is an organism consisting of a hollow sphere composed of a single layer of simple flagellate cells.

The four organisms just mentioned do not, it is true, constitute a lineal series, a series, namely, in which the more complex is genetically derived from the simpler. But they prove, nevertheless, that all the earlier temporary stages of the amphioxus, the several curious embryonic conditions through which it passes, can be paralleled by organisms which have an actual permanent existence as adults, and which are classed as so many distinct species. This, to students of embryology, is a very remarkable fact, and to the evolutionist, who believes that the history of the individual is but a recapitulation of the history of the race, it is profoundly suggestive and significant and seems to indicate unmistakably the derivative origin of higher from lower forms of life.

But this recapitulation may be observed, not only in the organisms themselves, but likewise in their constituent parts. A striking illustration is afforded in the development of the eye of the *loligo*, one of the higher cephalopoda, as compared with the rudimentary eyes of various species of mollusca. Thus, as the late Mr. Marshall tells us: "In *solen* we find the simplest condition of the molluscan eye, merely a slightly depressed and slightly modified patch of skin, which can only distinguish light from darkness, and in which the sensitive cells are protected by being situated at the bottom of the fold of skin. In *patella* the next stage is found, where the eye forms a pit with a widely-open mouth. This is a distinct advance on the preceding form, for, owing to the increased depth of the pit, the sensory cells are less exposed to accidental injury. The next stage is found in *haliotis*, and consists of the narrowing of the mouth of the pit. This is a simple change but a very important step forward, for, in consequence of the smallness of the aperture, light from any one part of an object can only fall on one particular part of the pit or retina, and so an image, though a dim one, is formed. The next step consists in the formation of a lens at the mouth of the pit, by a deposit of cuticle; this form of eye is found in *fissurella*. The gain here is two-fold, viz., increased protection and increased brightness of the image, for the lens will focus the rays of light more sharply on the retina, and will allow a greater quantity of light, a larger pencil of rays from each part of the object, to reach the corresponding part of the retina. Finally, the formation of the folds of the skin, known as the iris and eyelids, provides for the better protection of the eye, and is a distinct advance on the somewhat clumsy method of withdrawal seen in the snail. This is found in the cephalopoda, such as *loligo*.

"If now we study the actual development of the eye of a cuttle-fish, we find that the eye, although a complicated one, yet passes in its own development through all the above series of stages from the slight depression in the skin, through the stages of the pit with large and small mouth, lens, and finally eyelids, being developed."[1]

In the case of the cuttle-fish, as well as in that of the lancelet, we have transitory stages paralleled by permanent conditions in lower forms of life. The eye of the cuttle-fish, as just stated, not only gives an epitome, as it were, of the history of development of the visual organ in several distinct species of mollusca, but also traces out for us, according to evolutionists, the gradual development of the eyes of the ancestral forms from which the cuttle-fish itself is descended. Each stage indicated in the development of the cuttle-fish's eye, marks a distinct advance on the one preceding, as each stage in the development of the amphioxus exhibits progress from the simple to the more complex, from the less highly to the more highly organized.

It is not, indeed, always possible to adduce such remarkable examples of recapitulation as those just

---

[1] "Lectures on the Darwinian Theory," by Arthur Milnes Marshall, pp. 106 et seq.

instanced, but this is a consequence of the newness of the science of embryology, and of our ignorance of details which shall be disclosed by future research, rather than of the non-existence of such recapitulatory illustrations. Nor is it necessary that we should be able to trace such parallelisms in all cases. The countless numbers which embryologists have already pointed out are abundantly ample for the purpose of the argument in question.

Meaning of Recapitulation.

The marvelous coincidences and analogies we have just considered, and it were easy to add others, suggest questions that clamor for an answer. Why, then, is it, that every complex organism thus epitomizes the history of its ancestors; that in its embryonic life it exhibits a series of forms characteristic of organisms lower in the series of which it is a member? Many of the stages through which it passes in the course of its development have no adaptation either to its embryonic or to its adult condition. Wherefore, then, the reason of the existence of these curious stages?

On the special creation hypothesis they admit of no rational explanation whatever. "What," queries Mr. Lewes, "should we say to an architect who was unable, or being able, was obstinately unwilling to erect a palace, except by first using his materials in the shape of a hut, then pulling it down, and rebuilding them as a cottage, then adding story to story and room to room, not with any reference to the ultimate purposes of the palace, but wholly with reference to the way in which houses were constructed in ancient times? What should we say to the architect who could not directly form a museum out of bricks and mortar, but was forced to begin as if going to build a mansion; and after proceeding some way in this direction, altered his plan into a palace, and that again into a museum? Yet this is the sort of succession on which organisms are constructed." On the theory of Evolution all this recapitulation of ancestral forms, so characteristic of higher organisms, admits of an explanation which is as beautiful as it is consonant with fact and reason. And, from the theistic point of view, it exhibits the Deity creating matter and force, and putting them under the dominion of law. It tells of a God who inaugurates the era of terrestrial life by the creation of one or more simple organisms, unicellular monads, it may be, and causing them, under the action of His Providence, to evolve in the course of time into all the myriad, complicated, specialized and perfect forms which now people the earth. Surely this is a nobler conception of the Creator than that which represents Him as experimenting, as it were, with crude materials, and succeeding, only after numerous attempts, in producing the organism which He is supposed to have had in view from the beginning. To picture the Deity thus working tentatively, is an anthropomorphic view of the Creator, which is as little warranted by Catholic dogma as it is by genuine science. It is rather on a par with the view of those theologians and scientists who fancied fossils to be "rejected models" of creatures subsequently perfected, or tentative and unfinished efforts toward the creation of organisms which were never endowed with vitality because the Creator was not satisfied with His work. This is, certainly, as we shall see in the sequel, not the Augustinian view of creation, and, to those who are familiar with even the elementary facts of embryology, it cannot be the scientific view. From the point of view of embryology the great body of facts make for the theory of Evolution, as against the theory of special creation, and it is not surprising, therefore, to find that those who are most competent to interpret the facts of the case, are disposed to regard the argument from embryology as of itself sufficient to demonstrate the derivation theory of all forms of animal life.

Geographical Distribution of Organisms.

There yet remains another testimony to be considered, and that is the argument based on the distribution of organisms in space and time, or in other words, the argument based on the facts of geographical distribution and geological succession.

One of the most striking facts of natural history is that which regards the marked diversity of the fauna and flora of regions widely separated, or of adjacent regions separated by impassable natural barriers. Thus, the animals and plants of Europe are to a great extent unlike those of America, while those of Africa and Australia are entirely different. Even in passing from one portion of the continent to another, the observant traveler cannot help being impressed with the divers new and strange organisms which are continually presented to his view. The fauna on the opposite sides of mountain chains are often quite unlike, although the conditions of existence may be essentially the same. The animals on the contiguous islands of an archipelago are specifically distinct from one another, and generically different from the animals on the nearest mainland. The marine fauna on the opposite sides of the Isthmus of Panama, although the conditions of existence on the eastern and western shores are appreciably the same, are almost wholly distinct, when, if we considered only their environment, we should expect them to be exactly alike.

Whithersoever we go, we observe that "barriers of any kind, or obstacles to free migration, are related in a close and important manner to the differences between the productions of various regions. We see this in the great difference in nearly all the terrestrial productions of the New and Old Worlds, excepting in the northern parts where the land almost joins, and where, under a slightly different climate, there might have been free migration for the northern temperate forms, as there is now for the strictly Arctic productions. We see the same fact in the great difference between the inhabitants of Australia, Africa and South America under the same latitude; for these countries are almost as much isolated from each other as is possible. On each continent, also, we find the same fact; for on the opposite side of lofty and continuous mountain ranges, of great deserts and even of large rivers, we find different productions; though as mountain chains, deserts, etc., are not as impassable, or likely to have endured so long as the oceans separating continents, the differences are very inferior in degree to those characteristic of distinct continents."[1]

An instructive illustration of the matter under discussion is afforded by Darwin, in his observations on the flora and fauna of the Galapagos Archipelago. This is a group of islands situated between five and six hundred miles west of South America, the constituent islands being separated from one another by straits from twenty to thirty miles in width. "Each separate island of the Galapagos Archipelago," says the great naturalist, "is tenanted, and the fact is a marvelous one, by many distinct species; but these are related to each other in a very much closer manner than to the inhabitants of the American continent, or of any other quarter of the world."[2]

From observations made by naturalists all over the world, it is learned that the foregoing is but one of countless similar instances that might be adduced. Hence the general conclusion reached by the distinguished German savant, Moritz Wagner, that "the limits, within which allied species are found, are determined by impassable natural barriers."

Facts of Geological Succession.

It is only, however, when we come to compare the facts of geographical distribution with those of geological succession, that we are able to appreciate

---
[1] Darwin's "Origin of Species," vol. II, pp. 130–131.
[2] Op. cit., vol. II, p. 190.

the full significance of the observations of Darwin, Wagner and their compeers. It is then found that the distribution of species in space is intimately connected with their succession in time ; that the animals which occur in a determinate locality at present, closely resemble extinct animals which inhabited the same locality in ages long past, and hence the inference the naturalist draws, that existing types in a given area are genetically related to antecedent types of the same area. Thus, the marsupials which now inhabit Australia are allied to their fossil predecessors in the same part of the world. Similarly, the sloths, ant-eaters and armadillos now found in South America, are intimately related to numerous fossil forms which have been brought to light in this part of the Western continent.

Indeed, it is just such facts as these which impelled Darwin and others to conclude, that existing species must have originated by derivation from antecedent species, and that the divers species of any given area are but modified descendants of species long extinct.

"I was so much impressed with these facts," declares Darwin, "that I strongly insisted, in 1839 and 1845, on this 'law of succession of types,' on this wonderful relationship in the same continent, between the dead and the living! Prof. Owen subsequently extended the same generalization to the mammals of the Old World. We have the same law exhibited in his restoration of the extinct and gigantic birds of New Zealand. We see it also in the birds of the caves of Brazil. Mr. Woodward has shown that the same law holds good with sea-shells, but from the wide distribution of most mollusca it is not well displayed by them. Other cases could be added, as the relation between the extinct and living brackish-water shells of the Aralo-Caspian sea."[1]

It is no explanation of the facts of geographical distribution to say that species are specially adapted to the habitats in which they are found; that South America, for instance, is especially fitted for edentates, and Australia for marsupials. "That it is not the suitability of organisms to the areas which they inhabit that has determined their creation upon these areas, is," says Romanes, "conclusively proved by the effects of the artificial transportation of species by man. For in such cases it frequently happens, that the imported species thrives quite as well in its new as in its old home, and indeed often supplants the native species. As the Maoris say: 'As the white man's rat has driven away the native rat, so the European fly has driven away our fly, so the clover kills our fern, and so will the Maori himself disappear before the white man.'"[2]

The Demonstrative Evidence of Evolution.

We come now to what Huxley designates specifically "the demonstrative evidence of Evolution," the evidence based on the lineal succession of several carefully-studied types, and above all, the

---

[1] "The Origin of Species," vol. II, p. 121.
[2] "Scientific Evidence of Organic Evolution," chap. IV.

evidence based on the ancestors of the horse discovered by Marsh and others. So strong, indeed, is this evidence considered, that it has been said that if the theory of Evolution had not existed before, "paleontology would have been compelled to invent it, so clearly are the traces of it to be seen in the study of Tertiary mammalia discovered since 1859."

According to Prof. Huxley, "the primary and direct evidence in favor of Evolution can be furnished only by paleontology." Again he avers that: "The only perfectly safe foundation for the doctrine of Evolution lies in the historical, or rather archæological evidence, which is furnished by fossil remains, that particular organisms have arisen by the gradual modification of their predecessors." He tells, too, that "On the evidence of paleontology, the Evolution of many existing forms of life from their predecessors is no longer a hypothesis, but a historical fact; it is only the nature of the physiological factor to which that Evolution is due which is still open to discussion."[1]

But what about the pedigree of the horse? What about those ancestral equine forms about which so much has been said and written?

The ancestors of the horse, as revealed by the discoveries of Marsh and others, are "*Protohippus* or *hipparion*, which is found in the Pliocene; *miohippus* and *mesohippus*, found in the Miocene; *orohippus* in the Eocene; and *eohippus*, at the base of the Eocene. In the *protohippus* each foot has three well-formed digits; *miohippus*, in addition to this, has a

---

[1] "Encyclopædia Britannica," vol. VIII, p. 751.

rudimentary metacarpal bone of a fourth digit in the fore-foot; in *mesohippus* this rudimentary metacarpal bone is more fully developed; in *orohippus* there are four well-developed digits in the fore-foot, three in the hind-foot; while in *eohippus* five digits are present. Thus, this series of fossil forms furnishes a complete gradation, from the older Tertiary forms with four toes, up to the horse with one toe. These forms differ not only as regards the number of toes, but also in other respects, chiefly in the gradual diminution and loss of independence of the ulna and fibula, and in the gradual elongation of the teeth and increasing complexity of the grinding surfaces."[1]

Another interesting example frequently cited, of transitionary forms, is the fossil, *planorbis*, found in the bed of an old lake near the small village of Steinheim, in Wurtemberg. In the successive strata of this lake bottom occur an immense number of shells of divers forms, and all from a few varieties of one and the same species. In passing from the lowest to the highest layers a great modification of forms is observed, so much so, indeed, that were it not for the countless intermediate forms one should unhesitatingly say that the extreme forms belong, not only to different species, but even to different genera. As it is, however, the gradations are so insensible that the conclusion is almost irresistible

---

[1] "Lectures on the Darwinian Theory," by Dr. A. M. Marshall, p. 67. For an interesting discussion with diagrams, of this remarkable series of ancestral equine forms, see the third of Huxley's "Lectures on Evolution," entitled The Demonstrative Evidence of Evolution.

that the various species observed are, at least in this case, originated by derivation with modifications.[1]

The case just adduced is frequently appealed to by evolutionists, not only because it has been exhaustively studied, but also because it tells so strongly in favor of the theory of derivation.

An equally striking instance, perhaps, is found in the case of another group of mollusca belonging to the *paludina*. At first, the six or eight known gradational forms of this mollusc were reckoned as entirely distinct species. Subsequently, however, numerous connecting forms were discovered, so that now over two hundred varieties are counted. But so gradual are the transitions of one form into another, that shells which otherwise would be considered as belonging to different genera are, by reason of the known connecting links, regarded as constituting but one and the same species.[2]

Similar gradations have been shown by Cope to exist among certain extinct mammalian forms, notably among the species of the generalized family, *oreontitæ*, but it is unnecessary to give further illustrations of this character, as those just instanced are quite sufficient to exhibit the nature and force of the argument which is based on the existence of such gradational forms.

---

[1] Cf. A. Hyatt's "Anniversary Memoir of the Boston Society of Natural History, 1880, on Genesis of Tertiary Species of Planorbis at Steinheim."

[2] Cf. Romanes' "Darwin after Darwin," vol. I, p. 19.

Generalized Types.

Confirmatory of the argument founded on the remarkable series of transitional forms we have just been considering, are those curious extinct animals called by Huxley generalized, and by Dana, comprehensive types; types which by Agassiz were variously designated as combining, connecting, synthetic and prophetic types, and which embrace those strange creatures that embodied the characters of two or more groups at present widely separated from each other. Among these were certain early vertebrates which possessed both fish-like and reptilian characters. At a later geologic epoch there existed other animals, which possessed the characters of reptiles and birds in such a curious combination, that we are yet unable to decide whether they should be called reptilian birds or bird-like reptiles. Among these generalized types there were, in the words of Grant Allen: "Lizards that were almost crows, marsupials that were almost ostriches, insectivores that were almost bats, rodents that were almost monkeys." "Just on the stroke, when they were most needed," declares the same writer, "connecting links turned up in abundance between fish and amphibians, amphibians and reptiles, reptiles and birds, birds and mammals, and all of these together in a perfect network of curious cross-relationships."

Among these generalized forms may be mentioned the *archæopteryx*, the *pterodactyl* and the *compsognathus*. "In the *archæopteryx*," says Huxley, "we have an animal which, to a certain extent, occupies a midway place between a bird and a reptile." The *pterodactyl* was a reptile which was avi-form and capable of flying. The *compsognathus*, like the *archæopteryx*, was intermediate in form between a reptile and a bird, but was probably rather an avian reptile than a reptilian bird.

Again we have such fossil vertebrates as Cuvier's *anoplotherium*, which was intermediate in character between pigs and ruminants; the *palæotherium* which connected together such dissimilar animals as the horse, the tapir, and the rhinoceros. More remarkable still are the generalized types known as the *condylarthra*, the primitive form of which Cope considers the common ancestor of all true mammalia.[1]

And so we might mention other synthetic types brought to light by Gaudry, Rütimeyer, and other paleontologists. It was, indeed, M. Gaudry's researches in Attica, where he discovered an extraordinary number of gradational forms among the higher vertebrates, which convinced him that Evolution is the only theory that is competent to explain the existence of those remarkable connecting types which are every day, thanks to the investigations now conducted throughout the world, becoming more numerous and marvelous. "A few strokes of the pick-axe at the foot of Mount Pentelicus," says the eminent French savant, "have revealed to us the closest connecting links between forms which before seemed very widely separated."

How much closer and more remarkable these links will become with the progress of research, when

---
[1] Cf. "Origin of the Fittest," pp. 343, et seq.

the as yet vast and unexplored regions of the earth shall have yielded up a portion of their fossil treasures, can easily be divined. Already the generalized fossil types which have been discovered, have completely revolutionized all systems of classification which were based on existing specialized forms. For, by tracing the widely separated groups of the present back to past geologic time, we find that the specialized types of our day gradually converge towards, and merge into, the generalized types long since extinct. Species the most diverse gradually approach each other, and eventually unite to form common branches, and these again coalesce in a common trunk.[1]

And this is just what the theory of Evolution demands. For, "If the theory of Evolution be true," says Huxley," it follows that however diverse the different groups of plants and of animals may be, they must all, at one time or other, have been connected by gradational forms; so that, from the highest animals, whatever they may be, down to the lowest speck of protoplasmic matter in which life may be manifested, a series of gradations, leading from one end of the series to the other, either exists or has existed."[2]

---

[1] "Hence," declares Huxley, in his article on Classification in the Encyclopædia Britannica, "it follows that a perfect and final zoölogical classification cannot be made until we know all that is important concerning: 1, the adult structure; 2, the personal development; 3, the ancestral development of animals. It is hardly necessary to observe that our present knowledge, as regards even the first and second heads, is very imperfect; while as respects the third it is utterly fragmentary."

[2] "Lectures on Evolution." Lecture II.

Probability of Evolution.

Such, then, in brief, is the argument in favor of Evolution from classification, morphology, embryology, geographical distribution and geological succession. The argument, as based on any one of these four classes of facts, is strong, and to many, if not most contemporary naturalists, conclusive. But when we consider the joint effect of the argument built on the four classes of facts, and note in detail the perfect harmony, the argument becomes still stronger and, to all appearances, irrefragable. The evidence furnished by one class of facts corroborates and explains those offered by the others, and thus the cumulative force of the testimony, given by all the four classes, renders the theory, to say the least, in the highest degree probable. We may not be prepared to admit that the theory has the force of a demonstration. If it had, organic Evolution would cease to be any longer a matter of scientific inquiry and would at once become a matter of scientific fact.

But although Evolution is but a theory, and not a demonstration, a probability and not a certainty, it nevertheless possesses for the working naturalist a value that can be fully appreciated only by those who have labored in the museum and in the laboratory. "Probability," Bishop Butler tells us, "is the guide of life." It is no less truly the guide of science, and a highly probable theory often contributes as effectually towards the advancement of science and the acquisition of truth as would a demonstrated fact.

From what precedes it is evinced, that Evolution as a theory, to claim no more for it, is in the highest degree probable. It is, in fact, the sole natural explanation of the facts discussed; the sole theory that is in accordance with what Sir William Hamilton calls the law of parsimony; a law which was fully recognized by Fathers and Scholastics when they taught that we should not invoke the action of supernatural causes, when natural agencies are adequate to account for the facts and phenomena observed.

Special Creation and Evolution.

Special creation, as an explanation of the multitudinous forms of life with which the earth teems, and has teemed during long æons past, is but an assumption, and an assumption, too, that has no warrant outside of the individual opinions of certain commentators of Scripture; opinions which, by the very nature of the case, can carry with them no greater weight than would attach to the views of their authors on any other question of natural science. As to Scripture itself, and the teaching of the Fathers and Doctors of the Church, we shall see in the sequel that their testimony is as strongly in favor of derivative creation, Evolution under the Providential guidance of natural causes, as it possibly can be in favor of the old and now almost universally discarded theory of special creations.[1]

---

[1] " En paléontologie," declared the Abbé Guillemet before the International Catholic Scientific Congress at Brussels last year, " les inductions évolutionistes expliquent sans peine par la descendance d'ancêtres communs ces *enchainements* si bien mis

As a theory, Evolution certainly reposes on as firm a foundation as do the atomic theory of matter and undulatory theory of light, or as does Newton's theory of universal gravitation. And as these theories have been of priceless service to the chemist, the physicist and the astronomer, in the study of their respective sciences, so also has Evolution been of untold value to the naturalist, in enabling him to coördinate a vast body of facts, that else were naught but a stupendous chaotic mass. It has proved to him to be an "open sesame" to many of nature's secrets, and like the clue of Ariadne, it has enabled him to find his way out of the bewildering labyrinth in which every true student of nature must pass at least a portion of his existence.

It is said that "a striking corroboration of a scientific theory is furnished when it enables us correctly to *predict* discoveries." Judged by this standard Evolution can compare favorably with the best accredited theories of modern science. It will suffice to refer to but two cases in point, although it were easy to adduce numerous others.

---

en evidence par des savants spiritualistes et chrétiens, tels que D'Omalius d'Halloy et Albert Gaudry, et dont M. de Nadaillac nous a concédé la réalité. Le fixisme, au contraire, en est réduit à invoquer une filiation intellectuelle dans la pensée du Créateur, une sorte d'évolutionisme idéal. On comprend cela pour un architecte humain, qui ne peut pas tirer une cathédrale d'une cathédrale sinon par imitation. Mais celui dont 'les dons sont sans répentance' detruira-t-il sans cesse ce qu'il a créé pour recréer à nouveau ? Ne préférera-t-il pas conserver à ses créatures une vie renouvelée et rajeunie dans une descendance qu'il perfectionnera de génération en génération, récompensant par l'ascension de fils la fidélité des progéniteurs à leur lois naturelles." "Compte Rendu," Section d'Anthropologie, p. 27.

In the first edition of his "Origin of Species" Darwin wrote: "We may thus account even for the distinctness of whole classes from each other—for instance, of birds from all other vertebrated animals, by the belief that many animal forms of life have been utterly lost, through which the early progenitors of birds were formerly connected with the early progenitors of other vertebrate classes."

At the time this prophecy was made there was no positive evidence of the existence of such intercalated forms as Darwin required. Three years later the *archæopteryx* was discovered, meeting completely all the requirements of theory. Subsequent discoveries, notably by Marsh, disclosed other transitional forms which "bridge over the gap between reptiles and birds, in this sense, that they enable us to picture to ourselves forms from which both birds and reptiles as we know them could have sprung."

In his lecture on the Evolution of the horse, in 1876, Prof. Huxley spoke as follows: "Thus, thanks to these important researches [those of Marsh and other paleontologists], it has become evident that so far as our present knowledge extends, the history of the horse type is exactly and precisely that which could have been predicted from a knowledge of the principles of Evolution. And the knowledge we now possess justifies us completely in the anticipation that, when the still lower Eocene deposits, and those which belong to the Cretaceous epoch, have yielded up their remains of ancestral equine animals, we shall find first, a form with four complete toes, and a rudiment of the innermost or first digit in front, with probably a rudiment of the fifth digit in the hind foot; while in still older forms the series of the digits will be more and more complete, until we come to the five-toed animals, in which, if the doctrine of Evolution is well founded, the whole series must have taken its origin."

Only a few months after this declaration, Prof. Marsh unearthed in the Eocene deposits of the West an equine animal, *eohippus*, having four complete toes and a rudimentary one in the front foot, thus making good the first part of the prophecy. As to the remaining part, it is, for men of science, only a question of time until it, too, sees its fulfillment.

But the theory of Evolution enables not only paleontologists, but also morphologists and embryologists, to predict the unseen and unknown. And this, to say no more, is certainly a strong substantiation of its truth. For we can ask no more of a theory than that it accord with the facts it is designed to explain. And the more perfectly the theory harmonizes with the facts observed, the more nearly is it demonstrated, so far as any purely inductive conclusion can be demonstrated.

The theory of organic Evolution may not, as yet, be susceptible of an experimental demonstration—although there are not wanting those who think such a demonstration is forthcoming, if, indeed, it has not already been furnished—but it unquestionably occupies a high rank among the best accredited theories of contemporary science. It seems, even now, to repose on as firm a basis as did the Copernican theory in the days of Galileo and Tycho Brahe. For Evolution, like the heliocentric theory, is in perfect harmony with all the manifold facts which it is designed to integrate and interpret. How long will it be before it passes from a theory to a demonstration? Or, will it ever be demonstrated in such wise as to command the assent of all who are capable of weighing evidence, and discriminating between a scientific fallacy and a legitimate scientific induction? These are questions which only the future can answer. Judging, however, by the progress which has been made during the past half century towards the solution of many of the problems which have been discussed in this chapter, it does not seem unreasonable to express the belief that it is only a question of time, and probably not a very long time, until the theory of organic Evolution shall be as firmly established as is now the Copernican one of the solar system.

CHAPTER VIII.

OBJECTIONS AGAINST EVOLUTION.

Declarations of Anti-Evolutionists.

HAVING considered some of the arguments which are usually adduced in support of Evolution, we may now proceed to examine certain of the objections which are urged against it. But as it would require a large volume for anything approaching a detailed presentation of the reasons advanced for the acceptance of Evolution, so, likewise, would it demand far more space than can here be afforded for even a cursory discussion of the difficulties which anti-evolutionists have raised against a theory which, they contend, is discredited both by sound philosophy and the incontestable facts of science. " The theory is easy," declared De Quatrefages, " but the application is difficult; hence it is that those transformists who have attempted this application have invariably found that their hypotheses have led to conditions which are inadmissible." [1]

---

[1] *Journal des Savants*, May, 1891.

It was in view of the hypothetical character of current evolutionary teachings, especially of natural selection, that Mgr. d'Hulst in referring to them expressed himself in the following forcible and epigrammatic manner: " Le besoin de vivre créant la vie, le besoin d'organes créant les organes, le besoin d'ordre créant l'harmonie." *Le Correspondant*, Dec. 25, 1889.

The distinguished French savant, Dr. Charles Robin, is even more pronounced in his views. Evolution, he asserts, is at best but "a poetical accumulation of probabilities without proofs, of seductive explanations without demonstration."

As to the defenders of the theory of Evolution, they are accused of drawing universal conclusions from particular premises; of mistaking resemblance for blood relationship; of confounding variability with transmutability, and of falsely proclaiming the existence of a genealogical succession where there is nothing more than a hierarchy of organic forms. Anti-evolutionists may not, indeed, deny the possibility of the derivation of higher from lower forms of life; they impugn the reality of such derivation. They love to descant on the dictum of the Scholastics, *a possibili ad actum non valet consecutio*—possibility is far from implying existence. They charge their opponents with making species of what are only races, and confidently challenge them to indicate a single instance in which one species has been changed into another species, either in historic or in geologic time.¹ Species, they insist on it, are Divine

---

[1] A few years ago, in 1888, M. Émile Blanchard, a distinguished naturalist and a member of the French Institute, wrote as follows in the preface to his interesting work, "La Vie des Êtres Animés:" "J'ai souvent déclaré autour de moi que si un investigateur parvenait à faire la démonstration scientifique d'une certaine transformation chez quelques représentants d'un groupe du règne animal, je me tenais à sa disposition pour présenter ce résultat à l'Académie des Sciences, pour affirmer, pour proclamer le triomphe de l'auteur." So far, it seems, no one has accepted his challenge; a challenge made not in the spirit of animosity or party, but solely in the interests of truth. For as yet, the eminent savant contends, the theory of transformism is not supported by a single serious and logical argument. And

and immutable. With Linnæus, they declare species and genera to be the work of nature,[1] and contend that the ingenuity of man is incompetent to produce anything beyond races and varieties.

The spider, they will have it, still spins its web as it did in the time of Aristotle, and the ant collects its store of provisions in precisely the same manner as was its wont in the days of Solomon.

For the sake of brevity, I shall limit myself to the consideration of three of the chief objections urged by anti-evolutionists against the theory of derivation. The first refers to the alleged absence of all evidence regarding the transmutation of

---

hence, he continues, " Plus que jamais je renouvelle mon appel, je déclare ma bonne volonté, assurant que je ne souffrirais en aucune façon de me trouver vaincu. Avant pour me consoler la perspective d'un progrès scientifique dont l'importance serait immense, c'est de toutes les forces de mon âme que je jette cette parole à tous les amis des sciences naturelles: *Montrez-nous une fois l'exemple de la transformation d'une espèce.*"

[1] " Naturæ opus semper est species et genus; culturæ sæpius varietas; artis et naturæ classis et ordo." Elsewhere he writes " Classes and orders are the inventions of science, species the work of nature — Classis et ordo est sapientiæ, species naturæ opus." In his " Philosophia Botanica," § 59, he declares that genera, like species, are primordial creations. " Genus omne est naturale, in primordio tale creatum."

In contradistinction, however, to the above dogmatic statements, Linnæus, as we have already learned, was not averse from the idea that certain closely allied species had a common origin and were the products of extended variation or hybridization. Such species he called " the daughters of time "—temporis filiæ. He seemed also to have a presentiment that the day would come when botanists would regard all the species of the same genera as descended from a common parent " Tot species dici congeneres quot eadem matre sint progenitæ," he writes in vol. VI, p. 12, of the "Amœnitates Academicæ." Nay, more, in this same work, vol. I, p. 70, he suggests that not only species but even genera, may have arisen from hybrids. " Novas species immo et genera, ex copula diversarum specierum in regno vegetabili oriri."

species in times past, whether historic or geologic; the second to the imperfection of the geological record; while the third is based on the infecundity among individuals of different species. All three objections are obvious and popular ones, and they are, it must be admitted, not without their difficulties. Men of science, however, are satisfied that they have met these difficulties, and flatter themselves that they have long since given adequate, if not complete, answers to the three objections mentioned. But the objectors themselves are not so minded. They still persist in asserting that their difficulties remain unexplained, and that their objections have lost little, if any, of their original cogency.

Historical and Archæological Objections.

The first objection, then, is based on certain well-known facts of history, prehistoric archæology, and paleontology.

As to history and archæology we are informed, that all their indications positively negative the contention of evolutionists that there is not the slightest evidence, from the earliest dawn of civilization until the present time, that there has ever been a single instance of the transmutation of any one species, whether plant or animal, into another species. On the contrary, it is averred, all the well-attested facts of history bearing on the subject, make unmistakably for the absolute stability and immutability of species in both the great kingdoms of nature, animal and vegetable.

Regarding animals, the testimony elicited is as interesting as it is apparently conclusive. Thus, a collection of shells has been unearthed in the house of a painter in Pompeii, and all of them, even in their minutest details, are identical with shells of the same species now existing. As Pompeii was buried in ashes A. D. 79, we have, therefore, certain proof that the shells of the species in question have undergone no change during the last eighteen hundred years. The anatomical descriptions given by Galen of the monkeys which he dissected in Alexandria, in the second century of our era, enabled Camper not only to recognize the species to which they belonged, but to affirm that the species had, during the long period elapsed, remained perfectly immutable. Aristotle, who lived in the fourth century B. C., has left us accounts of many marine and terrestrial animals, and so accurate is he in his statements that naturalists are able to assert positively, that the species described have undergone no change during the long centuries which have intervened between the days of the Stagirite and our own.

But the monuments of the Nile valley permit us to extend our observations far beyond the times of Galen and Aristotle. In the numerous paintings, sculptures and bas-reliefs of this marvelous land, we have to hand an astonishing mass of evidence and apparently of such a character as to satisfy the objections of even the most critical and skeptical.

Egyptian Mummies.

The attention of the scientific world was first directed to the value of these monuments in the

OBJECTIONS AGAINST EVOLUTION. 145

beginning of the present century. During the French occupation of Egypt, from 1797 to 1801, the men of science who accompanied the army made a large collection of the embalmed bodies of consecrated animals and sent them home to swell the treasures of the museums of Paris. Some idea of the enthusiasm excited by the reception of these precious remains of an age long past, may be formed from the following passage of an official report regarding them drawn up by Cuvier, Lamarck and Lacépède, professors in the Museum of Natural History.

"It seems," they write, "as if the superstition of the ancient Egyptians had been inspired by nature with a view of transmitting to after ages a monument of her history. That extraordinary and eccentric people, by embalming with so much care brutes which were the objects of their stupid adoration, have left us, in their sacred grottoes, cabinets of zoölogy almost complete. The climate has conspired with the art of embalming to preserve the bodies from corruption, and we can now assure ourselves by our own eyes what was the state of a great number of species three thousand years ago. We can scarcely restrain the transports of our imagination on beholding thus preserved, with their minutest bones, with the smallest portions of their skin, and in every particular most perfectly distinguishable, many an animal, which at Thebes or Memphis, two thousand or three thousand years ago, had its own priests and altars."[1]

---

[1] "Annales du Muséum d'Histoire Naturelle," Tom. I, p. 234.
E.—10

Among the mummies thus collected were those of wild as well as those of domestic animals. "My learned colleague, M. Geoffroy Saint-Hilaire," writes Cuvier in his great work, " Discours sur les Révolutions de la Surface du Globe,"[1] "has collected in the temples of upper and of lower Egypt all the mummies of animals he was able to procure. He has brought back ibises, birds of prey, dogs, monkeys, crocodiles, the head of a bull, all embalmed; and one does not discern any greater difference between them and those we now see, than is observed between human mummies and the skeletons of men of the present day."

Interesting, however, as are the mummified remains of wild animals, those of domestic animals have a greater value in all discussions bearing on the question of transmutation of species. Among the animals frequently embalmed were the dog, the cat and the bull. But since the times when these animals were worshipped on the banks of the Nile, representatives of their species have been transported by man to almost every portion of the Old and New Worlds, and have been exposed to every extreme of climate and to the most diverse conditions of life. And yet, notwithstanding all these great changes of environment, the cat and the dog have undergone little or no mutations, and the bull Apis which was such a special object of worship among the Egyptians, was in no wise different from representatives of the same species now living.

---

[1] P. 132, edition of 1830.

Testimony of the Monuments.

The testimony afforded by mummies is corroborated by that of the monuments; by the paintings, sculptures and bas-reliefs which adorned the temples and tombs of the Pharaohs. Thanks to the researches of Nott, Broca and others, we are now able to assert positively that the greyhound and the terrier of the days of Rameses II., and even of an earlier date, were the same in form and appearance as they are at present, and that, consequently, they have suffered no perceptible change during the last four thousand or more years.[1]

And what holds good for the dog holds good also for other animals which are represented on the monuments of the Nile valley. "I have," says Cuvier, "examined with care the figures of animals and of birds engraved on the numerous obelisks brought from Egypt to ancient Rome. In their *ensemble*, which alone was the object of special attention on the part of the artists, these figures bear a perfect resemblance to species now in existence. Anyone may examine the copies of them given by Kircher and Zoega. Without preserving the defini-

---

[1] There is in Egypt an indigenous type of dog, the *parias*, formerly in a domestic, now in a semi-wild state, which can claim a much greater antiquity than the greyhound or the terrier. It is the image of this dog that constitutes the sole and invariable sign for the word "dog" in all hieroglyphical inscriptions, even the most ancient. This dog, there is reason to believe, existed in a domestic state as early as the time of Mena, of the first dynasty, a date which, according to Brugsch, would carry us back over an interval of more than six thousand years. And yet, despite all the vicissitudes through which they have passed, the parias of to-day, so far as observation can discern, are exactly what they were in the days of Egypt's first ruler.

tion of the original engravings, they nevertheless offer figures which are readily recognizable. Among them one may distinguish the ibis, the vulture, the screech-owl, the falcon, the Egyptian goose, the lapwing, the rail, the asp, the horned viper, the long-eared Egyptian hare and the hippopotamus.[1]

The monuments of Chaldea and Babylonia tell the same story as those of Egypt. On a magnificent bas-relief found among the ruins of Babylon, dating, it is said, from the time of Nabuchodonosor, is depicted the figure of a noble mastiff, which in form, proportions and physiognomy is so like unto that of the finest type of a modern mastiff, that one would say the engraving was made from a photograph of one of our prize exhibition dogs. Similarly, Layard gives us, in his " Nineveh and Babylon," a drawing of a type of dog of which the characteristics are so marked that naturalists have had no difficulty in identifying it with a race still occurring in Thibet.

Evidence From Plants.

What has been said of animals may also be iterated, and with equal truth, of plants both wild and cultivated. There is no certain evidence that even one of them has undergone any specific change since the earliest dawn of history. More than this. as far back even as paleobotany will serve as a guide, we are unable to point to a single well-attested instance of transmutation in a single species of plant.

---

[1] Op. cit.

Thus, the woods used in mediæval buildings, as well as those found in the buried ruins of British and Roman villages, differ in no appreciable feature from existing woods. Again, chestnuts, almonds and other fruits found in the shop of a fruit-dealer in Herculaneum, under the lava deposits made eighteen centuries ago, are identical with those still grown in the vicinity of Vesuvius.

But it is Egypt which supplies us with the best preserved vegetable, as it has furnished the best animal specimens of an ancient date. Recent explorations, particularly in the Nileland, have put us in possession of materials which are far better for purposes of comparison than anything which had been previously known. "And happily," says Mr. Carruthers, "the examination of these materials has been made by a botanist who is thoroughly acquainted with the existing flora of Egypt, for Dr. Schweinfurth has been a quarter of a century exploring the plants of the Nile valley. The plant remains were included within the mummy-wrappings, and being thus hermetically sealed, have been preserved with scarcely any change. By placing the plants in warm water, Dr. Schweinfurth has succeeded in preparing a series of specimens, gathered four thousand years ago, which are as satisfactory for the purposes of science as any collected at the present day. These specimens, consequently, supply means for the closest examination and comparison with their living representatives. The colors of the flowers are still present, even the most evanescent, such as the violet of the larkspur and the knapweed, and the scarlet of the poppy; the chlorophyll remains in the leaves, and the sugar in the pulp of the raisins. Dr. Schweinfurth has determined no less than fifty-nine species, some of which are represented by the fruits employed as offerings to the dead, others by flowers and leaves made into garlands, and the remainder by branches on which the body was placed and which were inclosed within the wrappings." [1]

Among the fruits used as votive offerings, dates, figs and palm fruits are common, and are identical with those which are still seen in the markets of Egypt. Branches of the sycamore, one of the sacred trees of Egypt, which had been used for the bier of a mummy belonging to the twelfth dynasty, a thousand years B.C., "were moistened and laid out by Dr. Schweinfurth, equaling," he says, "the best specimens of this plant in our herbaria, and consequently permitting the most exact comparison with living sycamores, from which they differ in no respect."

Very large quantities of linseed, found in tombs three thousand and four thousand years old, differ in nowise from the linseed still cultivated in the Nile valley. And from the seeds examined it has also been evinced, that the weeds which infest the cultivated fields of today were not absent from the

---

[1] See opening address before the Biological Section of the British Association for the Advancement of Science, as reported in *Nature*, Sept. 9, 1886. Mr. Carruthers is recognized as one of the most eminent of contemporary English botanists, and hence, his words in the matter under discussion have special weight.

I have myself examined Dr. Schweinfurth's wonderful collections in Cairo, and can testify that Mr. Carruthers' account of them is in no way exaggerated.

gardens and plantations of the Pharaohs. The spiny medick and the charlock, for instance, were as much of a pest to the growers of barley and flax during the age of the pyramid-builders, as they are to the fellahin of the last quarter of the nineteenth century.

"It is difficult," continues Mr. Carruthers, "without the actual inspection of the specimens of plants employed as garlands, which have been prepared by Dr. Schweinfurth, to realize the wonderful condition of preservation in which they are. The color of the petals of *papaver rheas*, and the occasional presence of the dark patch at their bases, present the same peculiarities as are still to be found in this species growing in Egyptian fields. The petals of the larkspur not only retain their reddish violet color, but present the peculiar markings which are still found in the living plant. A garland composed of wild celery and small flowers of the blue lotus, fastened together by fibers of papyrus, was found on a mummy of the twelfth dynasty, about three thousand years old. The leaves, flowers and fruits of the wild celery have been examined with the greatest care by Dr. Schweinfurth, who has demonstrated in the clearest manner their absolute identity with the indigenous form of this species now abundant in most places in Egypt. The same may be said of the other plants used as garlands, including two species of lichens."

Nor is this all. The evidence afforded by archæology and paleobotany is as direct and as unequivocal as that of history. The cereals cultivated in prehistoric times, during the Roman occupation of Britain, during the times of the mound-builders in the Mississippi valley, and during the reign of the Incas in Peru, were specifically the same and of as good quality as those harvested by the scientific farmer of to-day.

And yet more. We may even go so far back as the Glacial and pre-Glacial periods—periods so remote that, according to the calculations of Lyell, Ramsay and others, they antedate our own era by fully two hundred and fifty thousand years—and we fail to find from an examination of the vegetable remains of the time, that there has been any transition from one species to another. Scores of trees and plants are known to have existed during pre-Glacial times, which were in every respect, even in the venation of the leaf, identical with their living representatives of the present day. And yet, it is urged by anti-transmutationists, this is not what one should expect if the teachings of Evolution be true. For as Mr. Carruthers pertinently observes: "The various physical conditions which necessarily affected these species, in their diffusion over such large areas of the earth's surface, in the course of, say, two hundred and fifty thousand years, should have led to the production of many varieties, but the uniform testimony of the remains of this considerable pre-Glacial flora, as far as the materials admit of a comparison, is that no appreciable change has taken place."

Views of Agassiz, Barrande and Others.

One of the favorite arguments of Professor Louis Agassiz against the transmutation of species, was, as is well known, based on the observed permanence of divers species of the marine forms which contributed towards the production of the coral reefs of Florida. In his charming work, "Methods of Study in Natural History,"[1] the illustrious Swiss savant declares that "upon the lowest calculation, based upon the facts thus far ascertained as to their growth, we cannot suppose that less than seventy thousand years have elapsed since the coral reefs already known to exist in Florida began to grow." And as there is reason to believe that the entire peninsula of Florida is formed " of successive concentric reefs, we must," the same authority asserts, "believe that hundreds of thousands of years have elapsed since its formation began."

Continuing, he writes: "So much for the duration of the reefs themselves. What, now, do they tell us, of the permanence of the species of which they were formed? In these seventy thousand years has there been any change in the corals living in the Gulf of Mexico? I answer, most emphatically, *No*. Astræans, porites, mæandrinas, and madrepores were represented by exactly the same species seventy thousand years ago as they are now. Were we to classify the Florida corals from the reefs of the interior, the result would correspond exactly to a classification founded upon the living corals of the outer reefs to-day. Every species, in short, that lives upon the present reef is found in the more ancient one. They all belong to our own geological period, and we cannot, upon the

[1] Chap. XII.

evidence before us, estimate its duration at less than seventy thousand years, during which time we have no evidence of any change in species, but, on the contrary, the strongest proof of the absolute permanence of those species whose past history we have been able to trace."

But strong as is the evidence just adduced, against the mutability of species, that based on the investigation of the eminent French paleontologist, Joachim Barrande, is, so we are told, even more conclusive, and that for the reason that it extends over a vastly longer period of time. Barrande was undoubtedly one of the most careful and most successful inquirers into the life-history of certain periods of the remote, geologic past, whom the world has yet known. In Bohemia he had an exceptionally favorable area for the study of the fossiliferous strata of the Silurian Age, and his masterly work, "Système Silurien de la Bohème," the most complete production of the kind in existence, will ever remain a noble monument to his untiring industry and his incomparable genius for research in the domain of the earlier forms of terrestrial life.

The conclusion which this eminent man of science arrives at, after long years of patient investigation, and after the most careful examination of many thousands of specimens, is, to quote his own words, as follows: "Among the three hundred and fifty species (of trilobites) of Bohemia, there is not a single one which can be considered as having produced by its variations a new specific form, distinct and permanent. Thus, the traces of transformation by way of filiation, are completely imperceptible among the trilobites of the Silurian Age in Bohemia."[1]

Concerning cephalopods, of which more than a thousand distinct forms are described, M. Barrande declares, that there is not one among them, however long the species may have lasted, which, during the different stages of its existence, presents more marked differences than do those which coëxist on the same horizon; that not a single one of the countless cephalopods which were examined by him, can be considered as even the first step towards transformation, for all these forms disappear simultaneously, without any recognizable posterity.

---

[1] In view of the importance of M. Barrande's testimony, I here present his conclusions in full, as found in his work entitled, "Défense des Colonies," p. 155.

"1. Les Trilobites de Bohème qui offrent dans leurs formes la trace de quelques variations sont au nombre de 10. Comme nous connaissons aujourd'hui 350 espèces de cette tribu, dans notre bassin, on voit qu'il en reste environ 340 qui paraissent conserver une forme invariable, pendant toute la durée de leur existence.

"2. Les variations signalées dans les espèces qui ont joui de la plus grande longévité, sont relatives seulement aux dimensions du corps, à la grosseur des yeux, au nombre correspondant des lentilles, au nombre des articulations visibles du pygidium, et au nombre des pointes ornementales.

"3. Ces variations ne sont pas permanentes, mais *purement temporaires*, et, dans la plupart des cas, nous avons constaté *le retour des derniers représentants de l'espèce à la forme typique ou primitive*. Ainsi ces variations ne semblent être que des *oscillations transitoires*. Elles se manifestent quelquefois parmi des individus contemporains, et, par conséquent, sans l'influence des ages géologiques.

"4. Parmi les 350 espèces de Bohème, il n'en existe aucune qui puisse être considérée comme ayant produit, par ses variations, une nouvelle forme spécifique, distincte et permanente. Ainsi, les traces de la transformation, par voie de filiation, sont conplètement imperceptibles parmi les trilobites du Silurien de Bohème."

Davidson's exhaustive researches on the brachiopods of the English formations, lead him to the same conclusions as those arrived at by Barrande after his prolonged studies of the trilobites and cephalopods of Bohemia, viz., that there is not the slightest trace of any tendency towards development on the part of the species examined.

Similar testimony is given by Mr. Williamson regarding fossil plants. After forty years of patient study of the vegetable remains of different geological ages, he does not hesitate to affirm that the ferns whose imprints are of such frequent occurrence in certain strata of the Carboniferous Age, have retained their essential characteristics until the present time. For, if we compare those which now abound in our forests with those which gave beauty to the landscape in Paleozoic time, we find that they have neither advanced nor retrograded.

It were easy to add to the list of persistent types of animals and plants, of those, namely, which endured unchanged during long geologic periods. I might speak of the terebratulæ and globigerinæ which take us back to the Cretaceous Period; of certain types of scorpions which flourished during the Carboniferous Age and which are scarcely distinguishable from modern scorpions; of the lingulæ and lingulellæ which, appearing in the lower Silurian rocks, have persisted practically unchanged through all the grand climacterics of the world.[1]

---

[1] For able and dignified discussions of the questions here considered, see "Paléontologie et Darwinisme," by the eminent Belgian geologist, Charles de la Vallée Poussin, in the "Revue

OBJECTIONS AGAINST EVOLUTION. 157

In the preceding pages I have presented fully, and somewhat in detail, one of the stock arguments of anti-evolutionists against the transmutation of species. I have allowed the ablest and most noted opponents of the Evolution theory to present their objection in their own words, and have endeavored to select what have always been considered the most telling arguments against transpeciation. What, now, is the answer to the objection, or is any answer possible? What explanation can be given of facts which seem so utterly irreconcilable with the cardinal principles of Evolution, and so antagonistic to the fundamental tenets of the leading exponents of transformism.

Misapprehension of the Nature of Evolution and Answer to Objections.

The objection, as presented, rests on a total misapprehension of the nature of Evolution. It assumes that when an animal or a vegetable form once comes into existence, it must necessarily and continuously undergo progressive modifications. It assumes, too, that such modifications as may occur, must take place at the same rate in one form of life as in another. Both these postulates are equally unwarranted, for they are both totally at variance with Evolution as understood by its founders and approved spokesmen.

An answer, however, to the objection, was indicated nearly a century ago by Cuvier's great con-

---

de Questions Scientifiques" for January, 1877, and "Le Transformisme et la Discussion Libre," in the same review for January and April, 1889, by De. Kirwan, who writes under the pseudonym of Jean d' Estienne.

temporary, Lamarck. Replying to the argument based on the unchanged condition of the fauna and flora of Egypt, he observed that "the animals and plants referred to had not experienced any modification in their specific characters, because the climate, soil and other conditions of life had not varied in the interval. But if," he continued, "the physical geography, temperature and other natural conditions of Egypt, had altered as much as we know they have done in many countries in the course of geological periods, the same animals and plants would have deviated from their pristine types so widely as to rank as new and distinct species."[1]

This answer of Lamarck's is, with some modifications, the answer which is now given by men of science to the objection under consideration. Whenever the environment remains unchanged, where the conditions of life are always identical, the fauna and flora of a given area may persist without any specific mutations for an indefinite period of time. Regarding Egypt it is notorious, that its climate and soil are to-day precisely what they were during the reign of the first of the Pharaohs, and precisely what they were when the bull Apis was led in solemn procession to the temples of Memphis and Heliopolis. As to other examples of animals and plants which have resisted specific change, not only during thousands, but also millions of years, the same answer may be given. The environment may have been modified more or less, but not sufficiently to effect

---

[1] "Philosophie Zoölogique," pp. 70, et seq.

transmutation of the species named. For it must be borne in mind, that all species are not equally susceptible of change in consequence of mutations of climate and physical geography. Some are more stable and more cosmopolitan than others, and hence are capable of accommodating themselves within certain limits to quite considerable changes in surrounding conditions, without exhibiting the slightest indications of specific transmutations.

Then, too, we have "elastic types," those types, namely, which as M. Gaudry tells us, have the power of undergoing greater or less modifications and of returning sooner or later to their original condition. The rhynconella is a case in point. When the ocean bed is in anywise modified, rhynconella exhibits a corresponding change; when the ocean returns to its original state, rhynconella reverts to its pristine condition. Thus, in virtue of its elasticity, of its facility of accommodating itself to changes of environment, this marvelous brachiopod has been able to pass unscathed through mutations and catastrophes innumerable.

Again, it may be observed, that the changes of environment are not always so great as they are sometimes imagined to be. Thus, the conditions of life in a given area of the ocean may remain practically unchanged for long geological periods. The temperature and depth of the water might easily remain constant for untold æons, and, in such an event, there is no reason why the ocean fauna should not endure without variation for an indefinite time.

Even in the case of the vegetable organisms which Mr. Carruthers puts in evidence, there is reason to believe that the variations in climate to which they have been subject, have been far less than is usually thought. We can say of these what Darwin asserts of certain Arctic forms, that "they will not have been exposed to any great diversity of temperature and, as they all migrated in a body together, their mutual relations will not have been much disturbed."[1] Where, however, Arctic species have been left stranded on Alpine areas by the retreat of glaciation, and where the species thus isolated have been subsequently exposed to differences of climate, and to the influences of foreign plants and insects, we would expect to discover evidences of transmutation, to find the stranded species to differ, not only from their parent Arctic forms, but to differ also from those of the same origin occurring on neighboring mountain ranges. And this is what Darwin tells us is the fact, "for if," he says, "we compare the present Alpine plants and animals of the several great European mountain ranges, one with another, though many of the species remain identically the same, some exist as varieties, some as doubtful forms or sub-species, and some as distinct, yet closely allied species, representing each other on the several ranges."[2]

In the instance just quoted, as in countless others that might be adduced, we have an illustration of a phenomenon with which all naturalists are

---
[1] "The Origin of Species," vol. II, p. 154.
[2] Op. cit. vol. II, p. 155.

familiar, to-wit, that some types, both of animals and plants, are more plastic than others. Those which are the most plastic most readily undergo specific transformation, whilst, on the contrary, those which are rigid experience little or no change, even when exposed to very considerable mutations of environment.

Existence and Cause of Variations.

Of the existence of variations, numerous and important, there can then be no reasonable doubt. This fact, long known, is daily corroborated by evidence which cannot be gainsaid. But the existence of variations must not be confounded with the cause which originates them, for this, as yet, is shrouded in mystery. Huxley admits this without hesitation and refers to it as follows: "The cause of the production of variations is a matter not at all properly understood at present. Whether variation depends upon some intricate machinery, if I may use the phrase, of the living organism itself, or whether it arises through the influence of conditions upon that form, is not certain, and the question for the present may be left open. But the important point is that, granting the existence of the tendency to the production of variations, then, whether the variations which are produced shall survive and supplant the parent, or whether the parent form shall survive and supplant the variations, is a matter which depends entirely on those conditions which give rise to the struggle for existence. If the surrounding conditions are such that the parent form is more competent to deal with them, and flourish in them, than the derived forms, then in the struggle for existence the parent form will maintain itself and the derived forms will be exterminated. But if, on the contrary, the conditions are such as to be more favorable to a derived than to a parent form, the parent form will be extirpated and the derived form will take its place. In the first place there will be no progression, no change of structure, through any imaginable series of ages; and in the second place there will be modification and change of form." [1]

Paucity of Transitional Forms.

The second objection, like the preceding, is an obvious one, and at first sight equally plausible. It is based on the paucity of transitional forms, or "missing links," in the various sedimentary strata of the earth's crust. At first blush the objection seems to be fatal to the theory of Evolution, as it certainly would be fatal, if well founded, to the theory of natural selection, which supposes that species have advanced from lower to higher forms by infinitesimal increments. So much importance, indeed, does Darwin attach to this objection, that he devotes a whole chapter in his "Origin of Species" to its solution. And although he frankly admits that the geological record, so far as at present known, still opposes insuperable difficulties to his theory of natural selection, it does not follow, as we shall see farther on, that such difficulties can validly be urged

---

[1] "Science and Hebrew Tradition," pp. 83 and 84.

against the general theory of organic Evolution, as distinguished from Evolution through natural selection.

In the first place it is to be observed, that transitional forms are the first to become extinct in the struggle for existence; for it is well known that competition is more marked and devastating among intermediate or intercalated forms, than among forms which are more widely divergent. Thus, in philology it is remarked, that among a large number of dialects, certain closely allied ones die out, whilst others, more widely differentiated, become the dominant forms of speech. The means perish, while the extremes wax strong and end by attaining supremacy. Hence, of the countless dialects which in Italy, France and Spain had their origin in the Latin tongue, but three have attained to the dignity of a dominant language, and of being the vehicle of a national literature. These three are what are now known as the Italian, French and Spanish languages, the competing dialects having been worsted in the struggle for existence, and condemned to an earlier or later extinction.

A process quite analogous to this goes on among the divers forms of animated nature, the means showing themselves the weaker, and the extremes exhibiting themselves the stronger in the contest for supremacy. Commenting on this fact, Darwin writes as follows: "As the species of the same genus usually have, though by no means invariably, much similarity in habits and constitution, and always in structure, the struggle will generally be more severe between them, if they come into competition with each other, than between the species of distinct genera. We see this in the recent extension over the United States, of one species of swallow, having caused the decrease of another species. The recent increase of the missel-thrush in parts of Scotland has caused the decrease of the song-thrush. How frequently we hear of one species of rat taking the place of another species under the most different climates! In Russia, the small, Asiatic cockroach has everywhere driven before it its great congener. In Australia, the imported hive-bee is rapidly exterminating the small, stingless, native bee. One species of charlock has been known to supplant another species; and so in other cases. We can dimly see why competition should be most severe between allied forms which fill nearly the same place in the economy of nature; but probably in no one case could we precisely say why one species had been victorious over another in the great battle of life."[1]

Variations and the Formation of Fossiliferous Deposits.

Then again, it must be observed that it is not probable that variation has been going on at a uniform rate during the long course of the life-history of the earth. On the contrary, it is more likely that long periods of stability have alternated with brief periods of disturbance of greater or less extent. During the former periods specific forms would experience comparatively little change, whereas, during the latter, variations would rapidly accumulate and be strongly

---

[1] "The Origin of Species," vol. I, pp. 93 and 94.

accentuated. Such being the case, the number of gradational forms will be far less numerous than the forms contained in the species which persist with little or no modifications during long cycles of time.

Furthermore, it is now generally admitted that the strata which are richest in fossils were usually, if not always, deposited during eras which were least favorable for the development of transitional forms, that is, during eras when variation and extinction were least rapid. On the theory that natural selection has been the dominant factor in Evolution; on the theory, namely, that progress has resulted solely, or at least chiefly, in consequence of the accumulation of infinitesimal increments, a condition of things must have existed during the formation of fossiliferous strata, which it is certain could have obtained only at extremely rare intervals. For, as Darwin points out: " In order to get a perfect gradation between two forms in the upper and lower parts of the same formation, the deposit must have gone on continuously accumulating during a long period sufficient for the slow process of modification; hence the deposit must be a very thick one, and the species undergoing change must have lived in the same districts throughout the whole time. But we have seen that a thick formation, fossiliferous throughout its entire thickness, can accumulate only during a period of subsidence; and to keep the depth approximately the same, which is necessary that the same marine species may live on the same space, the supply of sediment must nearly counterbalance the amount of subsidence. But this same movement of subsidence will tend to submerge the area whence the sediment is derived, and thus diminish the supply whilst the downward movement continues. In fact, this nearly exact balancing between the supply of sediment and the amount of subsidence is probably a rare contingency; for, it has been observed by more than one paleontologist, that very thick deposits are generally barren of organic remains, except near their upper or lower limits."[1]

The foregoing are but a few of the reasons that might be assigned for the paucity of intermediate forms which characterizes the earth's fossil-bearing strata. When we come to reflect on the matter, however, the wonder is not that there is such a small number of gradational forms, but rather that there are any fossils at all. For everything has tended to render their formation impossible; and in the comparatively few instances in which circumstances have been favorable to the fossilization of animal or vegetable forms, a variety of circumstances has intervened to compass their destruction. Such being the case, therefore, we should be surprised, not at the existence of such extensive tracts that are utterly devoid of any traces of organic life, but rather at the fact that there are so many formations in different parts of the world which contain such a wealth of fossil remains.

For let us consider for a moment under what adverse conditions the slight vestiges of the fauna and flora of the ancient world have been preserved; what are a few of the agents of destruction, how

---

[1] Op. cit., vol. II, pp. 68 and 69.

continuous their action, and how inevitable their effect. We shall then learn that evolutionists have reason for insisting so strongly on the imperfection of the geological record, and for appealing to the results of future research and discovery for a confirmation of certain facts of their theory, and for an explanation of certain difficulties which, as matters now stand, are admittedly insoluble.

As to the formation of fossils, it is, as is well known, only the hard portions of organisms which are ever fossilized. But even these, as well as the softer parts, soon suffer disintegration unless in some way screened from sub-ærial agencies competent to decompose them, and unless they are protected from the solvent action of salt water, or fresh water holding carbonic acid in solution.

Again, as Darwin remarks, "we probably take a quite erroneous view, when we assume that the sediment is being deposited over nearly the whole bed of the sea at a rate sufficiently thick to embed and preserve fossil remains. Throughout an enormously large proportion of the ocean, the bright blue tint of the water bespeaks its purity. The many cases on record of a formation conformably covered, after an immense interval of time, by another and later formation, without the underlying bed having suffered in the interval any wear and tear, seem explicable only on the view of the bottom of the sea not rarely lying for ages in an unaltered condition."[1] "In regard to the mammiferous remains," the same authority continues, "a glance at

[1] Op. cit., vol. II, p. 58.

the historical table published in Lyell's 'Manual' will bring home the truth, how accidental and rare is their preservation, far better than pages of detail. Nor is their rarity surprising when we consider how large a proportion of the bones of Tertiary mammals have been discovered either in caves or in lacustrine deposits; and that not a cave or true lacustrine bed is known belonging to the age of our secondary or Palæozoic formations."[1]

But if the formation of fossils be rare and something wholly exceptional, when we consider the myriad organisms which are never fossilized; if shells and bones are always disintegrated unless adequately protected from the countless unfavorable and destructive agencies to which they are exposed, their preservation, after having been formed, is something which, when the facts of the case are known, must appear even more remarkable.

Romanes on Difficulties Attending Preservation of Fossils.

Mr. George Romanes, Darwin's favorite and most ardent disciple, has so accurately and picturesquely described the divers agencies which contribute to the annihilation of fossil forms, that I need make no apology for quoting him at length.

"But of even more importance," he writes, "than this difficulty of making fossils in the first instance, is the difficulty of preserving them when they are made. The vast majority of fossils have been formed under water, and a large proportional number of these, whether the animals were marine, ter-

---

[1] Ibid, pp. 59 and 60.

restrial, or inhabitants of fresh water, have been formed in sedimentary deposits either of sand, gravel or other porous material. Now, where such deposits have been afterwards raised into the air for any considerable time, and this has been more or less the case with all deposits which are available for exploration, their fossiliferous contents will have been, as a general rule, dissolved by the percolation of rain-water charged with carbonic acid. Similarly, sea-water has recently been found to be a surprisingly strong solvent of calcareous material; hence, Saturn-like, the ocean destroys its own progeny as far as shells and bones of all kinds are concerned, and this to an extent of which we have probably no adequate conception.

"Of still greater destructive influence, however, than these solvent agencies in earth and sea, are the erosive agencies of both. Anyone who watches the pounding of the waves upon the shore; who then observes the effect of it upon the rocks broken into shingle, and on the shingle reduced to sand; who, looking behind him at the cliffs, sees there evidence of the advance of this all-pulverizing power—an advance so gradual that no yard of it is accomplished until within that yard the 'white teeth' have eaten well into the 'bowels of the earth;' who then reflects that this process is going on simultaneously over hundreds of thousands of miles of coast-lines throughout the world; and who finally extends his mental vision from space to time, by trying dimly to imagine what this ever-roaring monster must have consumed during the hundreds of millions of years that slowly rising and slowly sinking continents have exposed their whole areas to her jaws; whoever thus observes and thus reflects must be a dull man, if he does not begin to feel that in the presence of such a destroyer as this we have no reason to wonder at a frequent silence in the testimony of the rocks.

"But although the erosive agency of the sea is thus so inconceivably great, it is positively small as compared with erosive agencies on land. The constant action of rain, wind and running water, in wearing down the surfaces of all lands into 'the dust of continents to be;' the disintegrating effects on all but the hardest rocks of winter frosts alternating with summer heats; the grinding power of ice in periods of glaciation, and last, but not least, the wholesale melting up of sedimentary formations whenever these have sunk any considerable distance beneath the earth's surface — all these agencies taken together constitute so prodigious a sum of energies, combined through immeasurable ages in their common work of destruction, that when we try to realize what it must amount to, we can scarcely fail to wonder, not that the geological record is highly imperfect, but that so much of the record has survived as we find to have been the case. And, if we add to these erosive and solvent agencies on land the erosive and solvent agencies of the sea, we almost begin to wonder that anything deserving the name of geological record is in existence at all."[1]

---

[1] "Darwin and After Darwin," vol. I, pp. 423-425. For an exhaustive discussion of the disintegrating and destructive ef-

That the effects of denudation are not exaggerated in the preceding quotation, is manifest from a number of facts to which Darwin has directed attention, and of which he was the first to realize the true import in their bearings on Evolution. In Europe, but especially in North and in South America, there are immense areas, embracing many thousands of square miles, in which the surface rocks are entirely granitic or metamorphic. This implies that denudation has here taken place on a tremendous scale. And the utter absence of fossils in such rocks shows conclusively how completely the work of destruction was accomplished, so completely, indeed, that of the animal and vegetable remains which must have originally existed in these portions of the earth not a vestige now remains. In view of such facts Darwin considers it "quite probable, that in some parts of the world whole formations have been completely denuded, with not a wreck left behind."

Small Percentage of Fossil Forms.

But this is not all. We have positive evidence that during certain periods many species existed in countless numbers, although, so far, not a fragment of bone has been found within the area in which they once flourished. The strange, bird-like forms that once inhabited the Connecticut valley are instances in point. Although more than a score of

---

fects of aqueous, glacial and igneous agencies, the reader may consult with profit the pages of Lyell's admirable "Principles of Geology."

species of this character had their habitat in the district, and in its vicinity, the only tangible evidences which we yet possess that they ever existed, are the tracks and foot-prints which they left in the shales and sandstones of Connecticut and New Jersey.

In other cases, again, all that has so far been discovered of what, in their time, were manifestly important species, is a single tooth, or a single bone, or even only a small fragment of bone. That future research will disclose remains of these species, in larger quantities or in greater numbers, there is reason to believe, but however rich the finds may be, it will always be true that the fossils which have been preserved are but an insignificant portion of those which were actually formed, and that the remains of organisms which were fossilized were but an infinitesimal part of those which were completely destroyed before fossilization was possible.

Darwin's observations on sessile cirripeds corroborate in the most striking manner what has been stated in the preceding paragraphs, and show how a large group of animals, represented by an extraordinary number of individuals all over the world, in every latitude and "inhabiting various zones of depths from the upper tidal limit to fifty fathoms," may fail to leave even a trace of their existence during long geological periods. "Not long ago, paleontologists maintained that the whole class of birds came suddenly into existence during the Eocene Period; but now we know, on the authority of Prof. Owen, that a bird certainly lived during the Upper Greensand; and still more recently that strange bird, the archæopteryx, with a long lizard-like tail bearing a pair of feathers on each joint, and with its wings furnished with two free claws, has been discovered in the Oölitic slates of Solenhofen. Hardly any recent discovery shows more forcibly than this how little we as yet know of the former inhabitants of the world."[1]

Another important fact we should not lose sight of is, that as yet but a comparatively small portion of the earth has been explored by geologists. The formations of the earth in North America are fairly well known, but even in these portions of the world there is still much to be learned. As to South America, Asia, Africa, Australia, they are for the most part *terræ incognitæ* to the paleontologist. Such being the case it were foolish in the extreme to dogmatize on the sequence of organic forms in past geologic time, or to attempt to base an argument against Evolution on the absence of certain transitional types and on the consequent imperfection of the record so far at our disposal.

It has been estimated that not so much as one per cent., of the countless species of animals which have flourished since the first dawn of life, has left the slightest trace of its past existence. Marine forms, as might be expected, are better represented than land forms. Indeed there are not wanting those who assert, that of terrestrial types not more than one species in a thousand is represented by known fossils.

---
[1] "The Origin of Species," vol. II, pp. 79 and 80.

Extraordinary Intercalary Forms.

But in spite of the rarity of fossils in comparison with the almost infinite number of individuals represented; in spite of the paucity of fossil species as compared with the total number which must have existed since the advent of life; in spite of the limited area of the earth which has so far been explored by the paleontologist, there are, as indicated in the preceding chapter, many examples of intercalary forms of the most extraordinary character. And all the instances adduced, be it remembered, constitute so much positive evidence in behalf of the theory of organic Evolution. The absence of transitional varieties in certain formations is, at best, but negative evidence, and such evidence is of but little value, or rather it is of no value, in face of all the positive evidence which recent research has brought to light. Thanks to the discoveries of Gaudry, Marsh, Cope and others, the number of intermediate forms has, within the past few years, been wonderfully augmented, and there is every reason to believe that future exploration will, in like manner, contribute towards filling up many of the lacunæ which at present are pointed to as difficulties in the way of yielding rational assent to the current theory of transformism.

"Indeed, it may be asserted," Prof. Fiske truthfully observes, "as one of the most significant truths of paleontology, that extinct forms are almost always intercalary between forms now existing. Not only species, genera and families, but even orders of contemporary animals, apparently quite distinct, are now and then fused together by the discovery of extinct intermediary forms. In Cuvier's time, horse, tapir, pig and rhinoceros were ranked as a distinct order from cow, sheep, deer, buffalo and camel. But so many transitional forms have been found in Tertiary strata, that pachyderms and ruminants are now united in a single order. By numerous connecting links the pig is now seen to be closely united with the camel and the antelope. Similar results relating to the proboscidians, the hyena family of carnivora, the apes, the horse and the rhinoceros, have been obtained from the exploration of a single locality near Mount Pentelicus in Greece. Among more than seventy species there discovered, the gradational arrangement of forms was so strongly marked, that the great paleontologist, M. Gaudry, became a convert to Mr. Darwin's theory in the course of the search."[1] Indeed, so much was M. Gaudry, who renews in our own day the triumphs of Cuvier in paleontology, impressed by the fossil remains of Greece and the transitional forms of other lands, that he did not hesitate thirty years ago to declare, that " the more we advance and fill up the gaps, the more we feel persuaded that the remaining voids exist more in our knowledge than in nature. A few blows of the pick-axe at the foot of the Pyrenees, of the Himalayas, of Mount Pentelicus; a few diggings in the sand-pits of Eppelsheim or in the Mauvaises Terres of Nebraska, have revealed to us the closest connecting links

[1] "Cosmic Philosophy," vol. II, pp. 40 and 41.

between forms which seemed before so widely separated. How much closer will these links be drawn when paleontology shall have escaped from its cradle."[1]

Imperfection of the Geological Record.

What precedes supplies us with an answer regarding two great difficulties on which anti-evolutionists have always laid special stress. These difficulties, briefly stated, are the sudden apparition of whole groups of allied species in certain formations, even in the lowest fossiliferous strata, without any previous transitional forms leading up to such groups, and the occurrence in geological time of numerous animal forms of a much higher grade than an evolutionist should antecedently expect.

From what has already been said not only respecting the absence of countless species, but also of the denudation of immense areas which must at one time have been rich in important fossiliferous deposits, it is manifest that the objection is at best but a neutral one, and as such may be dismissed as in nowise seriously affecting the contention of evolutionists. Regarding the appearance in the earlier strata of animals which are zoölogically of a higher grade than the principles of Evolution would lead one to look for, it may be said in reply that the objection urged proves, at most, that the imperfection of the geological record is even more extensive than it has usually been thought to be, and, likewise, that the advent of

---

[1] "Les Animaux Fossiles de Pikermi," p. 34.

life on the earth must date back much farther than is commonly thought. Not long since, it was the general opinion, that the first living organisms had their origin in the lower strata of the Silurian Age, but since then the Cambrian, the Huronian, and the Laurentian formations have been discovered, the united thickness of which, according to the eminent geologist, Sir W. Logan, "may possibly far surpass that of all the succeeding rocks from the base of the Palæozoic series to the present time," and may, therefore, carry us back to a period so remote, that the oldest Silurian fauna may in comparison be regarded as comparatively modern. So far as the information of paleontologists now extends, *Eozoön Canadense*, found even in the lowest deposits of the Laurentian, was the earliest form of life, but it is not impossible that in yet lower strata, beneath the ocean's floor perhaps, there are still more primitive types which as much antedate the time of *Eozoön Canadense*, as it antedates the advent of the last highest vertebrate.

Time, Change and Equilibrium.

But, it will be objected that the existence of such formations implies far more time than geologists can reasonably claim, far more than can be allowed by the almost certain conclusions of thermodynamics and astronomical physics. In reply it will suffice to observe, that much, very much, yet remains to be learned, concerning the time which has elapsed since the earth became a fit abode for the lower forms of life, and that until physicists, astronomers and mathematicians can agree among themselves, as to the data on which they base their calculations, and until they can furnish more satisfactory results than they have hitherto offered, geologists will be quite within their right in regarding the objections urged as negative or indifferent.

In all discussions relating to the ascent of life and the paucity of transitional forms, we should not lose sight of the fact that ours is a period of tranquility, and that, therefore, in accordance with the principles of Evolution, there should now be fewer changes in the fauna and flora of the earth than during periods of change and widely-extended disturbance. But the earth has not always been so stable and tranquil. During the inconceivably long interval which has elapsed since the first beginnings of life on our globe, there have been countless periods of equilibrium alternating with changes which were more or less paroxysmal. The last of these critical epochs was during that long stretch of time, known as the Glacial Period, when ice and snow reigned supreme over a great portion of Europe and North America. And during these long geologic rhythms, these alternations of upheaval and subsidence, of denudation and sedimentation, during these periods of comparative tranquility and almost cataclysmal mutation, there were alternately periods which in the one case favored the permanence of species, and in the other were conducive to their rapid metamorphosis, and to the speedy production of intercalary forms which connected all the links of living organisms in one grand unbroken chain.

OBJECTIONS AGAINST EVOLUTION. 179

Paleontology Compared with Egyptology and Assyriology.

The work of the paleontologist resembles in great measure the work of those who, from fragmentary and unpromising materials, have revived for us the histories, so long buried in oblivion, of those great nations of the Orient which erstwhile flourished amid such splendor on the banks of the Nile, the Tigris and the Euphrates. In the beginning of the present century the history of Egypt was almost a sealed book, and as to Chaldea, Assyria and Babylonia, it could be affirmed, and with truth, scarcely yet a generation ago, that many of the most important features of their respective histories had little more for a basis than myth and conjecture. But thanks to the labors and discoveries of Champollion, Lassen, Burnouf, Rawlinson, Layard, George Smith, Mariette, Maspero, and their compeers, the mysterious hieroglyphics and curious cuneiform characters have been deciphered, and the treasures of knowledge so long concealed by them have been opened up to the world. In Egypt, temples and tombs have been searched for records bearing on the past. Pyramids and obelisks, sphinxes and cartouches, have been carefully scrutinized and compelled to give up their secrets to the persistent and determined votaries of history and science. And so, too, it has been in Mesopotamia and in the territory adjacent. From the Persian Gulf to the site of ancient Nineveh, from Tyre and Sidon to glorious Palmyra, the pick and the spade of the archæologist have been busy, especially during the past four decades, and the result has been that we now have more complete and more accurate information respecting peoples who lived four and five thousand years ago, than we have in regard to the inhabitants of many of the most powerful nations of Europe during periods which carry us back but a few hundred years. Rolls of papyrus and mummy cases, tablets and cylinders, which were once but so many meaningless objects for the curious, have been converted into trustworthy records regarding an almost forgotten past. Seti and Rameses, Sennacherib and Assurbanipal live again, and in all their salient features they come before us with fully as much distinctness as do the historic and romantic figures of Charlemagne and Cœur de Lion.

Thus, likewise, is it in respect of paleontology. Thanks to the discoveries and labors of Cuvier, Smith, Sedgwick, Hugh Miller, Murchison, Hall, Barrande, Gaudry, Marsh, and a host of other successful students of nature, who have consecrated their lives to the work of collecting and coördinating the testimony of the rocks, we have now light where before all was darkness; we have knowledge where all was mystery. And though paleontology, like Egyptology and Assyriology, is still in its infancy, it has, nevertheless, already achieved marvels. From a few scattered fragments, the *disjecta membra* of organisms long since extinct, it has constructed for us a history which embraces periods of such duration, that in comparison with them the long dynasties of the Pharaohs sink into positive insignificance. It tells us the story of life from its humblest beginnings till the advent of man, the paragon of God's visible universe. It shows us the grand unity of plan which has characterized the fauna and flora of the world, and exhibits to our view the direction Evolution must have taken in its progress from the simple to the complex, from the general to the special, from the primitive monad to the highest vertebrate. Like the records of the Egyptologist and the Assyriologist, those of the student of the past history of the earth have been imperfect and fragmentary in the extreme, but, notwithstanding this, and notwithstanding the enormous gaps which are everywhere discernible, the paleontologist has been able to give us an account which, considering the difficulties under which it has been written, all thoughtful minds must recognize as singularly complete and satisfactory, even in many of its details.

Darwin, in closing his interesting chapter on the imperfection of the geological record, makes a comparison which so beautifully illustrates the character of the materials from which the paleontologist must weave his story of the earth and its former inhabitants, that I reproduce it here in his own words: " For my part, following Lyell's metaphor, I look at the geological record as the history of the world, imperfectly kept and written in a changing dialect. Of this history we possess the last volume alone, relating only to two or three countries. Of this volume, only here and there a short chapter has been preserved; and of each page, only here and there a few lines. Each word of the slowly-changing language, more or less different in the successive chapters, may represent the forms of life, which are entombed in our consecutive formations, and which falsely appear to have been abruptly introduced. On this view the difficulties above discussed are greatly diminished, or even disappear." [1]

Sterility of Species when Crossed.

The third objection against Evolution, the last one we shall consider, is based on the sterility of species when crossed and on the infertility of hybrids. The argument as usually advanced appears well-founded, and is, it must be confessed, not without its difficulties.

According to anti-evolutionists species have been rendered barren by a special provision of nature, in order thereby to prevent confusion which would result from intercrossing. So convinced, indeed, was Frederick Cuvier, the brother of the illustrious paleontologist, of this view, that he did not hesitate to declare: "Without the employment of artificial means or without derogation to the laws of Providence, the existence of hybrids would never have been known." And Dufrénoy affirmed that "animals instinctively mate with individuals of their own species only, and avoid those of others, as they instinctively select food and eschew poison."

"In fact," writes De Quatrefages, who to the day of his death was opposed to the transmutation theory, "if in the organized world there exists anything which ought to strike the superficial observer, it is the order and constancy which we see there reigning during the past ages; it is the distinction which is maintained among those groups of beings

---

[1] "The Origin of Species," vol. II, p. 88.

which Darwin and Lamarck, like ourselves, call species, even when in general form, function, instinct and habit, they resemble one another so closely that their discrimination is a matter of difficulty. Certainly the cause which maintains this order, this constancy over the entire surface of the globe, is of far greater importance than any mere particularity affecting individual life, or the simple local existence of a domestic race.

"Now, this cause is simple and unique. Suppress infecundity among different species; suppose that the unions among wild species were to become in every way fertile, and indefinitely so, as they are in our dove-cotes, cow-houses and dog-kennels among domestic races. And instantly what comes to pass? Barriers separating species and genera are taken away; crosses are effected in all directions; everywhere intermediate types make their appearance, and everywhere existing distinctions are gradually effaced. As for myself, I cannot see where the confusion would end. Entire orders and probably even classes would, after a few generations, present nothing but a group of bastard forms of doubtful characters, irregularly allied and intercrossed, among which disorder would go on increasing, thanks to the mixture rendered more and more complete, and thanks to atavism which would doubtless struggle for a long time with direct heredity. This is not an imaginary picture. Every reader, when asked what will be produced by promiscuous unions among the one-hundred-and-fifty races of pigeons recognized by Darwin, and the one-hundred-and-eighty races of dogs shown at our expositions, will certainly give the same answer as I do.

"Infertility among species, therefore, has, in the organic world, a rôle which is almost analogous to gravitation in the sidereal world. It preserves the zoölogical or botanical distance among species, as attraction maintains the physical distances among the stars. Both have their perturbations, their unexplained phenomena. But, has anyone called in question the great fact which fixes in their respective places both satellites and suns? No. And can one, on this account, deny the fact which assures the separation of species the most closely allied, as well as of groups the most widely separated? By no means. In astronomy we should reject incontinently every hypothesis in opposition to the first. And, although the complication of phenomena is much greater in botany and zoölogy, serious study will always lead us to discard all doctrines that are at variance with the second."[1]

Infertility among distinct species, as De Quatrefages here views the matter, is thus seen to be demanded by the fitness of things. It is required for the harmony of animated nature, and is rendered necessary by the hopeless confusion which would result if such infertility did not exist.

But the argument from infertility, as urged against evolutionists, has even greater force when regarded from another point of view—I mean from the standpoint of fact. Evolution, it is alleged, is disproved, not because it seems fit and necessary

---

[1] "Darwin et ses Précurseurs Français," pp. 259 and 260.

that species should be reciprocally sterile, but because of the fact of infecundity; because, so it is said, not a single instance can be cited of continued fertility among the hybrid offspring of any two species, however closely related. Here is the core of the difficulty, "*le fait*," as the Marquis de Nadaillac phrases it, "*qui domine toute la question.*"[1] Evolutionists, say their opponents, confound species with race, assert of one what is true only of the other, pile hypothesis upon hypothesis, and ultimately deny the reality of species, or see in this fundamental group only an artificial combination.

Morphological and Physiological Species.

As is evident, we are here again confronted with the old question of the reality and permanence of species. And, unfortunately, most of the reasoning one is asked to follow on the subject is carried on in a vicious circle, or is based on assumptions which are wholly unwarranted. What is species? This is a question which again comes to the fore. Morphologically, many of the domesticated pigeons, of which Darwin makes mention, notably the pouter, the tumbler, the fantail, and the carrier, are so unlike

---

[1] For a masterly presentation of the Marquis de Nadaillac's objections against Évolution, see his "Problème de la Vie," and "Le Progrès de l'Anthropologie," in the Compte Rendu of the International Catholic Scientific Congress at Paris, in 1891. For a critical examination of his views, see a paper on "Création et Évolution," by Dr. Maisonneuve, in the same Compte Rendu, Section of Anthropology, as also a paper entitled, "Pour la Théorie des Ancêtres Communs," by the Abbé Guillemet, in the Compte Rendu of the same Congress, held at Brussels in 1894.

each other that they would be regarded as belonging not only to different species, but even to different genera, did we not know that they are all descended from the ordinary rock pigeon, *columbia livia*. For these birds, Huxley tells us, "not only differ most singularly in size, color, and habit, but in the form of the beak and the skull; in the number of tail feathers; the absolute and relative size of the feet; in the presence or absence of the uropygial gland; in the number of the vertebræ in the back; in short, in precisely those characters in which the genera and species of birds differ from one another." And so it is with the different races of dogs. Whether they are all originally descended from one or more species is yet a moot question, although there is reason to believe that most, if not all of them, are descended from the wolf and the jackal. But be this as it may, when we compare the divers races of the domestic dog, when we observe how they differ in the number of their teeth, toes and vertebræ, and note the divergencies in the form and disposition of other portions of the body, we see that they are so unlike that if found in a state of nature they would unhesitatingly be pronounced distinct species. Even Cuvier was forced to admit, that the differences in the forms of the skulls of certain canine races are so great, as to justify one in assigning them to distinct genera.

What has been said of pigeons and dogs may also, in great measure, be iterated in respect of sundry races of fowls, rabbits, sheep and horses. Morphologically their differences are so marked, that they should be reckoned not only as distinct species, but also as distinct genera, but because they are fertile when crossed *inter se*, they must be regarded, anti-evolutionists insist, as all belonging to one and the same species. And for this reason, too, we are told that the species of any given organism is to be determined, not by its form, but by its filiation. According to this view, therefore, the determining characteristic of species is not something morphological, as Tournefort opined, but rather something, as Ray and Flourens taught, which is physiological.

But even physiological species is not the constant quantity it is represented to be by anti-transformists. Infertility of species and of their hybrid progeny does not constitute the positive line of demarcation, so often claimed by the advocates of the immutability of specific forms. On the contrary, as Darwin and others have shown, "neither sterility nor fertility affords any certain distinction between species and varieties." Long-continued experiments, of the most ingenious character, have demonstrated beyond question that sterility in animals is not to be regarded as an indelible characteristic, but as one capable of being removed by domestication. And, observations on numberless groups of plants and animals have disclosed the remarkable fact, that "the degree of fertility, both of first crosses and of hybrids, graduates from zero to perfect fertility."

From the foregoing, then, it is evinced that physiological species present as many and as grave difficulties as do morphological species. If it be true, as is so often contended, that species have been endowed with sterility in order thereby to prevent their becoming confounded in nature, why is it that we find so many exceptions to what is said to be an invariable law? "Why," asks Darwin, "should the sterility be so extremely different in degree when various species are crossed, all of which we must suppose it would be equally important to keep from blending together? Why should the degree of sterility be innately variable in the individuals of the same species? Why should some species cross with facility, and yet produce very sterile hybrids; and other species cross with extreme difficulty, yet produce fairly fertile hybrids? Why should there often be so great a difference in the result of a reciprocal cross between the same two species? Why, it may even be asked, has the production of hybrids been permitted? To grant to species the special power of producing hybrids, and then to stop their further propagation by different degrees of sterility, not strictly related to the facility of the first union between their parents, seems a strange arrangement."[1]

To show to how great absurdities a too strong insistence on physiological species, as an absolute criterion as to what is a true species and what is but a simple variety, may sometimes lead, I need only refer to a large number of groups of flowers, in which individuals of a given species can be more easily fertilized by pollen from a different plant, or even by the pollen of a different species, than by

---

[1] "The Origin of Species," vol. II, p. 17.

their own pollen. The *corydalis cava* is a striking illustration of this strange phenomenon. According to Hildebrand, the flowers of this species are absolutely incapable of being fecundated by their own pollen, and are rendered but imperfectly fertile by pollen from other flowers of the same stem. They are, however, always perfectly fecundated when the pollen is brought from a flower of a different stalk, or from the flower of a closely allied species. In this case we are absolutely certain that the stamens and carpels of any given flower, came from the same seed; that they have, consequently, a common parentage. Wherefore, then, their sterility; and why is it that the carpel of the given flower can be perfectly fecundated only by pollen from the flower of an independent stem, or of a different species? The only answer which can consistently be given by anti-evolutionists, who pin their faith to the usually-accepted definition of physiological species, is that the stamens and carpels, not only of the different flowers of the same stem, but also those of the same flower of the given stalk, belong to distinct species, and that only the stamens and carpels of flowers of independent plants, or of different species, belong to the same species. It is scarcely necessary to observe that a more perfect *reductio ad absurdum* can hardly be imagined.

Strictly speaking, the infertility of hybrids is rather an objection against the theory of natural selection than against that of Evolution. From what is known of the extreme sensitiveness of the reproductive system of most forms of life, and of the intimate dependence of this system on the organism to which it belongs, it appears *a priori* quite natural that species or races, which in the beginning were reciprocally fertile, should, in the course of time, owing to some change in the conditions of existence, or to protracted subjection to different sets of circumstances, become completely infertile. Many causes have been assigned for this infecundity, but the answers given are, it must be confessed, far from satisfactory. "He who is able," says Darwin, "to explain why the elephant, and a multitude of other animals, are incapable of breeding when kept under only partial confinement in their native country, will be able to explain the primary cause of hybrids being so generally sterile. He will, at the same time, be able to explain how it is that the races of some of our domesticated animals, which have often been subjected to new, and not uniform, conditions, are quite fertile together, although they are descended from distinct species which would probably have been sterile if originally crossed."[1]

True Significance of the Term "Species."

From what precedes, then, it is manifest that whether viewed from the standpoint of morphology, or from that of physiology, species is something which is extremely vague, and pregnant with difficulties of all kinds. But it is also equally manifest that the sterility of species, and of their hybrid progeny, is something which establishes different groups

---

[1] Op. cit., p. 28.

of organisms that require to be designated by a special term. Evolutionists are willing to accept the term "species," provided, however, it be understood that this term does not imply specific immutability during all time. That species may be immutable during a relatively brief period, or during the time it may have been possible to study them, evolutionists are ready to concede, but they decline to admit, that because certain forms are known to have been permanent for a limited period, they must, therefore, have been immutable during an indefinite past time. This indefinite immutability is what De Quatrefages and his school demand, but it is, as is obvious, a simple begging of the question.

Even more than a third of a century back, the eminent comparative anatomist, Richard Owen, although never in sympathy with the dominant school of contemporary Evolution, felt himself constrained to write regarding species as follows: " I apprehend that few naturalists, nowadays, in describing and proposing a name for what they call a new species, use that term to signify what was meant by it thirty years ago; that is, an originally distinct creation, maintaining its primitive distinction by obstructive generative peculiarities. The proposer of the new species now intends to state no more than he actually knows, as, for example, that the differences on which he founds the specific characters are constant in individuals of both sexes, so far as observation has reached; and that they are not due to domestication, or to artificially superinduced circumstances, or to any outward influence within his cognizance;

that the species is wild, or is such as it appears in nature."[1]

Nothing could better illustrate the uncertain character of species and the impossibility of distinguishing species from varieties, or one species from another species, even when they are widely divergent, than certain experiments made some years ago by a Russian naturalist, Schmankewitsch, upon a species of crustacean known as *artemia Mühlhausenii*. Normally, this organism lives in water which is slightly saline. By increasing the salinity of the water, this experimenter was enabled to transform the species in question into an entirely different one, *artemia salina*. Reversing the process, the original species was obtained. But this was not all. By continuing to diminish the amount of salt in the water, a species was finally obtained that was so entirely different from the original one, that it had previously been regarded as belonging to a distinct genus, *branchippus*. The changes mentioned took place slowly, the complete transformation being effected only after several generations. And all the types here referred to as having been artificially produced, were known before, and had always been considered as distinct species and genera. Now, however, that their genetic relationship has been demonstrated, anti-transformists assert that all the three forms spoken of are but varieties of one and the same species. And so they must assert, for

---

[1] Cf. contribution "On the Osteology of the Chimpanzees and Orangs," in the Transactions of the Zoölogical Societies for 1858.

otherwise they would be confronted with what they have always challenged their opponents to produce—a tangible instance of the transmutation of species. Here, then, we have another illustration of the impossibility of satisfying those who, in spite of all evidence to the contrary, persist in affirming specific immutability. They group organisms into species and genera, in accordance with their preconceived notions of species and genus, but when it is shown that these organisms are genetically related to one another, they hasten to proclaim that such forms of life are all only varieties of the same species. Such being the case, it is obviously impossible to give an experimental proof of Evolution, for just the moment that organisms, however widely divergent they may appear, are proved to be connected by filiation, they are forthwith pronounced to be but simple varieties, no matter what views taxonomists may have previously held regarding them. Phantom-like, the proof desired vanishes, just at the moment it is thought to be established. And such, doubtless, will continue to be the case, until naturalists shall discover some infallible method of distinguishing species, a highly improbable event, or until they shall be willing to agree that species, as ordinarily understood—that is, something permanently immutable—has, in nature, no real existence.

Factors of Evolution.

In this and the preceding chapters I have considered the arguments for and against Evolution in general, aside from any of the numerous theories which have been advanced to account for the commonly accepted fact of Evolution. But, before closing this protracted discussion, it is important, for a proper understanding of our subject, to make a few brief observations respecting the factors which have been operative in the origination and development of species, and to say a few words regarding some of the most popular theories concerning the *modus operandi* of Evolution.

As has incidentally been observed in the foregoing pages, the principal factors of Evolution are: 1, the physical environment; 2, the use or disuse of organs; 3, natural selection. The first two of these were recognized by Lamarck;[1] while the third owes its prominence to the labors and speculations of Charles Darwin. In addition to these three factors, two others have attracted some attention, namely, sexual selection, suggested by Darwin, and physiological selection, which was especially insisted on by the late Professor Romanes.

By physical environment are understood, among other things, the external conditions of life, such as temperature, nature of the soil, humidity, dryness and rarity of the atmosphere. That organisms, whether animal or vegetable, are markedly affected by changes of environment has long been admitted, and it suffices here to refer to the well-known results

---

[1] The action of the environment was not unknown to Buffon, and hence some of his admirers are wont to speak of this factor as "Buffon's factor." It was, however, reserved for Lamarck to demonstrate the important rôle which environment plays in causing variation of organic forms.

of adaptation due to changes of climate. Thus, to go no further, "*pigs with fleece* are to be found on the cold plateaus of the Cordilleras, *sheep with hair* in the warm valleys of the Madeleine, and *hairless cattle* in the burning plains of Mariquita." That use and disuse are factors in Evolution is evinced by facts within the experience of everybody, such, for instance, as the general development of the body of the athlete, the highly delicate senses of touch and hearing of the blind, or the atrophied limb of the paralytic.

The Lamarckian factors were deemed of little importance by Darwin, but recently they have, with some modifications, come into special prominence in America, and constitute the basis of the new theory of Neo-Lamarckism. According to Cope and Hyatt, two of the most prominent exponents of this theory, the Lamarckian factors, especially the activities of animals in their constant endeavor to accommodate themselves to their environment, have been the chief agencies in producing varieties and species, and consequently, the chief agencies also in the Evolution of higher from lower forms of life.

Natural selection, or the "survival of the fittest," as Spencer loves to call it, is an abbreviated expression for several well-recognized causes of evolutionary change. Among the more prominent of these are heredity, variation and struggle for existence. Darwin, however, did not teach, as is sometimes imagined, that natural selection is the sole factor of Evolution, although he did, indeed, contend that it is the chief factor. He frankly admitted, especially in his later works, that it left much unexplained, and that he had at first over-estimated its importance. Sexual selection, and the two Lamarckian factors just referred to, he always considered as quite secondary and subordinate to natural selection. But some of Darwin's disciples, notably Wallace, Hæckel, and Ray Lankester, attribute a far greater potency to natural selection than did Darwin himself, and are disposed to regard it as the sole and sufficient cause of all organic development. So different, indeed, are their views from those of their master, that they have given rise to a new school of thought known as Neo-Darwinism.

Evolutionary Theories and Their Difficulties.

But all the theories of Evolution connected with the above-named factors, Lamarckism and Darwinism, Neo-Lamarckism and Neo-Darwinism, involve numerous and grave difficulties, which, so far, have not been satisfactorily answered. Thus, it is not yet positively demonstrated that the effects of use and disuse are inherited. To obtain direct evidence of the inheritance of acquired variations of this kind has hitherto been attended with insuperable difficulties. As to natural selection, it labors under difficulties which are apparently even more serious, and to such an extent is this true, that it may well be questioned if there is a single pure Darwinian now living.[1]

---

[1] Many years ago, it will be remembered, Mivart characterized natural selection as "a puerile hypothesis." Time seems to have confirmed him in his opinion, for in a recent magazine article he refers to natural selection as an "absurd and childish theory."

OBJECTIONS AGAINST EVOLUTION. 197

Why do animals tend to vary? Why do they transmit their characteristics to their offspring? How can chance, irregular, infinitesimal variations, give rise to all the countless species which are known to have existed since the dawn of life, and that within the interval of time which astronomers and physicists are willing to allow? Why, if species have originated by minute, indefinite and irregular variations, are there not more transitional forms than the geological record actually discloses? And how can variations be of any avail in the production of a new species, if these variations, as seems to be the case, are always eliminated by crossing, and if acquired characters are not transmitted by inheritance? Why is it that certain features, which are demonstrably useless to the individual, are preserved, and how is it that organs which are useful only when highly developed, could ever have had a beginning? These are but a few of the many questions which might be asked, to which the advocates of natural selection have not as yet given satisfactory answers.

Many attempts, it is true, have been made to overcome the objections against natural selection, but the success of all such attempts is still open to question. Thus, Moritz Wagner, observing that isolation is favorable to the development of varieties, formulated his theory of isolation by migration. To overcome the difficulty embodied in the slow and irregular variations which Darwin postulated, Mivart and others have formulated their theory of extraordinary births. They deny the truth of Leibnitz' aphorism, *natura non facit saltum,* and contend that species are always formed by what has been designated as saltatory Evolution, that is, Evolution which effects such notable change in an organism that it is constituted a distinct species from the beginning. Among the extraordinary births which are appealed to as evidence of the existence of saltatory Evolution, are the Ancon and Mauchamp breeds of sheep, Niata cattle, pug dogs, tumbler pigeons, hook-bill ducks, and a large number of vegetable forms that have suddenly appeared with essentially the same characteristic features which they now exhibit.[1]

To the objection that we have no evidence that wild species ever originate in this way, it is replied that "we have never witnessed the origin of a wild species by any process whatever; and if a species were to come suddenly into being in a wild state, as the Ancon sheep did under domestication, how could you ascertain the fact? If the first of a newly-begotten species were found, the fact of its discovery would tell nothing about its origin. Naturalists would register it as a very rare species, having been only once met with, but they would have no means

---

[1] The real author of the theory of saltatory Evolution was Geoffroy Saint-Hilaire. It has, however, been specially developed and supported by such eminent authorities as Mivart, Owen, Kölliker, and the Duke of Argyll. Even Huxley is inclined to take a favorable view of it. "We greatly suspect," he says, "that she (nature) does make considerable jumps in the way of variation now and then, and that these saltations give rise to some of the gaps which appear to exist in the series of known forms." Mr. Bateson's recent theory of "discontinuous variations," is essentially only a modification of the theory of saltatory Evolution as held by Mivart and others.

of knowing whether it were the first or the last of its race."

Regarding the laws governing such extraordinary births, Mivart is unable to vouchsafe any information. He is, however, of the opinion, that sufficiently numerous instances of such births are known to justify one in accepting the theory. If it could be demonstrated to be true, it would at once remove all the difficulties presented by the lack of geological time, the absence or paucity of transitional forms, the origin of rudimentary organs, and the elimination of variations by crossing; difficulties which natural selection has been thus far impotent to remove. As is manifest, Mivart's theory does not explain the facts it deals with; it simply refers the sudden changes demanded to the action of unknown internal forces. This, at bottom, is not unlike the theory of the German botanist, Nägeli, who would account for development by assuming that there exists in all organisms an internal tendency towards progression. But this is obviously only another way of expressing the action of the "perfecting principle" of Aristotle, as Darwin's theory of chance variations is but a modification of the conjecture of "fortuity in nature," of old Empedocles.

Concerning Weismann's theory of heredity, Hæckel's speculations on perigenesis, Jäger's notions regarding soul-stuff, and Brooks' hypothesis respecting both heredity and variation, we need say nothing except that Weismann's theory has many points of weakness, that the views of Hæckel and Jäger are based mostly on fancy, and that the hypothesis of

Brooks is an attempt to combine the theories of some of his predecessors, especially those of Darwin and Weismann.

From the preceding paragraphs, therefore, it is clear that, as yet, we have no theory of Evolution which is competent to coördinate all the facts that Evolution is supposed to embrace. Neither singly nor collectively do the theories just discussed meet the many objections urged against them. All of them, doubtless, contain an element of truth, but how far they can be relied upon as guides in research it is still impossible to say. The same may be said concerning the so-called factors of Evolution. All of them, there is reason to believe, are more or less potent in organic development, but it is generally admitted that other factors, factors probably more important than any of those yet mentioned, remain to be discovered before we can properly understand the working of Evolution, and account for numberless phenomena of the organic world which are still involved in mystery.

The Ideal Theory.

The discovery of a true, comprehensive, irrefragable theory of Evolution; of a theory of the "ordained becoming" of new species by the operation of secondary causes; of a theory which will admit a preconceived progress "towards a foreseen goal;"[1] of a theory which in its "broad features" will disclose the unmistakable evidence and the certain impress of a Divine intelligence and purpose—this is something

---

[1] Cf. Owen's "Anatomy of Vertebrates," vol. III, ch. XL.

which still remains to be accomplished, but something which can scarcely be realized before many years shall have elapsed, and until much serious labor shall have been expended on the vast, and as yet but partially explored, domain of animated nature.[1] Such a theory, when fully worked out, will do for biology what the heliocentric theory has achieved for astronomy. It will place in the clear light of day what is now veiled in darkness, and render certain what at present can but vaguely be surmised. The lack of this perfected theory, however, does not imply that we have not already an adequate basis for a rational assent to the theory of organic Evolution. By no means. The arguments adduced in behalf of Evolution in the preceding chapter, are of sufficient weight to give the theory a degree of probability which permits of little doubt as to its truth.

Whatever, then, may be said of Lamarckism, Darwinism and other theories of Evolution, the fact of Evolution, as the evidence now stands, is scarcely any longer a matter for controversy. Hence, it is the factors which have been operative during the long course of organic development, and a theory that can be brought into harmony with these factors, and which is at the same time in consonance with the phenomena observed, that men of science

---

[1] In the *American Naturalist* for May, 1895, Professor Osborn, in concluding an interesting article on the "Search for the Unknown Factors of Evolution," pertinently observes: "My last word is that we are entering the threshold of the Evolution problem instead of standing within its portals. The hardest tasks lie before us, not behind us, and their solution will carry us well into the twentieth century."

are now seeking. Whether the divers conjectures which at present obtain, regarding the method according to which Evolution has acted in past time, and according to which it must still act, be true or false, matters little so far as Evolution itself is concerned. The true, the all-embracing theory, which is now the object of the earnest quest of so many ardent investigators the world over, and which, as Professor Owen believed, should constitute the chief end and aim of biological research, is something which we must look to the future to supply. And when such a theory shall have been elaborated, as every advance in science leads us to believe it will be, then will it be found to be as superior in simplicity, beauty and comprehensiveness, to all current theories of Evolution, as the grand and far-reaching conceptions of Copernicus and Newton are superior to the almost forgotten speculations of Ptolemy and Aristarchus.

PART II.

EVOLUTION AND DOGMA.

Εἶναι γὰρ πάσης πλάνης καὶ ψευδοδοξίας αἴτιον, τὸ μὴ δύνασθαι διακρίνειν, πῇ τε ἀλλήλοις τὰ ὄντα κοινωνεῖ, καὶ πῇ διενήνοχεν. Εἰ δὲ μὴ κατὰ διωρισμένα τις τὸν λόγον ἐφοδεύοι, λήσεται συγχέας τά τε κοινὰ καὶ τὰ ἴδια τούτου δὲ γινομένου, εἰς ἀνοδίαν καὶ πλάνην ἐμπίπτειν αναγκαῖον.

"For the cause of all error and false opinion, is inability to distinguish in what respect things are common, and in what respect they differ. For unless, in things that are distinct, one closely watch speech, he will inadvertently confound what is common and what is peculiar. And where this takes place, he must of necessity fall into pathless tracts and error."
Clement of Alexandria.—" Stromata." Book VI, chap. x.

PART II.

EVOLUTION AND DOGMA.

CHAPTER I.

MISCONCEPTIONS OF THEORY, ERRORS IN DOCTRINE AND MISTAKES IN TERMINOLOGY.

Evolution of the Evolution Theory.

IN the preceding pages we have considered what might be termed the evolution of the theory of Evolution. We traced its development from its earliest germs, as disclosed in the speculations of Hindu and Greek philosophy, and reviewed some of the evidence ordinarily adduced in its support, as well as the objections which are commonly urged against its acceptance. We also adverted to some of the many attempted explanations of Evolution, which have been proposed since the publication of Darwin's "Origin of Species," and noted the wide divergence of views which obtains respecting some of the most fundamental elements of the theory. We learned that the great majority of contemporary scientists are believers in some theory of organic Evolution; that the controversy is no longer about the fact of Evolution—that being assumed, if not demonstrated—but rather regarding the factors which have been operative in the onward march of animal and vegetable life, and the processes which have characterized organic development in its divers phases and epochs. We may not be prepared to go the same lengths as do Spencer, Huxley and Fiske, in the demands which they make for Evolution as the one controlling agency in the world of phenomena; we may refuse assent to the theories of Darwin, Mivart, Cope, Brooks, Weismann, Nägeli and others; but it seems difficult, if not impossible, to ignore the fact that some kind of Evolution has obtained in the formation of the material universe, and in the development of the divers forms of life with which our earth is peopled.

The question now is: How are we to envisage this process of Evolution, and what limits are we to assign to it? Is it as universal in its action as it is usually claimed to be, or, is the sphere of its activity restricted and confined within certain definite, fixed limits, beyond which it may not extend? And then, a far more important question comes to the fore, a question to which all that has hitherto been said is but a preamble—a long one, it is true, but still only a preamble—and that is, how is faith affected by Evolution, or, in other words, what is the attitude of Dogma towards Evolution?

Evolution and Darwinism.

To this last question various answers have been given, many of them contradictory, more of them absurd, few of them satisfactory or philosophical. All remember the storm that was raised against Darwinism on its first appearance, a few decades ago. Darwinism, however, is not Evolution, as is so often imagined, but only one of the numerous attempts which have been made to explain the *modus operandi* of Evolution. Nevertheless, for a long time Darwinism and Evolution were regarded as synonymous—as in the popular mind they are still synonymous—even by those who should have been better informed. The objections which were advanced against Darwinism were urged against Evolution, and *vice versa*. And in most of the controversies relating to these topics there was a lamentable, often a ridiculous, ignorance of the teachings of the Church, and this, more than anything else, accounts for the *odium theologicum*, and the *odium scientificum*, which have been so conspicuous in religious and scientific literature during the past third of a century.

During the first few years after the publication of "The Origin of Species," there were but few, even among professed men of science, who did not condemn Darwinism as irreligious in tendency, if not distinctly atheistic in principle. "Materialistic" and "pantheistic," were, however, the epithets usually applied both to Evolution and the theory so patiently elaborated by Darwin. Prof. Louis Agassiz, as we have already seen, did not hesitate to denounce "the transmutation theory as a scientific mistake, untrue in its facts, unscientific in its method, and mischievous in its tendency." Certain others of Darwin's critics characterized his theory as "an acervation of endless conjectures," as an "utterly rotten fabric of guess and speculation," and reprobated his "mode of dealing with nature" as "utterly dishonorable to natural science," and as contradicting "the revealed relation of the creation to its Creator."[1]

Darwinism was spoken of as "an attempt to dethrone God;" as "the only form of infidelity from which Christianity has anything to fear;" as doing "open violence to everything which the Creator Himself has told us in the Scriptures of the methods and results of His work." It was declared to be "a dishonoring view of nature;" "a jungle of fanciful assumption;" and those who accepted it were said to be "under the frenzied inspiration of the inhaler of mephitic gas." "If the Darwinian theory is true," averred another, "Genesis is a lie, the whole framework of the Book of Life falls to pieces, and the revelation of God to man, as we Christians know it, is a delusion and a snare."

Evolution naturally shared in the denunciations hurled against Darwinism. It was designated as "a philosophy of mud;" as "the boldest of all the philosophies which have sprung up in our world;" as "a flimsy framework of hypothesis, constructed upon imaginary or irrelevant facts, with a complete

---

[1] M. Flourens, perpetual secretary of the French Academy of Sciences, thus wrote of Darwin's "Origin of Species," shortly after its appearance :

"Enfin l'ouvrage de M. Darwin a paru. On ne peut qu'être frappé du talent de l'auteur; mais que d'idées obscures, que d'idées fausses! Quel jargon métaphysique jeté mal-à-propos dans l'histoire naturelle, qui tombe dans le galimatias dès qu'elle sort des idées claires, des idées justes. Quel langage prétentieux et vide! Quelles personifications puériles et surannées! O lucidité! O solidité de l'esprit français, que devenez-vous?"

departure from every established canon of scientific investigation." It was stigmatized as "flatly opposed to the fundamental doctrine of creation," and as discharging God " from the governing of the world." The distinguished Canadian geologist, Sir J. W. Dawson, in speaking of the subject, affirms that "the doctrine [of Evolution] as carried out to its logical consequences excludes creation and Theism. It may, however, be shown, that even in its more modified forms, and when held by men who maintain that they are not atheists, it is practically atheistic, because excluding the idea of plan and design, and resolving all things into the action of unintelligent forces."[1]

Evolution, Atheism and Nihilism.

To judge from the declarations of some of the most ardent champions of Evolution, it must be admitted that orthodoxy had reason to be at least suspicious, of the theory that was heralded forth with such pomp and circumstance. For it was announced with the loudest flourish of trumpets, not only that Evolution is a firmly established doctrine, about whose truth there can no longer be any doubt, but it was also boldly declared, by some of its most noted exponents, to be subversive of all religion and of all belief in a Deity. Materialists, atheists, and anarchists the world over, loudly proclaimed that there is no God, because, they would have it, science had demonstrated that there is no

---

[1] "Story of the Earth and Man," p. 348.

longer any *raison d'être* for such a Being. Evolution, they claimed, takes the place of creation, and eternal, self-existent matter and force exclude an omnipotent personal Creator. "God," we are told, "is the world, infinite, eternal, and unchangeable in its being and in its laws, but ever-varying in its correlations." A glance at the works of Hæckel, Vogt, Büchner, and others of this school, is sufficient to prove how radical and rabid are the views of these "advanced thinkers."

It is in accordance with the spirit of such teaching that "science," as Caro observes, "conducts God with honor to its frontiers, thanking Him for His provisional services." It is such science that declares that "faith in a personal and living God is the origin and fundamental cause of our miserable social condition;" and that advances such views as these: "The true road to liberty, to equality, and to happiness, is Atheism. No safety on earth, so long as man holds on by a thread to heaven. Let nothing henceforth shackle the spontaneity of the human mind. Let us teach man that there is no other God than *himself;* that *he* is the Alpha and Omega of all things, the superior being, and the most real reality."

It was in consequence of the circulation of such views among the masses, that Virchow and others declared Evolution responsible, not only for the attempts made by Hödel and Nobeling on the life of the emperor of Germany, but also for all the miseries and horrors of the Paris Commune. For the theory of Evolution, in its atheistic form, is one of the cardinal tenets of nihilists, and their device is: "Neither God, nor master," *Ni Dieu, ni maître.* It is at the bottom of the philosophy of the Krapotkins and Réclus, who "see in the hive and the ant-hill the only fundamental rule of right and wrong, although bees destroy one class of their number and ants are as warlike as Zulus." And we all remember how Vaillant, the bomb-thrower in the Chamber of Deputies, boastfully posed as the logical executant of the ideas of the Darwins and the Spencers, whose teachings, he contended, he was but carrying out to their legitimate conclusions.[1]

Evolution and Faith.

But all evolutionists have not entertained, and do not entertain, the same opinions as those just mentioned. America's great botanist, Prof. Asa Gray, was not so minded. One of the earliest and most valiant defenders of Darwinism, as well as a professed Christian believer, he maintained that there is nothing in Evolution, or Darwinism, which is incompatible with Theism. In an interesting chapter on Evolution and Theology, in his "Darwiniana,"[2] he gives it as his opinion, arrived at after long consideration, that "Mr. Darwin has no atheistical intent, and that, as respects the test question of design in nature, his view may be made clear to the theological mind by likening it to that of the

---

[1] Ravachol, another dynamitard, of the same school as Vaillant, confessed on his way to the guillotine: "*Si j'avais cru en Dieu, je n'aurais fait ce que j'ai fait.*"

[2] P. 258.

'believer in general, but not in particular, Providence.'" So far, indeed, was Darwin from having any "atheistical intent," that when interrogated regarding certain of his religious views he replied: "In my most extreme fluctuations I have never been an atheist in the sense of denying the existence of God."[1] And the late Dr. McCosh declared, that he had "never been able to see that religion, and in particular that Scripture, in which our religion is embodied, is concerned with the absolute immutability of species."[2]

The Rev. Doctor Pohle thus expresses himself in an able and interesting article on Darwinism and Theism: "I feel bound to confess that I never could prevail upon myself to believe, that Darwinism contains nothing short of a hot-bed of infidelity and iniquity, brought into a system, and is, therefore, irreconcilable on principle with a sincere and pious belief in a First Cause and Designer of the world."[3]

The illustrious Dominican *conférencier*, Father Monsabré, records it as his opinion that the theory of Evolution, " far from compromising the orthodox belief in the creative action of God, reduces this action to a small number of transcendent acts, more in conformity with the unity of the Divine plan and the infinite wisdom of the Almighty, who knows how to employ secondary causes to attain his ends."[4] This is in keeping with the view of the dis-

---

[1] " Life and Letters of Charles Darwin," vol. I, p. 274.
[2] " The Religious Aspect of Evolution," p. 27.
[3] *American Ecclesiastical Review*, Sept. 1892; p. 163.
[4] " L'Évolution des Espèces Organiques, par le Père M. D. Leroy, O. P.," p. 4.

tinguished German Catholic writer, Doctor C. Güttler, who asserts that " Darwin has eliminated neither the concept of creation, nor that of design; that, on the contrary, he has ennobled both the one and the other. He does not remove teleology, but merely puts it farther back." [1]

Evolution and Science.

But there are yet others to be heard from. According to Huxley, who is an avowed agnostic, the "doctrine of Evolution is neither anti-theistic nor theistic. It simply has no more to do with Theism than the first book of Euclid has." [2] It will be observed that with Huxley, Evolution is neither a hypothesis nor a theory, but a doctrine. So is it with many others of its advocates. It is no longer something whose truth may be questioned, but something which has been established permanently on the solid foundation of facts. It has, we are assured, successfully withstood all the ordeals of observation and experiment, and is now to be counted among those acquisitions of science which admit of positive demonstration. Thus, a few years ago, in an address before the American Association for the Advancement

---

[1] "Lorenz Oken und sein Verhältniss zur modernen Entwickelungslehre," p. 129.

"Transformismus Darwinianus," declares the Rev. J. Corluy, S. J., "dicendus est sensui Scripturæ *obvio* contradicere, non tamen *aperte* textui sacro adversari; tacet enim Scriptura *modum* quo terra varietatem illam specierum produxerit, an statim an decursu temporum, an cum specierum firmitate an cum relativa duntaxat. Sed et de sensu disputari posset quem Scriptura hic assignet nomini ק מין," Min., "Specilegium Dogmatico-Biblicum," tom. I, p. 198.

[2] "Life and Letters of Darwin," vol. I, p. 556.

of Science, Prof. Marsh said: "I need offer no argument for Evolution, since to doubt Evolution is to doubt science, and science is only another name for truth." "The theory of Evolution," writes M. Ch. Martins, in the *Revue de Deux Mondes*, "links together all the questions of natural history, as the laws of Newton have connected all the movements of the heavenly bodies. This theory has all the characters of Newtonian laws." Prof. Joseph Le Conte, however, goes much further: "We are confident," he declares, "that Evolution is absolutely certain, not indeed Evolution as a special theory— Lamarckian, Darwinian, Spencerian—but Evolution as a law of derivation of forms from previous forms; Evolution as a law of continuity, as a universal law of becoming. In this sense it is not only certain, it is axiomatic."[1]

Ignorance of Terms.

But, wherefore, it may be asked, have we such diverse and conflicting opinions regarding the nature and tendency of Evolution? Why is it that some still persist in considering it a "flimsy hypothesis," while others as stoutly maintain that it is a firmly established doctrine? Why is it that some believe it to be neutral and indifferent, so far as faith is concerned, and others find in its tenets illustrations and corroborations of many of the truths of Dogma; that there are so many who see, or fancy they see in it, the negation of God, the destruction of religion, and the subversion of all order, social and political?

---

[1] "Evolution, and Its Relation to Religious Thought," p. 65.

These are questions which are frequently asked, and that press themselves upon even the most superficial reader. Are they insoluble? Must they be relegated forever to the domain of paradox and mystery, or is there even a partial explanation to be offered for such clashing opinions and such glaring contradictions? With all due deference to the judgment of those who see nothing good in Evolution, nothing which must not incontinently be condemned as false and iniquitous, I think that the enigma may be solved, and that it may be shown that the contradictions, as is usually the case in such matters, are due mostly, if not wholly, to an *ignoratio elenchi*, a misapprehension of terms, or to a deliberate intention of exploiting a pet theory at the expense of religion and Dogma, which are ostentatiously repudiated as based on superstition and falsehood.

The two words most frequently misunderstood and misemployed are "creation" and "nature." They are of constant occurrence in all scientific treatises, but no one who is not familiar with the writings of modern evolutionists has any conception of the extent to which these terms are misapplied. For this reason, therefore, it is well, before proceeding further, briefly to indicate the meaning which Catholic theology attaches to these much-abused words.

Materialism and Dualism.

From the earliest times, the dogma of creation has been a stumbling-block to certain students of science and philosophy. The doctrines, however, which have met with most general acceptance regarding the origin and constitution of the universe, can be reduced to a few typical and comprehensive classes.

First of all, comes the Materialism of Leucippus and Democritus, of Heraclitus and of Empedocles, of Epicurus and the philosophers of the Ionian school. The only reality they recognized was matter. Simple atoms, infinite in number, eternal and uncreated, moving eternally in a void infinite in extent, are, of themselves, the only postulate demanded by materialists to explain the universe and all the phenomena which it exhibits. It excludes the intervention of an intelligent cause, and attributes all life and thought to the mere interaction of the ultimate atoms of brute matter. Morality, according to this teaching, is but "a form of the morality of pleasure," religion is the outcome of fear and superstition, and God the name of a being who has no existence outside of the imaginations of the ignorant and the self-deceived.

Materialism, as is obvious, is but another name for Atheism, and is a blank negation of creation as well as of God. "Rigorously speaking," as M. Caro well observes, "Materialism has no history, or, at least, its history is so little varied that it can be given in a few lines. Under what form soever it presents itself, it is immediately recognized by the absolute simplicity of the solutions which it proposes. Contemporary Materialism has in nowise changed the framework of this philosophy of twenty centuries' standing. It has never deviated from its original program; it has but been enriched with scientific notions; it has been transformed in appearance only, by being surcharged with the data, the views, the hypotheses, infinite in number, which are the outgrowth of the physical, chemical, and physiological sciences. Democritus would easily recognize his teaching, if he were to read the works of M. Büchner; even the language used has undergone but a trifling change."[1] Indeed, "the history of Materialism," as has well been remarked, "may be reduced to indicating the influence which it has exercised at divers epochs, and to recording the names of its most famous representatives."

The advocates of Dualism, like the defenders of Materialism, taught the eternity of matter, but in addition to eternal, uncreated matter, recognized the existence of a personal God. Many of the philosophers of antiquity, who escaped the errors of Materialism and Pantheism, fell headlong into those of Dualism, which possessed as many forms as Proteus himself. Thus, the Manicheans asserted the existence of two principles, one good, the other evil; the former, the creator of souls, the latter, the creator of bodies. According to the gnostics, the world is the work of the angels, and not the immediate result of Divine creative action. Even according to J. Stuart Mill, matter is uncreated and eternal. God, he will have it, but fashioned the universe out of self-existent material, and far from being the Crea-

---

[1] "Le Matérialisme et la Science," p. 136.

tor of the world, in the strict acceptation of the term, is but its architect and builder.

Both Materialism and Dualism are one in asserting the eternity of matter. Materialism, however, is atheistic, in that it excludes a Creator, while Dualism, although rejecting creation, properly so called, admits the existence of a Supreme Being. But God, according to dualists, is little more than a demiurge. He is powerful, but not omnipotent. The eternal, self-existent matter which is postulated, and which exists outside of God, rebels against His action, and becomes a cosmic power against which He is powerless.

Pantheism.

Pantheism is the opposite of Materialism. According to the latter, as we have seen, everything is matter; according to the former, as the word indicates, everything is God. The finite and the infinite; the contingent and the necessary; beings, which appear in time, and God, who is from eternity, are, according to the teachings of pantheists, but different aspects of the same existence. Whether we consider the emanation of the Brahmans, the Pantheism of the Eleatics, or that of the neo-Platonists of Alexandria, or that of Spinoza, Fichte, Schelling and Hegel, the doctrines so taught issue in the negation of creation as well as in the negation of the true nature of God. For to predicate, in what manner soever, an identity of God with the world, or to conceive God as the material principle, or the primal matter, from which everything emanates, as pantheists do, is to negative completely not only the Christian idea of God, a Being eternal, spiritual in substance, and distinct from the world in reality and essence, but also the Christian and the only true idea of creation.

Having briefly adverted to some of the principal philosophical doctrines which exclude creation in the Christian and Scriptural sense, and having given a hasty glance at some of the more widely-spread errors respecting the nature of the Creator and His creatures, we are now prepared to consider the teachings of Catholic philosophy and theology as to creation, and as to the origin and nature of the material universe.

Dogma of Creation.

Creation, in its strictest sense, is the production, by God, of something from nothing. The universe and all it contains was called into existence *ex nihilo*, by an act of the Creator, which was not only supernatural, but also absolute and free. It was, therefore, in no wise formed from preëxisting material, for none existed, nor by any emanation from the Divine substance. God alone is necessary and eternal; the world of matter and the world of spirit, outside of God, are contingent, and have their existence in time. But, notwithstanding that the nature of the world of created things is finite, and entirely different from the Divine nature, which alone is infinite and necessary, nevertheless, all the creatures of God have a real existence, although limited in its duration and dependent entirely on Divine Providence for its continuance.

A secondary meaning of the word "creation," is the formation, by God, of something from preëxisting material. This is the natural action of God in the ordaining or administering of the world, as distinguished from the supernatural act of absolute creation from nothing. In this sense God is said to create derivatively, or by the agency of secondary causes. He creates potentially; that is, He gives to matter the power of producing or evolving, under suitable conditions, all the manifold forms it may ever assume. In the beginning He created matter directly and absolutely, once for all; but to the matter thus created He added certain natural forces—what St. Augustine calls *rationes seminales*—and put it under the action of certain laws, which we call "the laws of nature." Through the operation of these laws, and in virtue of the powers conferred on matter in the beginning, God produces indirectly, derivatively, by the operation of secondary causes, all the various forms which matter may subsequently assume, and all the divers phenomena of the physical universe.

In another sense, also, the word "creation" may be employed, as when we speak of the creations of genius, or refer to creations of Raphael, Michael Angelo, or Brunelleschi. In these cases, the work of the artist or of the architect consists simply in making use of the laws, and powers and materials of nature, in such wise as to effect a change in form or condition. The action of the intelligent agents in this case being natural, but more than physical, may conveniently be designated as hyperphysical.

With hyperphysical creation we shall have little to do. Our chief concern will be with absolute, or direct creation, and with secondary or derivative creation, both of which are so often misunderstood and confounded, if not positively denied. It would, indeed, seem that the sole aim and purpose of a certain school of modern scientists, is to discover some means of evading the mystery of creation. For they not only deny creation, but also deny its possibility, and all this because they, with "the fool," persist in saying in their hearts " There is no God." So great, indeed, is their hatred of the words " Creator" and " creation," that they would, if possible, obliterate them from the dictionary, and consign all works containing them to eternal oblivion.[1]

The Vatican Council on Creation.

For a clear and succinct statement of Catholic doctrine, in respect of God as Creator of all things, as well for an expression of the Church regarding the errors of Materialism and Pantheism now so rife, we can have nothing better or more pertinent to our present subject than the constitution and canons of the Vatican Council: *De Deo Rerum Omnium Creatore.*

The "Dogmatic Constitution of the Catholic Faith," in reference to " God, the Creator of all things," reads as follows: " The Holy Catholic Apostolic Roman Church believes and confesses, that

---

[1] " In properly scientific works," says Büchner, who declares that "science must necessarily be atheistic," " the word [God] will seldom be met with; for, in scientific matters the word 'God' is only another expression for our ignorance." " Man in the Past, Present, and Future," p. 329.

there is one true and living God, Creator and Lord of heaven and earth, Almighty, Eternal, Immense, Incomprehensible, Infinite, in intelligence, in will, and in all perfection, who, as being one, sole, absolutely simple and immutable spiritual substance, is to be declared as really and essentially distinct from the world, of supreme beatitude in and from Himself, and ineffably exalted above all things which exist, or are conceivable, except Himself.

"This one only true God, of His own goodness and Almighty power, not for the increase or acquirement of His own happiness, but to manifest His perfection by the blessings which He bestows on creatures, and with absolute freedom of counsel, created out of nothing, from the very beginning of time, both the spiritual and the corporeal creature, to wit, the angelical and the mundane, and afterward the human nature, as partaking in a sense of both, consisting of spirit and body."

But the canons of the Council relating to God as Creator of all things, are, if anything, stronger and more explicit than what precedes.

They are as follows:

"1. If anyone shall deny one true God, Creator and Lord of things visible and invisible, let him be anathema.

"2. If anyone shall not be ashamed to affirm that, except matter, nothing exists; let him be anathema.

"3. If anyone shall say that the substance and essence of God and of all things is one and the same; let him be anathema.

"4. If anyone shall say that infinite things, both corporeal and spiritual, or at least spiritual, have emanated from the Divine substance; or that the Divine Essence by the manifestation and evolution of Itself becomes all things; or lastly, that God is universal or indefinite being, which by determining itself constitutes the universality of things, distinct according to genera, species and individuals; let him be anathema.

"5. If anyone confess not that the world and all things which are contained in it, both spiritual and material, have been, in their whole substance, produced by God out of nothing; or shall say that God created, not by His will free from all necessity, but by a necessity equal to the necessity whereby He loves Himself; or shall deny that the world was made for the glory of God; let him be anathema."

We have here in a nutshell the Catholic doctrine of creation, as well as an authoritative pronouncement, which cannot be mistaken, respecting the attitude of the Church towards the Atheism, Materialism and Pantheism which have infected so many minds in our time, and exerted such a blighting influence on contemporary science.

Meaning of the Word "Nature."

Knowing, now, in what sense we may interpret the word "creation," in what sense it must be understood according to Catholic teaching, we next proceed to the discussion of the word "nature," about which so much crass ignorance prevails, even among those who employ it most frequently, and whom it behooves to have clear ideas as to its import.

"Nature" is frequently employed to designate "the material and spiritual universe as distinguished from the Creator;" to indicate the "world of substance whose laws are cause and effect;" or to signalize "the aggregate of the powers and properties of all things." It is used to signify "the forces or processes of the material world, conceived as an agency intermediate between the Creator and the world, producing all organisms, and preserving the regular order of things." In this sense it is often personified and made to embody the old gnostic notion of a demiurge, or an archon; a subordinate, creative deity who evolved from chaos the corporeal and animated world, but was inferior to the infinite God, the Creator of the world of spirits. It is made to refer to the "original, wild, undomesticated condition of an animal or a plant," or to "the primitive condition of man antecedent to institutions, especially to political institutions," as when, for instance, we speak of animals and plants being found, or men living in a state of nature. It likewise distinguishes that which is conformed to truth and reality "from that which is forced, artificial, conventional, or remote from actual experience."

These are only a few of the many meanings of the word "nature," and yet they are quite sufficient to show us how important it is that we should always be on our guard lest the term, so often ambiguous and so easily misapplied, lead us into grave mistakes, if not dangerous errors. In works on natural and physical science, where the word "nature" is of such frequent occurrence, and where it possesses such diverse meanings, having often different significations in a single paragraph, there is a special danger of misconception. Here, unless particular attention be given to the changed meanings of the term, it becomes a cloak for the most specious fallacies, and a prolific source of the most extravagant paralogisms.

Any one of the diverse meanings of the word "nature," as just given, is liable to be misconstrued by the unwary. But the chief source of mischief with incautious readers arises from the habit scientific writers have, of indiscriminately personifying nature on all occasions; of speaking of it as if it were a single and distinct entity, producing all the various phenomena of the visible universe, and of referring to it as one of the causes that "fabricate this corporeal and sensible world;" as a kind of an independent deity "which, being full of reasons and powers, orders and presides over all mundane affairs."

When poets personify nature there is no danger of misconception. In their case the figurative use of the term is allowed and expected. Thus, when Bryant tells us that nature speaks "a various language," or when he bids us —

"Go forth under the open sky, and list
To nature's teachings;"

or when Longfellow declares that—

"No tears
Dim the sweet look that nature wears,"

we understand at once that "nature" is but a

poetical fiction; and that the term is to be interpreted in a metaphorical and not in a literal sense.

With naturalists, however, and philosophers, who are supposed to employ a more exact terminology, such a figurative use of language cannot fail, with the generality of readers, to be both misleading and mischievous.

Darwin, and writers of his school, are continually telling us of the useful variety of animals and plants given to man "by the hand of 'nature,'" and recounting how "'nature' selects only 'for the good of the being which she tends,'" how "every selected character is fully exercised by her," and how "natural selection entails divergence of character and extinction of less improved forms." Huxley loves to dilate on how "'nature' supplied the club-mosses which made coal," how she invests carbonic acid, water, and ammonia "in new forms of life, feeding with them the plants that now live." He assures us that "thrifty 'nature,' surely no prodigal! but the most notable of housekeepers," is "never in a hurry, and seems to have had always before her eyes the adage, 'Keep a thing long enough, and you will find a use for it;'" that "it was only the other day, so to speak, that she turned a new creature out of her workshop, who, by degrees, acquired sufficient wits to make a fire."

Nature and God.

Now, there is no doubt but that all these quotations can be understood in an orthodox sense, but the fact, nevertheless, remains, that they are not always so construed, and for the simple reason that both the writers from whom these citations are made, are avowed agnostics. So far as Huxley and Darwin are concerned, there *may* be a personal God, the Creator of the universe; but, they will have it, there is no evidence of the existence of such a Being. On the contrary, according to their theory, there is nothing but matter and motion, and if they do not, like King Lear, say: "Thou, nature, art my goddess," their teachings tend to incline others to the belief that there does really exist an entity subordinate to God, if not independent of Him, that produces all existing phenomena, not only in the world of matter, but also in the world of spirit.

It is, then, against this constant misuse of the word "nature," and especially against the many false theories which are based on the misapprehension of its true significance, that it behooves us to be constantly on our guard. Errors of the most dangerous character creep in under the cover of ambiguous phraseology, and the poison of false doctrine is unconsciously imbibed, even by the most cautious. We may, if we will, personify nature, but, if we do so, let it not be forgotten that nature, with all her powers and processes, is but a creature of Omnipotence; that far from being merely an inward, self-organizing, plastic life in matter, independent of God, as was asserted by the hylozoist, Strato of Lampsacus, nature, as good old Chaucer phrases it, is but "the vicar of the Almightie Lord."

"What else," asks Seneca, "is nature, but God, and a certain Divine purpose manifested in the world?

You may, at pleasure, call this Author of the world by another name."[1] Again, in referring to the Deity, under the name of Jupiter, he inquires, "Wilt thou call Him nature? Thou wilt not sin. For it is from Him that all things are born, and by whose Spirit we live."[2] All this, and more, is affirmed with equal beauty and terseness by the "Christian Cicero," Lactantius: "If nature," he asks, "does all that she is said to do; if she everywhere displays evidences of power, intelligence, design, wisdom; why call her nature, and not God?"[3]

Having explained the meaning of the words "creation," and "nature," we are now prepared to consider the subject of Evolution in relation to the teachings of faith. Here, however, we must again distinguish, and explain. There are evolutionists, and evolutionists. There are evolutionists who give us in a new guise the old errors of Atheism, Materialism and Pantheism; there are others who assert that our knowledge is confined to the phenomenal world, and that, consequently, we can know nothing about the

---

[1] "Quid enim aliud est natura quam Deus et divina ratio toti mundo et partibus ejus inserta? Quoties voles, tibi licet aliter hunc auctorem rerum nostrarum compellare." Seneca, "De Beneficiis." Lib. IV, chap. 1.

[2] "Vis illum naturam vocare? non peccabis. Est enim ex quo nata sunt omnia, cujus Spiritu vivimus." "Natural. Quæst." Lib. II.

[3] "Natura, quam veluti matrem esse rerum putant, si mentem non habet, nihil efficiet umquam, nihil molietur. Ubi enim non est cogitatio, nec motus est ullus; nec efficacia. Si autem concilio suo utitur ad incipiendum aliquid, ratione ad disponendum, arte ad efficiendum, virtute ad consummandum, potestate ad regendum, et continendum, cur natura potius quam Deus nominetur." "De Ira Dei," cap. x.

absolute and the unconditioned; and there are others still, who contend that Evolution is not inconsistent with Theism, and maintain that we can hold all the cardinal principles of Evolution without sacrificing a single jot or tittle of Dogma or revelation.

For the sake of simplicity, we shall designate these three classes of evolutionists as: 1, monists; 2, agnostics; and 3, theists. Their doctrines are clearly differentiated, and naturally distinguish three schools of contemporary thought, known respectively as: 1, Monism; 2, Agnosticism; and 3, Theism. This is the most convenient and comprehensive grouping we can give, of the tenets of the leading representatives of modern science and philosophy, and, at the same time, the most logical and satisfactory. In order to secure as great exactness, and make my exposition as concrete and tangible as possible, I shall, when feasible, allow the chief exponents of Monism, Agnosticism, and Theism, to speak for themselves, and to present their views in their own words. This will insure not only greater accuracy, but will also be fairer, and more in keeping with the plan I have followed in the preceding pages.

CHAPTER II.

MONISM AND EVOLUTION.

Hæckel and Monism.

HISTORICALLY considered, Monism, as a system of philosophy, is as old as speculative thought. It has, however, had various and even contradictory meanings. Etymologically, it indicates a system of thought, which refers all phenomena of the spiritual and physical worlds to a single principle. We have, accordingly, idealistic Monism, which makes matter and all its phenomena but modifications of mind; materialistic Monism, which resolves everything into matter; and, finally, the system of those who conceive of a substance that is neither mind nor matter, but is the underlying principle or substantial ground of both. In each and all of its forms, Monism is opposed to the philosophical Dualism which recognizes two principles — matter and spirit.

The Monism, however, with which we have to deal here, is not the idealism of Spinoza, Berkeley, Hume, Hegel or Schopenhauer, nor the atheistic Materialism of D'Holbach and La Mettrie, which was but a modified form of Epicureanism, but rather a later development of these errors. An outgrowth of recent speculations in the natural and physical sciences, its origin is to be traced to certain hypotheses connected with some of the manifold modern theories of Evolution.

The universally-acknowledged protagonist of contemporary Monism is Ernst Hæckel, professor of biology in the University of Jena. He is often called "the German Darwin," and is regarded, with Darwin and Wallace, as one of the founders of the theory of organic Evolution. From the first appearance of Darwin's "Origin of Species," he has been a strong and persistent advocate of the development theory, and did more than anyone else to popularize it in Germany and throughout the continent of Europe. He has, however, gone much further than the English naturalist, in his inductions from the premises supplied by the originator of the theory of natural selection. He draws conclusions from Darwinism at which many of its advocates stand aghast, and which, if carried out in practice, would not only subvert, religion and morality, but would sap the very foundations of civilized society. Anti-monists, of course, contend that Hæckel's conclusions are not valid, and that there is nothing either in Darwinism, or Evolution, when properly understood, which warrants the dread inductions which have been drawn from them by the Jena naturalist.

To understand the nature of Hæckel's doctrines, and to appreciate the secret of his influence, we must consider him in a three-fold capacity — as a scientist, as a philosopher, and as the hierophant of a new form of religion, "the religion of the future."

Hæckel as a Scientist.

As a scientist, especially as a biologist, he deservedly occupies a high place. Of unquestioned ability, of untiring industry, and of remarkable talent for original research, he is distinguished also for a certain intrepidity and assertiveness in promulgating his views, which have given him, not only a reputation, but a notoriety which is world-wide. His best work, probably, has been done in connection with his investigations of some of the lower forms of life, especially the protista, the radiolaria, and the calcareous sponges. His researches in this direction would alone have been sufficient to make him famous in the world of science. But concerning these researches the general public knows little or nothing. The works of Hæckel which have made his name familiar the world over, are his popular expositions of evolutionary doctrines, viz., his "Natürliche Schöpfungsgeschichte," or "Natural History of Creation," and "Anthropogenie,"or "Evolution of Man." In these works, his chief endeavor is to present the theory of Evolution in a popular form, and to give the evidences on which it is founded.

Hæckel's Nature-Philosophy.

But he does more than this. Not satisfied with being an expounder of the truths of science, he promulgates views on philosophy and religion which are as radical as they are irrational. He appears not only as a professor of biology, but poses as the founder of a new school of philosophy, and as the high-priest of a new system of religion. He commits the error into which so many have fallen, of confounding the methods of metaphysics with those of experimental science, and of mistaking *a priori* reasoning for strict inductive proof.

The name which Hæckel gives his nature-philosophy, as he loves to call it, is, as already stated, Monism. The word "Monism" is often attributed to the Jena professor, but erroneously, as it was coined by Wolf long before. Hæckel has, however, given it a new meaning, and the one which is now generally understood when Monism is in question. He has, as he tells us, chosen this term so as to eliminate the errors attaching to Theism, Spiritualism, and Materialism, as well as to the Positivism of Comte, the Synthetism of Spencer, the Cosmism of Fiske, and other like evolutionary systems of philosophy. But here I shall let Hæckel speak for himself.

In his "Evolution of Man,"[1] he declares that "this mechanical or monistic philosophy asserts that everywhere the phenomena of human life, as well as those of external nature, are under the control of fixed and unalterable laws; that there is everywhere a necessary causal connection between phenomena, and that, accordingly, the whole knowable universe forms one undivided whole, a 'monon.' It further asserts that all phenomena are produced by mechanical causes, *causæ efficientes*, not by prearranged, purposive causes, *causæ finales*. Hence, there is no such thing as 'free-will' in the usual sense. On the contrary, in the light of this monistic conception of nature, even those phenomena which we have been

---
[1] Vol. II, p. 455.

accustomed to regard as most free and independent, the expressions of the human will, appear as subject to fixed laws as any other natural phenomenon. Indeed, each unprejudiced and searching test applied to the action of our free will, shows that the latter is never really free, but is always determined by previous causal conditions, which are eventually referable either to heredity or to adaptation. Accordingly, we cannot assent to the popular distinction between nature and spirit. Spirit exists everywhere in nature, and we know of no spirit outside of nature." Elsewhere, he tells us that "unitary philosophy, or Monism, is neither extremely materialistic, nor extremely spiritualistic, but resembles rather a union and combination of these opposed principles, in that it conceives all nature as one whole, and nowhere recognizes any but mechanical causes. Binary philosophy, on the other hand, or Dualism, regards nature and spirit, matter and force, inorganic and organic nature, as distinct and independent existences."[1]

Again, he assures us that the theory of development of Darwin must, "if carried out logically, lead us to the monistic, or mechanical, causal, conception of the universe. In opposition to the dualistic, or teleological conception of nature, our theory considers organic, as well as inorganic bodies, to be the necessary products of natural forces. It does not see in every species of animal and plant the embodied thought of a personal Creator, but the expression, for the time being, of a necessarily active cause, that is, of a mechanical cause, *causa efficiens*.

---

[1] Op. cit., vol. II, p 461.

Where teleological Dualism seeks the thoughts of a capricious Creator in the miracles of creation, causal Monism finds in the process of development the necessary effects of eternal, immutable laws of nature."[1]

Five Propositions of Hæckel.

These quotations would seem to be sufficiently explicit, but Hæckel, not satisfied with such general statements, has been pleased to lay down five theses, respecting the theory of Evolution, which admit neither doubt nor ambiguity. They are worded as follows:

1. "The general doctrine [of Evolution] appears to be already unassailably founded.

2. "Thereby every supernatural creation is completely excluded.

3. "Transformism and the theory of descent are inseparable constituent parts of the doctrine of Evolution.

4. "The necessary consequence of this last conclusion is the descent of man from a series of vertebrates.

5. "The belief in an 'immortal soul,' and in 'a personal God' are therewith—i. e., with the four preceding statements — completely ununitable [*völlig unvereinbar*]."[2]

Such, then, in brief compass, is Monism as expounded by its latest and most applauded doctor and prophet. Such is Hæckelism, about which so

---
[1] "History of Creation," vol. I, p. 34.
[2] "Evolution in Science, Philosophy and Art," p. 454

much is said, but concerning which there is so little accurate knowledge. As is manifest from the above five propositions, it is but a neologistic formulation of old errors; a recrudescence, in modern scientific terminology, of the teachings of the Ionian and Greek materialistic schools; a rechauffé of the well-known atomic theory of Leucippus and Democritus of Abdera; a *mixtum compositum* of science, philosophy and theology; an *olla podrida* compounded of the most glaring errors and absurdities of Atheism, Materialism and Pantheism, ancient and modern.

God, and the Soul.

God, according to Hæckel, is but a useless hypothesis. A personal "Creator is only an idealized organism, endowed with human attributes; a gross anthropomorphic conception, corresponding with a low animal stage of development of the human organism." Hæckel's idea of God, an idea which, he assures us, "belongs to the future," is the idea which was expressed by Giordano Bruno when he asserted that: "A spirit exists in all things, and no body is so small but contains a part of the Divine substance within itself, by which it is animated." In the words of one of Hæckel's school, the true God is the totality of the correlated universe, the Divine reality, and there is, therefore, "no possible room for an extra-mundane God, a ghost, or a spook, anyway or anywhere."

The atom, eternal and uncreated, is the sole God of the monist. Hæckel's atom, however, is not the atom of the chemist—an infinitesimally small particle of inorganic matter, the smallest constituent part of a molecule. It is far more. It is a living thing, endowed not only with life but also possessed of a soul. And this is no mere hypothesis with him. It is, he will have it, a demonstrated doctrine, an established fact. "An atom soul," "a molecule soul," "a carbon soul," are among the first corollaries of Monism, which, one of its advocates tells us, is now "irrefragable, invincible, inexpugnable."

Organic and Inorganic Matter.

There is, in Hæckel's estimation, no essential difference between inorganic and organic matter; no impassable chasm between brute and animated substance. All vital phenomena, especially the fundamental phenomena of nutrition and propagation, are but physico-chemical processes, identical in kind with, although differing in degree from, those which obtain in the formation of crystals and ordinary chemical compounds. Like D'Holbach, he identifies mental operations with physical movements; and, like Robinet, he attributes the moral sense to the action of special nerve-fibres. His *Weltseele* is not like that of Schelling, a spiritual principle or intelligence, but a blind unconscious force which always accompanies, and is inseparably connected with, matter.

According to his views, sensation is a product of matter in movement, and consciousness is but a summation of the rudimentary feeling of ultimate sentient atoms. The genesis of mind is thus entirely a mechanical process, and the conceptions of genius are but the result of the clash of atoms and the impact of molecules. Intellectual work is the correlative of certain brain-waves; thrills of gratitude, and love of friends and country, are mere oscillations of infinitesimal particles of brute matter. Pleasure and pain, joy and sorrow, are the direct product of vibratory motion, and the difference in the nature of these emotions arises solely from the difference in the character of the generating shakes and quivers. Like Cabanis, Hæckel makes thought a secretion of the brain, and holds, with Vogt, that the brain secretes thought as the liver secretes bile. With Moleschott, he would assert that thought is dependent on phosphorus, and with Büchner he would declare it to be a product of nervous electricity. In the words of Caro, he teaches that: "In matter, resides the principle of movement; in movement, is the reason of life; in life, is the reason of thought." Hence, in returning to the first term of the series, we observe that thought and life are only forms of movement, which is the original inherent property of eternal matter.[1]

With Hugo, Hæckel would exclaim:
"Learn that everything knows its law, its end,
    its way; . . .
That everything in creation has consciousness.
    . . . . Winds, waves, flames,
Trees, reeds, rocks, all are alive! All have
    souls . . .
Compassionate the prisoner, but compassionate
    the bolt;

---

[1] "Le Matérialisme et la Science," p. 116.

Compassionate the chain, in dark, unhealthy prisons;
The axe and the block are two doleful beings,
The axe suffers as much as the body, the block
as much as the head." [1]

The Religion of the Future.

Such, in brief outline, are the leading conclusions of Hæckel's teachings in science and philosophy. What, now, are his views on religion? For his friends and disciples assert that he is not only a great scientist, and a great philosopher, but that he is also to be saluted as the prophet and high-priest of the religion of science, which means, we are assured, the religion of the future. According to a recent exponent of Hæckelism, "We find the religious history of our race to consist of a gradual Evolution of its leading peoples from a broad base of general Animism and Fetichism, thence to astrology, thence to Polytheism, thence to Monotheism, and thence to Scientism, expressed chiefly to us in the Pantheism of Goethe, the Positivism of Comte, the Synthetism of Spencer, the Cosmism of Fiske, and finally by the Monism of Hæckel." [2] His new form

---

[1] "Sache que tout connait sa loi, son but, sa route; . . .
Que tout a conscience en la création . . .
. . . . Vents, ondes, flammes,
Arbres, roseaux, rochers, tout vit! Tout est plein d'âmes.
Ayez pitié! Voyez âmes dans les choses . . .
Plaignez le prisonnier, mais plaignez le verrou;
Plaignez la chaîne au fond des bagnes insalubres;
La hache et le billot sont deux êtres lugubres;
La hache souffre autant que le corps, le billot
Souffre autant que la tête."
"Les Contemplations." Tom. II, p. 315.

[2] "Evolution in Science, Philosophy and Art," p. 41.

of religion, we are told, "rises above all religions as the culmination of all. If anything can be, it is, the universal faith," and this because "it is based upon verified science."

Truth to tell, however, Hæckel's own views concerning religion are as crude and as extravagant as many of his expressed opinions respecting philosophy and science. The monistic religion of nature, he informs us, "which we should regard as the veritable religion of the future, is not, as are all the religions of the churches, in contradiction, but in harmony with a rational knowledge of nature. While the latter have no other source than illusions and superstitions, the former reposes on truth and science. Simple, natural religion, based on a perfect knowledge of nature and its inexhaustible treasure of revelations, will, in the future, impress on Evolution a seal of nobility, which the religious dogmas of divers peoples have been incapable of giving it. For these dogmas rest on a blind faith in obscure mysteries, and in mythical revelations formulated by priestly castes. Our epoch, which shall have had the glory of achieving the most brilliant result of human research, the doctrine of Evolution, will be celebrated in coming ages as having inaugurated a new and fecund era for the progress of humanity; an era characterized by the triumph of freedom of investigation over the domination of authority, through the noble and puissant influence of monistic philosophy."[1]

"[1] Schöpfungsgeschichte," 7th edition, p. 681.

MONISM AND EVOLUTION.   241

This brief extract from Hæckel's inept statements about religion, concerning which, it is manifest, he is crassly ignorant, will relieve us from the necessity of following further this trumpeted reformer of religion and omniscient seer of Monism. It would be difficult to collect together, in the same space, a greater number of misstatements of fact, more glaring absurdities, or more preposterous propositions, than those contained in the foregoing quotation from one of his best-known and most popular works. I shall not attempt categorically to refute his errors of history and philosophy, of science and theology, as this is beyond the scope of the present work. Neither shall I waste time in indicating wherein he has put himself, especially in matters of theology and religion, against the unanimous teaching of the saints and sages of all time. A mere presentation of his errors, in a clear light and in bold relief, is a sufficient, if not the best refutation, for all reasonable men. Hæckel's vagaries but emphasize once more a fact which has often been signalized — the danger incurred by specialists, particularly by mere physicists and biologists, when they attempt to discuss matters of which they are not only ignorant, but which are entirely foreign to their ordinary trend of thought, and when they pass the frontiers with which they may be familiar, and, entering upon a domain of knowledge with which they are entirely unacquainted, seek the discussion of topics for which both their temper and education totally disqualify them.

Such a congeries of errors, scientific, philosophic and theologic, error personified, as it were, as that which we have just been contemplating, forcibly reminds one of the words of the Mantuan bard when he describes the giant Polyphemus, whose solitary orb was burnt out by Hercules,

"Monstrum horrendum, informe, ingens, cui lumen ademptum."[1]

But if Hæckel is the accomplished biologist he is reputed to be, if he is one of the leading representatives of contemporary science, and even his enemies will not deny that he is all this, how comes it, it will be asked, that he has fallen into so many errors and that he has so many enthusiastic followers?

---

[1] "A frightful, misshapen, huge monster deprived of sight."

In his latest work, "The Confession of Faith of a Man of Science," Hæckel gives expression to absurdities which are almost incredible. It would, indeed, seem impossible that any sane man, much less one who pretends to be a leader in science and philosophy, should be guilty of such utterances as the following:

"The Monistic idea . . . can never recognize in God a 'personal being,' or, in other words, an individual of limited extension in space, or even of human form. . . . Every atom is . . . animated, and so is the ether; we might, therefore, represent God as the infinite sum of all natural forces, the sum of all atomic forces, and all ether vibrations. . . . 'Homotheism,' the anthropomorphic representation of God, degrades this loftiest cosmic idea to that of a gaseous vertebrate." Pp. 78–79.

Again, on p. 92 of the same work, he says: "As the simpler occurrences of inorganic nature, and the more complicated phenomena of organic life, are alike reducible to the same natural forces, and as, further, these in their turn have their foundation in a simple primal principle pervading infinite space, we can regard this last [the cosmic ether] as all-comprehending Divinity, and upon this found the thesis: 'Belief in God is reconcilable with science.'"

Similar unphilosophical language, to use no stronger terms, is found in "The Religion of Science," by Paul Carus, the chief trumpet and propagandist of Hæckelism in the United States.

For those who are familiar with the life-work of the Jena professor, and know how blindly the multitude follow one who is looked upon as an authority in science, how prone they are to hero worship, there will be no difficulty in answering those questions and in reconciling what are, at least, apparent contradictions.

Hæckel's Limitations.

Hæckel, no one questions it, has achieved deserved eminence in his chosen field of work. But Hæckel is a specialist, an ardent specialist, and his limitations are very strongly marked. As a student of the lower forms of life, to which he has devoted the greater portion of his time, he has probably no superior, and but few peers. But the very ardor with which he has cultivated science, and forced everything to corroborate a pet theory, has made him one-sided and circumscribed in his views of the cosmos as a whole, so as practically to incapacitate him for the discussion of general questions of science and philosophy, and much more those of theology. Like all specialists, he suffers from intellectual myopia, and it is almost inevitable that such should be the case. He examines everything as he would a microbe or a speck of protoplasm, under the objective of his microscope. He applies the methods of induction to questions of metaphysics, and confounds the principles of metaphysics with the data of experimental science. The result, as might be anticipated, is to "make confusion worse confounded." For such a one, the only cure is a broader knowledge and a rigid and systematic drill in the fundamental rules of dialectics. Verily, for a specialist afflicted as Hæckel is, and he is but a type of the majority of specialists, it behooves him to purge—

> "With euphrasy and rue
> The visual nerve, for he hath much to see."

But is this the sole explanation of the manifold errors into which the German naturalist has lapsed, and will this account for his false declamation against religion, and his vehement denunciation of the Church, and of what she regards as most sacred? It is to be feared not. There is more than simple antipathy in his case. There is downright hatred. Only on this assumption can we explain the use of the violent and blasphemous language which is of such frequent occurrence in his more popular works.

As to the reading public, their position is not difficult to understand. They are, as it were, hypnotized, by what a German writer, Wiegand, aptly designates, "the confused movement of the mind of our age," and are, so far as their ability to think and judge for themselves goes, in a state of chronic catalepsy. They mistake assertions for proof, theories for science, and regard a conglomeration of neologisms, which explain nothing, as so much veritable knowledge.

Verbal Jugglery.

The secret of Hæckel's prestige and influence with his readers, is not due simply to the extent of his information in his special line of study, nor to the astonishing mass and variety of facts which he discusses and compares, but rather to his manner of presenting facts, and to his adroitness in drawing the conclusions which suit him, whether such conclusions are warranted by the facts or not. With Hæckel, especially when treating of his favorite topics, Evolution and Monism, the wish is always father to the thought, and he has a way of convincing his readers that he is right, even when they have reason to suspect, if they are not certain, that he is positively wrong.

One of the chief reasons for Hæckel's success as a theorist, is to be found in the fact that he is an expert in verbal jugglery, and a consummate master in the art of sophistry. Whether his use of sophism is intentional or not, is not for me to say. It does, however, seem almost incredible, that anyone endowed with ordinary reasoning powers could unconsciously fall into so great, and so frequent, errors of logic, as may be seen on almost every page of Hæckel's evolutionary works. He possesses in an eminent degree, as has been well said of him, what a French prestidigitator declared to be the leading principle of legerdemain, viz., "the art of making things appear and disappear." This is true. What Robert Houdin is among conjurers, that is Hæckel among what the Germans call the "nature-philosophers" of the present generation.

A striking illustration of adroitness in verbal jugglery is given in his genealogy of man. In his genealogical tree Hæckel recognizes twenty-two "form-stages," through which he traces human ancestry from monad to man, from the beginning of the Laurentian to the Quaternary Period, when *homo sapiens* first appeared on this planet.

In accordance with his theory of Monism, Hæckel, as might be supposed, is a strenuous advocate of spontaneous generation, to which he gives the new names, plasmogeny and autogeny. His chief reason for believing in autogeny is, that if we do not do so, we must believe in creation and a Creator, which, according to his notions, is both anti-scientific and anti-philosophical.

The first product of spontaneous generation was the moneron, a simple unicellular, structureless bit of slime or protoplasm, or, as Hæckel himself describes it, a form of life of such extreme simplicity as to deserve to be called an "organism without organs." It is due to the action of some natural force, heat, electricity, or what not, on brute matter, and is not only the simplest form of life that can exist, but also the simplest form conceivable. No one, it is true, has ever seen a moneron, not even Hæckel himself. But this matters not. The moneron, if it did not exist, should have existed — because theory demands it.

To confirm his views regarding this first form-stage of the human ancestral line, Hæckel appeals to the famous *bathybius*, over which Huxley and himself went into such ecstasies for awhile, but which eventually proved to be as imaginary as the moneron itself.

The immediate successor of the monera in the phylogeny of man were the amœbæ. These differed from the former in having a nucleus in the cell-substance or protoplasm. Both these stages existed as simple individuals. They were, however, succeeded by what are termed amœboid communities, "simple societies of homogeneous, undifferentiated cells." Under the action of a favorable environment, these amœbæ developed into various larval or gastrula forms, and these, in turn, by the action of inherent forces, evolved into worms, and into animals similar to our modern sea-squirts, lancelets, lampreys, sharks and mud-fish. The mud-fish, or its prototype, a kind of salamander fish, was followed by animals nearly related to existing sirens, axolotls, and by a cross between tailed amphibians and beaked animals, the precursor of the monotremata. The next in the order of succession were marsupials or pouched animals, semi-apes; tailed, narrow-nosed apes; tailless, narrow-nosed apes, or men-like apes; speechless men, or ape-like men; and finally, as the culmination of all, the crown and glory of the genealogical tree, whose germ was but a simple speck of slime, or plasson, we have *homo sapiens*—man, dowered with the power of reason and articulate speech.¹

The twenty-two parent forms of the human ancestral line indicated by Hæckel are, we are assured, but a few of those which actually existed. They are

---

¹ In marked contrast with the atheistic, mechanical theory of Hæckel are the views entertained by Darwin's great rival, Alfred Russel Wallace. Writing in his "Darwinism," chap. xv., of "the introduction of sensation or consciousness," as "constituting the fundamental distinction between the animal and vegetable kingdoms," he expresses himself as follows: "Here, all idea of mere complication of structure producing the result is out of the question. We feel it to be altogether preposterous to assume, that at a certain stage of complexity of atomic constitution, and as a necessary result of that complexity alone, an *ego* should start into existence—a thing that *feels*, that is *conscious* of its own existence. Here we have the certainty that

given only as typical stages, and are far from complete. In reality, instead of being only a score in number, there were thousands and tens of thousands of transitional forms, intermediate between the first moneron and primitive man.

I have said that the existence of the first form of life indicated in this genealogical tree is purely imaginary. So, likewise, are many others. So far as paleontology teaches, fully ten of the twenty-two groups mentioned by Hæckel are unknown as fossils, while a number of the others do not, so far as our present knowledge extends, belong to the periods to which he assigns them. But this matters not. *Se non è vero è ben trovato.* If the facts required for the support of the theory do not exist, they must be manufactured. And if facts are found which contravene the theory which has been elaborated with such care, *tant pis pour les faits.* The facts must be wrong, because, forsooth, the theory is right.

---

something new has arisen—a being whose nascent consciousness has gone on increasing in power and definiteness till it has culminated in the higher animals. No verbal explanation or attempt at explanation—such as the statement that life is the result of the molecular forces of the protoplasm, or that the whole existing organic universe from amœba up to man was latent in the fire-mist from which the solar system was developed—can afford any mental satisfaction, or help in any way to a solution of the mystery."

Referring to the origin of man he concludes: "We thus find that the Darwinian theory, even when carried out to its extreme logical conclusion, not only does not oppose, but lends a decided support to a belief in the spiritual nature of man. It shows us how a man's body may have been developed from that of a lower animal form under the law of natural selection; but it also teaches us, that we possess intellectual and moral faculties which could not have been so developed, but must have had another origin; and for this origin we only find an adequate cause in the unseen universe of spirit."

False Analogy.

Some of the most striking and characteristic of Hæckel's methods of ratiocination are specially displayed in the foregoing attempt to outline the genealogy of our species. Among these may be noted the fallacy of regarding analogous processes as identical. Thus, to his mind the development of the individual animal—man, for instance—from a simple germ, is but a repetition within a short space of time of what has actually occurred in the development of the species. Embryological facts in the life-history of the individual animal, ontogenesis, are considered as corresponding *exactly* with those which must have characterized phylogenesis, or the development of any species in geological time. The former being open to observation and study, while the latter are not, the facts which must have obtained in phylogeny are inferred from the known facts of ontogeny.

This fallacy of false analogy is one into which Hæckel is constantly lapsing, and one, therefore, against which the reader must always be on the alert. But it is by no means peculiar to Hæckel alone. It is a frequent occurrence in most of our current scientific literature, and has probably been more productive of error than any other one form of sophism. Instead of being employed in its strict sense, as it should always be used in science and philosophy, analogy is taken most loosely or given a meaning it will not bear. In lieu of being understood to imply a similarity of relations, which is its proper and specific meaning, it is used to signify essential resemblance, which is wholly inexact.

In order that the argument of analogy should be valid, the data given should be identical, and should refer to two different classes of beings viewed under the same bearings. When this is the case, the identical data given may be regarded as premises, from which conclusions may be drawn applicable to both classes of beings. Until, therefore, Hæckel and his school can demonstrate, that the causes which have operated and the conditions which have prevailed in phylogeny, are identical with those which exist in respect of ontogeny, his argument is inconclusive, if not worthless, and the theories based on his assumptions are at best but simple hypotheses and should be so considered.[1]

The suppositions which he continually makes, and the postulates which everywhere abound in his writings, show the looseness of his reasoning and the flimsiness of the structure which he has reared with such a flourish of trumpets, and to which he points with such evident feelings of arrogant exaltation. On almost every page of his "Evolution of Man," and his "History of Creation," we find such phrases as "there can be no doubt;" "which may

---

[1] It is not my purpose to minimize the force or plausibility of the argument in favor of Evolution which is based on the teachings of embryology. On the contrary, I am quite willing to accept the argument for what it is worth, and in the earlier part of this work I have endeavored to present it as fairly as possible within a brief compass. The facts of embryology *may* justify the conclusions which evolutionists draw from them, but so far there is no positive evidence that such is the case. The argument from analogy *may*, in this particular instance, be warrant-

safely be regarded;" "as is now very generally acknowledged;" "we can with more or less certainty recognize;" "it might be argued;" "a conception which seems quite allowable;" "we can, therefore, assume;" "we may assert;" "this justifies the conclusion;" and numberless others of similar import, which, like the paraphernalia of the magician, are designed to perplex and deceive. Attention, however, to the matter under discussion, will always reveal the imposture in Hæckel's case, and disclose the fact that his plausible statements are often nothing more than rhetorical artifices and tricks of dialectics; the reasonings of a special pleader who has before his mind but one aim, to give vraisemblance to an assumption that cannot be substantiated by fact.

Understanding his methods of reasoning, and the reckless manner in which he draws conclusions not contained in the premises, we need not be surprised to have Hæckel tell us, as he does in his fanciful pedigree of man, that we must "regard the amphioxus with special veneration, as that animal which alone, of all extant animals, can enable us to form an approximate conception of our earliest Silurian vertebrate ancestors." Neither need we be surprised, because we know the man's flippancy and cynicism,

---

ed, but this remains to be demonstrated. What I take exception to in Hæckel's argumentation are, the exaggerated importance he attaches to faint or imaginary resemblances, and his continual attribution to the argument from analogy of a value which it rarely, and which, as he ordinarily uses it, it never possesses and never can possess. As usually employed in biology, analogical reasoning can at best afford us nothing more than probability; Hæckel would have his readers believe, in the instances referred to, that it gives physical certainty, which it is very far from doing.

when he declares that "the amphioxus, skull-less, brainless and memberless as it is, deserves all respect as being of our own flesh and blood," and that this same brainless creature " has better right to be an object of profoundest admiration and devoutest reverence, than any of that worthless rabble of so-called 'saints,' in whose honor our 'civilized and enlightened' cultured nations erect temples and decree processions."

Type of a Class.

But we need not follow further the Jena professor in his extravagant speculations and his wild diatribes against religion and Christian philosophy. He has already been given more attention than his work deserves. He is, however, a type of a class, and of quite a large class of scientific men who hold similar views, and who reason in a similar manner. The saying, *ab uno disce omnes*, is specially applicable here, because to know one, and, especially, to know the leader, is to know all. The methods of all those belonging to the school of which Hæckel is such an outspoken exponent are identical. They are all experts in the "art of making things appear and disappear," and if not as adroit as their master in the use of sophism, they are, nevertheless, able to deceive the unwary and thus accomplish untold mischief.

Considering the nature of the teachings of Monism, it is not surprising that Hæckel and his school should have such a multitude of adherents and sympathizers as they are known to have.

"In the troublous times in which we live," observes the distinguished savant, the Marquis de

Nadaillac, "and in the midst of the confusion of ideas of which we are the sorrowful witnesses, human pride has attained proportions hitherto unknown. Science has become more dogmatic and more imperious than was ever theology. It counts, by thousands, adepts who speak with emphasis of modern science, without very often knowing the first word about it. But I am mistaken—they have been taught that modern science is the negation of creation, the negation of the Creator. God belongs to the old régime; the idea of his justice weighs heavily on our enervated consciences. Accordingly, when a hypothesis, or a discovery, seems to contravene Christian beliefs, it is accepted without reflection and promulgated with inexplicable confidence. It is in this fact, rather than in its scientific value, that we must seek the *raison d'être* of transformism."[1]

But probably no better explanation could be given of the confusion and perplexity which now reign supreme, especially among the masses, in matters of science, philosophy and theology, than is expressed by the old Epicurean poet when he affirms:

"Omnia enim stolidei magis admirantur amantque,
Inversis quæ sub verbis latitantia cernunt;
Veraque constituunt, quæ belle tangere possunt
Aureis, et lepido quæ sunt fucata sonore."[2]

---

[1] "Le Problème de la Vie," p. 64, et seq.

[2] "For fools rather admire and delight in all things which they see hid under inversions and intricacies of words, and consider those assertions to be truths which have power to touch the ear agreeably, and which are disguised with pleasantness of sound." Lucretius, "De Rerum Natura," Lib. I, 642–45.

CHAPTER III.

AGNOSTICISM AND EVOLUTION.

Nature and Scope of Agnosticism.

A MORE popular form of error than Monism, or scientific Atheism, and one which is more wide-spread and devastating in its effects, is the new-fangled system, if system it can be called, known as Agnosticism. To the superficial student it is not without color of plausibility, and by concealing the objectionable and repulsive features of Monism, it now counts more adherents, probably, than any other form of scientific error.

Like Monism, Agnosticism is a system of thought which has allied itself with the theory of Evolution, from which, as ordinarily understood, it is inseparable. Like Monism, it is a *mixtum compositum* of science, philosophy and theology, in which science and Evolution are predominant factors. And, like Monism, too, it is a new name for an old form of error. Unlike Monism, however, Agnosticism affects to suspend judgment, where Monism makes a positive assertion, or enters a point-blank denial. In many questions of fundamental importance, Agnosticism is ostensibly nothing more than simple doubt, or gentle skepticism, while Monism is always arrogant, downright affirmation, or negation. In its ultimate analysis, however, Agnosticism as well as Monism issues in a practical denial of a personal God, the Creator of the universe, and relegates Providence, the immortality of the soul, and the moral responsibility of man to a Divine Being, to the region of fiction.

Again, Agnosticism, like Monism, is peculiarly and essentially the product of a combination and a succession of causes and conditions. As no one individual can be pointed to as the father of Monism, so no one person can be singled out as the founder of Agnosticism. Both may have, and have had, their recognized exponents; both, like a Greek drama, have their choragi and coryphei, but these exponents, these choragi and coryphei, are not spontaneous growths. They do not, Minerva-like, leap suddenly into the intellectual arena, fully developed and armed cap-a-pie. On the contrary, they are the product of their environment, as affected by a series of antecedent factors and influences. They had their predecessors and prototypes; those who planted the seeds which lay dormant until new conditions favored germination and development. Then the fruit contained in the germ was made manifest, and the poison which had been so surreptitiously instilled, was discovered when it was too late to administer an antidote.

The word "agnostic" was invented by the late Prof. Huxley in 1869. He took it from St. Paul's mention, in the Acts of the Apostles, of the altar erected by the Athenians "to the unknown God," ἀγνώστῳ θεῷ, and, to the inventor's great satisfaction, the term took, and soon found a recognized position in the languages of all civilized nations.[1]

Late Developments of Agnosticism.

As a creed, or system of philosophy, Huxley derives Agnosticism from the teachings of Kant, Hume and Sir William Hamilton. At an early age his mind, he informs us, "steadily gravitated towards the conclusion" of Kant, who affirms, in his "Kritik der reinen Vernunft," that "the greatest and perhaps the sole use of all philosophy of pure reason is, after all, merely negative, since it serves not as an organon for the enlargement (of knowledge), but as

---

[1] Father Clarke, S. J., in a note to an interesting series of articles on Agnosticism in *The Month*, for June, July and August, 1882, declares that the term Agnosticism is "an impostor from the Greek vocabulary," and further that "the analogy of other Greek formations is fatal to its claims of recognition." "The word Agnosticism," he tells us, "is founded on a false analogy to Gnosticism. Gnosticism is the doctrine of those who are γνωστικοί, men professing γνῶσις, or knowledge. In the same way Agnosticism would be the doctrine of ἀγνωστικοί, or those who profess ἀγνωσία, or ignorance. But ἀγνωστικὸς is an impossible Greek word. The Greeks never prefix the privitive ἀ, or ἀν, to the adjective expressing the possession of a faculty to indicate its absence. If we are reminded of anæsthetic, ἀναισθητικός, as formed on the analogy of agnostic, we answer (1) that it is not a classical Greek word at all; (2) that it means not men who profess want of perception, but that which tends to destroy perception. By a parity of reasoning, agnostic would mean that which tends to destroy or banish knowledge. In this sense we admit the appropriateness of the name."

"Greek philosophers," says Max Müller, "called it [Agnosticism] with a technical name, *Agnoia*, or if they wished to express the proper attitude of mind towards transcendental questions, they called it *Epoche*, i. e., suspense of judgment. During the Middle Ages, exactly the same idea which now goes by the name of Agnosticism, was well known as *Docta Ignorantia*, i. e., the ignorance founded on the knowledge of our ignorance or impotence to grasp anything beyond what is phenomenal." See *Nineteenth Century*, for Dec., 1894, pp. 892–95.

a discipline for its delimitation; and instead of discovering truth, has only the modest merit of preventing error."

The writings of "that prince of agnostics," David Hume, and Sir William Hamilton's essay on The Philosophy of the Unconditioned, confirmed Huxley in this view, and stamped upon his mind "the strong conviction that, on even the most solemn and important questions, men are apt to take cunning phrases for answers; and that the limitations of our faculties, in a great number of cases, render real answers to such questions, not merely actually impossible, but theoretically inconceivable."[1]

Huxley, however, although the coiner of the word Agnosticism, and one of its most zealous and popular exponents, is not its coryphæus. This position is held by the philosopher of "the unknowable," Herbert Spencer, who has done far more than any other one person to establish what might be called a school of agnostic philosophy. When it is remembered that Spencer is likewise the philosopher of Evolution, "our great philosopher," as Darwin calls him, we can see what an intimate connection there must be between Evolution, as a scientific theory, and Agnosticism as a system of philosophy.

But if Spencer is the coryphæus of modern Agnosticism, who was his choragus, who was the teacher and the fautor-in-chief, of the system of thought which he has developed at such length in his numerous volumes on science and philosophy?

---

[1] "Collected Essays," by T. H. Huxley, vol. V, p. 236.

Strange as it may appear, Spencer's master was none other than an Anglican divine, whose orthodoxy and loyalty to the established church of England were never suspected, and who, at the time of his death, held the honorable position of dean of St. Paul's, London. The name of this divine was Dean Mansel, one of the most distinguished theologians and metaphysicians of England in the latter half of the nineteenth century.

The germs of modern Agnosticism, according to Spencer's showing, are unequivocally contained in Mansel's Bampton "Lectures on the Limits of Religious Thought," delivered in the University of Oxford in 1859. In one sentence he stated by implication, if not directly, all that Spencer has developed in his "First Principles," and supplied, as it were, the charter for all the extreme forms of Agnosticism which have had such a vogue during the past generation, and whose progress has been marked with such dire results to faith, not only in Great Britain, but also throughout the entire Christian world.

"Of the nature and attributes of God in his infinite being, philosophy," asserts Mansel, "can tell us nothing; of man's inability to apprehend that nature, and why he is thus unable, she tells us all that we can know, and all that we need to know."[1]

God being thus separated from His creatures by an impassable gulf, it is useless for us to attempt to investigate His nature and attributes. No knowledge that we can acquire of God will satisfy the demands

---
[1] Lecture VIII, p. 126.

of philosophy, or be capable "of reduction to an ultimate and absolute truth." The only response that may be given to our inquiries, "the only voice which sounds back from the abyss where dwells the Being whom we designate as the Absolute and the Infinite, is a solemn warning that we possess no faculties which qualify us for the attainment of any knowledge of God."

This, in brief, is Manselism, the elimination of God from the domain of human knowledge, and a substitution, in its place, of a dreary, hopeless, derisive skepticism; the abolition of theology as an aimless, bootless pursuit, and the virtual recognition of a dark, blighting, forbidding Atheism.

Mansel, Huxley and Romanes.

There is every reason to believe that Mansel never apprehended the full significance of the destructive principles enunciated in his Bampton lectures. Not so, however, with the enemies of Christianity. They saw, at a glance, the real bearing of the Oxford professor's teachings, and were not slow to give them all the publicity possible.

Spencer quotes from him, at length, in his "First Principles," and makes his declaration the basis of the agnostic philosophy. Huxley, Romanes and others followed in the wake of Spencer, and were not long in bringing the principles of Mansel, as expounded by Spencer, within the comprehension of the general reading public.

Huxley, indeed, has done more, probably, than anyone else to popularize Agnosticism, and by the majority of readers he is regarded as its chief exponent and defender. He, however, disclaims anything like a creed, and declares that agnostics are precluded from having one by the very nature of their mental status. He prefers to regard Agnosticism, not as a creed, but as "a method, the essence of which lies in the rigorous application of a single principle." "Positively," he informs us, "the principle may be expressed: In matters of the intellect, follow your reason as far as it will take you, without regard to any other consideration. And negatively: In matters of the intellect do not pretend that conclusions are certain which are not demonstrated or demonstrable. That I take to be the agnostic faith, which, if a man keep whole and undefiled, he shall not be ashamed to look the universe in the face, whatever the future may have in store for him."[1]

The profession of faith of G. J. Romanes is more explicit, at least in so far as it refers to God, and gives us in a few words the views entertained by the two leading classes of agnostics regarding the First Cause, or the Absolute or Unconditioned.

"By Agnosticism," asserts Romanes, "I understand a theory of things which abstains from either affirming or denying the existence of God. It thus represents with regard to Theism a state of suspended judgment; and all it undertakes to affirm is, that upon existing evidence the being of God is unknown. But the term Agnosticism is frequently used in a widely different sense, as implying belief

---

[1] "Science and Christian Tradition," p. 246.

that the being of God is not merely now unknown, but must always remain unknown."

Docta Ignorantia.

The agnostic creed, then, is a creed based on ignorance rather than on knowledge. We can know nothing that does not come within the range of sense; nothing which we cannot observe with our microscopes, spectroscopes and telescopes, or examine with our scalpels, or test in our alembics and crucibles. Our knowledge is and must be, by the very nature of the case, limited to things material and phenomenal. Every attempt to fathom the mysteries of the super-sensible or spiritual world, if

---

[1] *Contemporary Review*, vol. L, p. 59. In his posthumous "Thoughts on Religion," Romanes distinguishes two kinds of Agnosticism, pure and impure, the former held by Huxley, the latter by Spencer. "The modern and convenient term 'Agnosticism,'" writes Romanes, "is used in two very different senses. By its originator, Professor Huxley, it was coined to signify an attitude of reasoned ignorance touching everything that lies beyond the sphere of sense-perception, a professed inability to found valid belief on any other basis. It is in this, its original sense, and also, in my opinion, its only philosophically justifiable sense, that I shall understand the term. But the other, and perhaps more particular sense, in which the word is now employed, is as a correlative of Mr. H. Spencer's doctrine of the unknowable.

"This latter term is philosophically erroneous, implying important negative knowledge, that if there be a God, we know this much about him, that He *cannot* reveal Himself to man. *Pure* Agnosticism is as defined by Huxley." Pp. 107-108.

It is a matter of regret that the lamented author of these "Thoughts on Religion," did not live to complete his work. Not long before his premature death, it is pleasing to record, he recognized the weakness and fallacies of Agnosticism, and returned to "a full and deliberate communion" with the Church of England, from which he had so long been separated. "In his case," writes Canon Gore, "the 'pure in heart' was, after a long period of darkness, allowed in a measure, before his death, to 'see God.'"

there be such a world, or to trace a connection between noumenal cause or phenomenal effect, if there be such a connection, must, we are told, prove useless and abortive. There may or there may not be, a God; we hope there is a God, but we have no warrant for asserting His existence. We cannot affirm either that He is personal or impersonal, intelligent or unintelligent; we cannot say whether He is mind or matter. We cannot, by searching, find Him out, and our every assertion regarding Him is but a contradiction in terms. If there be a Supreme Being, a First Cause, an Absolute Existence, an Ultimate Power; if, in a word, there be a God, He not only is now, but ever must be, unknown and unknowable.

"There may be absolute Truth, but if there is, it is out of our reach. It is possible that there may be a science of realities, of abstract being, of first principles and *a priori* truths, but it is up in the heavens, far above our heads, and we must be content to grovel amid things of earth — to build up as best we can our fragments of empirical knowledge, leaving all else to that future world, in which, in a clear light, if there is ever to be a clearer light for us, we shall know, if there is such a thing as knowledge, the nature and attributes of God, if there is a God, and if His nature can be known, and if His attributes are anything more than a fiction of theologians."[1]

The Duke of Argyll in his interesting work, "The Unity of Nature" well observes that "This fundamental inconsistency in the agnostic philosophy,

---

[1] *The Month*, vol. XLV, p. 156.

becomes all the more remarkable when we find, that the very men who tell us that we are not one with anything above us, are the same who insist that we are one with everything beneath us. Whatever there is in us or about us which is purely animal, we may see everywhere; but whatever there is in us purely intellectual, or moral, we delude ourselves if we think we see it anywhere. There are abundant homologies between our bodies and the bodies of beasts; but there are no homologies between our minds and any Mind which lives and manifests itself in nature. Our livers and our lungs, our vertebræ and our nervous systems, are identical in origin and in function with those of the living creatures around us; but there is nothing in nature, or above it, which corresponds to our forethought or design or purpose, to our love of the good, or our admiration of the beautiful, to our indignation with the wicked, or to our pity for the suffering or the fallen. I venture to think that no system of philosophy that has ever been taught on earth, lies under such a weight of antecedent improbability; and this improbability increases in direct proportion to the success of science in tracing the unity of nature, and in showing step by step, how its laws and their results can be brought into more direct relation with the mind and intellect of man."[1]

Agnosticism as a Via Media.

Agnosticism professes to be a kind of *via media* between Theism and Atheism. It does not deny

---
[1] P. 166.

the existence of God, but declares that a knowledge of Him is unattainable. Whether He has personality or not; whether He has intelligence or not; whether He is just, holy, omnipotent, omniscient or not; whether He has a care for man and watches over him or not; whether He has created man and the earth he inhabits or not—all these are questions which are simply insoluble; are matters which are, and must forever be, beyond the ken and apprehension of the human intellect.

A very slight examination will suffice to convince anyone that such a *via media* cannot exist; that, notwithstanding what its advocates may assert to the contrary, Agnosticism is but Atheism in disguise. More than this; it is worse than Atheism. An atheist, although he may deny the existence of God, is nevertheless open to discuss the subject. An agnostic, however, takes away all matter for discussion by insisting that God, if there be a God, is unknowable, and being so, is beyond and above the reach of reason and consciousness. Far from being the Creator of heaven and earth and all things, as faith teaches, God, according to the agnostic, is but a creature of the imagination, a figment of theologians, and religion, even in its pure and noblest form, is but a development of fetichism or ghost-worship.

Our present concern, however, is not so much with Agnosticism as a system of belief or unbelief, as with Agnosticism in relation to the theory of the origin and Evolution of the visible universe.

Origin of the Universe.

The great and perpetual crux for agnostics, as well as for atheists, is the existence of the world. For the theist, the origin of the material universe offers no difficulty. He accepts as true the declaration of Genesis, that: "In the beginning God created heaven and earth," and with the acceptance of this truth, all difficulty, based on the fact of creation, vanishes forthwith. But to the agnostic, as well as to the atheist, the query: Whence the world and the myriad forms of life which it contains?—is constantly recurring, and with ever-increasing persistency and importance. It is, as all must acknowledge, a fundamental question, and no system of thought is worthy of the name of philosophy, that is not able to give an answer which the intellect will recognize as rational and conclusive.

According to Herbert Spencer, there are but "three verbally intelligent suppositions" respecting the origin of the universe. "We may," he says, "assert that it is self-existent; or that it is self-created; or that it is created by an external agency. That it should be self-existent is inconceivable, because this" implies the conception, which is an impossibility, of infinite past time. To this let us add, that even were self-existence conceivable, it would not in any sense be an explanation of the universe, nor make it in any degree more comprehensible. Thus the atheistic theory is not only absolutely unthinkable, but even if it were thinkable would not be a solution.

"The hypothesis of self-creation," the English philosopher continues, "which practically amounts to what is called Pantheism, is similarly incapable of being represented in thought. Really to conceive self-creation, is to conceive potential existence passing into actual existence by some inherent necessity; which we cannot do. And even were it true that potential existence is conceivable, we should still be no forwarder. For whence the potential existence? This would just as much require accounting for existence, and just the same difficulties would meet us." According to Spencer, therefore, both the pantheistic and the atheistic hypotheses must be dismissed, as utterly inadequate to explain the fact of the world's actual existence.

The third hypothesis, and the one generally received, is known as the theistic hypothesis; creation by an external agency. But "the idea," I am still quoting Spencer, "of a Great Artificer shaping the universe, somewhat after the manner in which a workman shapes a piece of furniture, does not help us to comprehend the real mystery; viz., the origin of the materials of which the universe consists. . . . But even supposing that the genesis of the universe could really be represented in thought as the result of an external agency, the mystery would be as great as ever, for there would still arise the question: How came there to be an external agent, for we have seen that self-existence is rigorously inconceivable? Thus, impossible as it is to think of the actual universe as self-existing, we do but multiply impossibilities of thought by every attempt we make to explain its existence."[1]

According to Spencer, then, the theistic hypothesis of creation is as unthinkable as the hypotheses of Atheism and Pantheism. The theistic, as well as the atheistic and the pantheistic views, he will have it, imply a contradiction in terms, and, such being the case, we must, perforce, resign ourselves to the acceptance of the agnostic position, which is one of ignorance and darkness.

Spencer's Unknowable.

But, strive as he may, Spencer cannot think of the world around him without thinking of it as caused — and hence he is forced to think of a First Cause, infinite, absolute and unconditioned. And in spite of his assertion that God is and must be unknowable, he is continually contradicting himself by assigning characteristics and attributes to that of which he avers we can know absolutely nothing. For He of whom nothing can be known, of whom nothing can be declared, is, Spencer affirms, the First Cause of all, the Ultimate Reality, the Inscrutable Power, that which underlies all phenomena, that which accounts for all phenomena, that which transcends all phenomena, the Supreme Being, the Infinite, the Absolute, the All-Being, the Creative Power, the Infinite and Eternal Energy, by which all things are created and sustained; a mode of being as much transcending intelligence and will as these transcend mechanical motion.

---

[1] "First Principles," chap. ii.

Max Müller on Agnosticism.

The distinguished philologist and orientalist, Max Müller, although not a philosopher by profession, reasons far more philosophically than Herbert Spencer, when he writes: "I cannot help discovering, in the universe an all-pervading causality or reason for everything; for even when, in my phenomenal ignorance, I do not yet know a reason for this or that, I am forced to admit that there exists some such reason; I feel bound to admit it, because, to a mind like ours, nothing can exist without a sufficient reason. But how do I know that? Here is the point where I cease to be an agnostic. I do not know it from experience, and yet I know it with a certainty greater than any which experience can give. This, also, is not a new discovery. The first step towards it was made at a very early time by the Greek philosophers, when they turned from the observation of outward nature to higher spheres of thought, and recognized in nature the working of a mind, or Νοῦς, which pervades the universe. Anaxagoras, who was the first to postulate such a Νοῦς in nature, ascribed to it not much more than the first impulse to the inter-action of his homoiomeries. But even his Νοῦς was soon perceived to be more than a mere *Primum Mobile*; more than the κινοῦν ἀκίνατόν. We, ourselves, after thousands of years of physical and metaphysical research, can say no more than that there is νοῦς, that there is mind and reason in nature. *Sa Majesté le Hasard* has long been dethroned in all scientific studies, and neither natural selection, nor struggle for life, nor the influence of environment, nor other aliases of it, will account for the *logos* within us. If any philosopher can persuade himself, that the true and well-ordered *genera* of nature are the results of mechanical causes, whatever name we may give them, he moves in a world altogether different from my own. To Plato, these genera were ideas; to the peripatetics, they were words, or *logoi;* to both, they were manifestations of thought."[1]

Sources of Agnosticism.

One of the chief sources of the Agnosticism now so rampant, is to be sought in the lamentable ignorance of the fundamental principles of true philosophy and theology everywhere manifest, and especially in the productions of our modern scientists and philosophers. And the only antidote for agnostic, as well as atheistic teaching, is that scholastic philosophy which contemporary thinkers ignore, if they do not positively contemn; for it alone can clear up the fallacies which are constantly admitted in the name of philosophy, and which have done so much to confuse thought and to make sound ratiocination impossible.

Another not unfrequent cause of error arises from a false psychology, from confounding or identifying a faculty — imagination — which is material, with a faculty — reason — which is immaterial. Mind is made a function of matter, and that which cannot be pictured to the imagination is regarded as impossible of

---
[1] *The Nineteenth Century*, December, 1894.

apprehension by the intellect. That, therefore, which the imagination cannot admit, cannot be accepted by reason; that which is unimaginable is, *ipso facto*, unthinkable. Such is the suicidal skepticism of those who confuse the immaterial thought, which is above and beyond sense, with the material imagination, which is always intimately connected with sense, and which, by its very nature, is incompetent to rise above the conditions and limitations of matter.

Again, probably no two terms are more prolific of fallacy and confusion than the much-abused words time and space.

Infinite Time.

One of the gravest objections against the existence of God, from Spencer's point of view, is that we cannot conceive of a self-existent being, because self-existence implies infinite past time, which is a contradiction in terms. We cannot conceive of God existing from all eternity, because eternity is but time multiplied to infinity, and we cannot conceive time multiplied to infinity.

The difficulty here indicated arises from a misapprehension of the nature of time, and from an anthropomorphic view of God, which subjects Him to the conditions and limitations of His creatures. God has not existed through infinite time, as is supposed. He does not exist in time at all. He exists apart from time; and before time was, God was. Time implies change and succession; but in God there is neither change nor succession. As the measure of the existence of created things, it is something relative;

but in God all is absolute. Eternity is not, as the agnostic has it, time raised to an infinite power, no more than the attributes of God are human attributes raised to an infinite power. God has existed from all eternity, but He is, by His very nature, above time, and before time, and beyond time, even infinite time. To make God exist through infinite past time, because He has existed from all eternity, would be tantamount to imposing on Him the conditions of created things, and to degrading Him as much as do the most extravagant of anthropomorphists.

Infinite Space.

And as God does not exist in time, so He does not exist in space. Infinite space, like infinite time, is a contradiction in terms. If there were nothing to be measured, if material objects could be annihilated, space would disappear. For space is not an independent entity, as agnostics suppose, not a kind of a huge box, which was created for the reception of material things, but the necessary and concomitant result of the creation of matter, of what is limited and capable of measurement. And as God is above and before and beyond time, so is He likewise above and before and beyond space. As time began only when God uttered His creative *fiat*, so space had no existence until the creation of the material universe. Neither space nor time, therefore, can be used as a foundation on which to base an argument against creation, or the existence of a First Cause, for both space and time imply limitation, and God, the Absolute, is above and independent of all limitation. Agnostics, who protest so strongly against Anthropomorphism, are, therefore, themselves anthropomorphists, when they attempt, as they do by their irrational theory, to tie down the Creator to the conditions of His creatures.

Mysteries of Nature.

I have said that one of the chief causes of Agnosticism is ignorance of Christian philosophy and theology. This is true. But there is also another reason. The mysteries of nature which everywhere confront us, and which baffle all attempts at their solution; the impossibility of lifting the veil which separates the visible from the invisible world, are other sources of skepticism, and contribute not a little to make Agnosticism plausible, and to give it the vogue which it now enjoys. "Hardly," says the Wise Man, "do we guess aright at things that are upon earth; and with labor do we find the things that are before us. But the things that are in Heaven, who shall search out?" The mysteries of the natural order, those which confront us on the threshold of the unseen, are great and often insoluble; but how much greater, how much more unfathomable, are those that envelop the world beyond the realm of sense, the world of spirit and soul, the world of angelic and Divine intelligence!

The difficulties indicated are grave indeed, but skeptics are not the only ones who have given them thought or fully appreciated their magnitude. There is a Christian as well as a skeptical Agnosticism, and all the difficulties suggested by the mysteries of the natural and supernatural orders, were long ago realized and taken into account by Christian philosophy and Christian theology. They were before the minds of Origen and Clement of Alexandria; they occupied the brilliant intellects of St. Basil, St. John Chrysostom, St. Gregory of Nyssa and St. Augustine; they entered into the disputations of the Schoolmen, and have found a prominent place in the writings of their successors up to the present day. No, these difficulties have not been ignored; neither have they been underrated nor dismissed without receiving the consideration their importance demands. Far from being new, as certain writers would have us believe; far from being the product of the research of these latter days; far from being the result of those deep and critical investigations which have been conducted in every department of knowledge, sacred and profane, they are as old as the Church, as old even as speculative thought.

Christian Agnosticism.

Unlike the Agnosticism of skepticism, however, Christian Agnosticism is on firm ground, and, guided by the principles of a sound philosophy, is able with unerring judgment to discriminate the true from the false, and to draw the line of demarcation between the knowable and the unknowable. Christian Agnosticism confesses aloud that God is incomprehensible, that we can have no adequate idea of His perfections, but, unlike skeptical Agnosticism, it brushes aside the false and delusive hope, that in the distant future, when our faculties are more highly developed, when the work of Evolution is farther advanced than it now is, we may perhaps be able to comprehend the Divine nature, and have an adequate notion of the Divine perfections. Christian Agnosticism tells us that not even the blessed in Heaven, who see the whole of the Divine nature, can ever have, even after millions and billions of ages, a knowledge which shall be commensurate in depth with the Divine Object of their adoration and love. They shall see God in the clear light of the Beatific Vision, *facie ad faciem*, and shall know as they are known. Nothing shall be hidden from them. Their intelligence will be illumined by the light of God's glory. The veil that now intervenes between the Creator and the creature will be removed, and the created intellect will be in the veritable presence of the Divine Essence. But even then, it will be impossible to have an adequate or a comprehensive knowledge of God. He will, as the Scholastics phrase it, be known *totus sed non totaliter*. The soul will always have new beauties undiscovered, fresh glories to arrest its enraptured gaze, and unfathomable abysses of love and wisdom to contemplate, whose immensity will be as great after millions of æons shall have elapsed, as when it was ushered into the Divine Presence, when it caught the first glimpse of the glory of the Beatific Vision, and experienced the first thrills of ecstasy in the contemplation of the fathomless, limitless ocean of God's infinite perfections. The soul will know God, but its knowledge will always be limited by the fact that it is created, that it is finite, that it is human, that its capacity is narrowed and restricted by its very nature, and is, therefore, incompetent to fathom the depths, or comprehend the immensity, of the ocean of Divine Wisdom and Divine Love, to comprehend, in a word, that which is immeasurable, and infinite, and eternal.

If, then, the blessed may drink for all eternity at the fountain of the Godhead, without exhausting or diminishing the infinitude of joy and love and knowledge which is there found, we should not be surprised to encounter difficulties and mysteries, in the natural as well as in the supernatural order, which are above and beyond our weak and circumscribed intellects. We admit, and admit frankly, that there is much that we do not know, much that we can never comprehend. But our ignorance of many things does not make us skeptics in all things beyond the range of sense and experiment. We may not know God adequately, but we do know much about Him, aside from what He has been pleased to reveal regarding Himself. With St. Paul, we believe that "the invisible things of God from the creation of the world are clearly seen, being understood by the things that are made: His eternal power also and divinity."[1]

---

[1] Romans, chap. i, 20. I take pleasure in again quoting from Max Müller, who, in speaking of the matter under discussion truthfully observes: "In one sense I hope I am, and have always been, an agnostic, that is, in relying on nothing but historical facts, and in following reason as far as it will take us in matters of the intellect, and in never pretending that conclusions are certain which are not demonstrated or demonstrable. This attitude of the mind is the *conditio sine qua non* of all philosophy. If in future it is to be called Agnosticism, then I am a true agnostic; but if Agnosticism excludes a recognition of an

Of the essence of God we can know nothing. Even of matter we are ignorant as to its essence. From the existence of the world, we infer the existence of God; for our primary intuitions teach us that there can be no effect without a cause. The evidences of order and design in the universe, prove the existence of a Creator who is intelligent, who has power and will, and who, therefore, is personal, and not the blind fate and impersonal energy and unknowable entity of the agnostic.

Gods of the Positivist and the Agnostic.

The gods of the heathen were manifold and grotesque, but what shall we say of the objects which the positivist and agnostic propose for our worship and love?

The Greeks and Romans gave Divine honors to demi-gods and heroes. Comte, one of the apostles of modern Agnosticism, affects to recoil before such gross idolatry; but is he more of a philosopher, or less of an idolator, when he proclaims that it is not man taken individually, or any particular man, but man taken collectively, man considered in the aggregate, that is to be regarded as the object of our cult? The Roman and the Athenian worshipped Apollo and Hercules, Jupiter and Venus; Comte

---

eternal reason, pervading the natural and the moral world, if to postulate a rational cause for a rational universe is called Gnosticism, then I am a gnostic, and a humble follower of the greatest thinkers of our race, from Plato and the author of the Fourth Gospel to Kant and Hegel." *The Nineteenth Century*, Dec., 1894; see also, "The Christian Agnostic and the Christian Gnostic," by the Very Rev. A. F. Hewit, D. D., C. S. P., in the *American Catholic Quarterly Review*, January, 1891.

says we must worship humanity in its entirety. Huxley, however, dissents from this view, and tells us that it is not humanity, but the cosmos, the visible material universe, which should constitute the object of our highest veneration and religious emotion. Herbert Spencer is even more nebulous and mystical. His deity is an unknowable energy, "impersonal, unconscious, unthinking and unthinkable." God is "the great enigma which he [man] knows cannot be solved," and religion can at best be concerned only with "a consciousness of a mystery which can never be fathomed." According to Mr. Harrison, however—the brilliant critic of the views propounded by Huxley, the doughty combatant who has so frequently run full atilt against the champions of Agnosticism—Spencer's Unknowable is "an ever-present conundrum to be everlastingly given up;" his Something, or All-Being, is a pure negation, "an All-Nothingness, an x^n and an Everlasting No." Verily it is of such, "vain in their thoughts and darkened in their foolish heart," that the Apostle of the Gentiles speaks when he declares that they "changed the truth of God into a lie; and worshipped and served the creature rather than the Creator."[1]

But it is not my purpose to dilate on the teachings of Agnosticism. My sole object is to indicate briefly some of its more patent and fundamental errors. A detailed examination and refutation of them does not come within the purview of our subject. For such examination and refutation, the

---
[1] "Romans," chap. i, 25.

reader is referred to works which treat of these topics *ex professo*.[1] It suffices for our present purpose to know the relation of Agnosticism to Evolution; to know that a particular phase of Evolution is so intimately connected with Agnosticism, that it cannot be disassociated from it, to realize that Agnosticism, and agnostic Evolution, are practically as synonymous as are Atheistic Evolution and Monism. It is enough for us to appreciate the fact that Agnosticism and Monism are fundamentally erroneous, to understand that both monistic and agnostic Evolution are untenable and inconsistent with the teaching of Theism and with the doctrines of Christianity; that they are illegitimate inductions from the known data of veritable science, and utterly at variance with the primary concepts of genuine philosophy. We need, consequently, consider them no further. Evolution, in the sense in which it is held by the Monist and Agnostic, is so obviously in positive contradiction to the leading tenets of Theism, that it may forthwith be dismissed as not only untenable, but as unwarranted by fact and experiment, and negatived by the incontestable principles of sound metaphysics and Catholic Dogma.

---

[1] See especially: "Agnosticism and Religion," by the Rev. George J. Lucas, D.D.; chaps. III and IV of "The Great Enigma," by W. S. Lilly, and the succinct and philosophical "Agnosticism," by the Right Rev. J. L. Spalding, D.D. The reader will likewise find many valuable and suggestive pages in Balfour's "Foundations of Belief," and in a review of this work by Mgr. Mercier, in the *Revue Neo-Scolastique*, for October, 1895.

CHAPTER IV.

THEISM AND EVOLUTION.

Evolution and Faith.

HAVING eliminated from our discussion the forms of Evolution held by the divers schools of monists and agnostics, there now remains but the third form, known as theistic Evolution. Can we, then, consistently with the certain deductions of science and philosophy, and in accordance with the positive dogmas of faith—can we as Christians, as Catholics, who accept without reserve all the teachings of the Church, give our assent to theistic Evolution? This is a question of paramount importance, one which is daily growing in interest, and one for an answer to which the reading public has long been clamoring. And with it must also be answered a certain number of cognate questions, of scarcely less interest and importance than the main question of Evolution itself.

I have elsewhere[1] shown that the principles of theistic Evolution—the Evolution, namely, which admits the existence of a God, and the development, under the action of His Providence, of the universe and all it contains—were accepted and defended by some of the most eminent Doctors of the early Greek and Latin Churches. It was a brilliant

---
[1] "Bible, Science and Faith," part I, chaps. III and IV.

luminary of the Oriental Church, St. Gregory of Nyssa, who first clearly conceived and formulated the nebular hypothesis, which was long centuries subsequently elaborated by Laplace, Herschel and Faye. The learned prelate found no difficulty in admitting the action of secondary causes, in the formation of the universe from the primal matter which the Almighty had directly created. According to Gregory and his school, God created matter in a formless or nebulous condition, but impressed on this matter the power of developing into all the various forms which it afterwards assumed. The universe and all it contains, the earth and all that inhabits it—plants, animals, man—were created by God, but they were created in different ways. The primitive material, the nebulous matter, from which all things were fashioned, was created by God directly and immediately; whereas, all the multitudinous creatures of the visible world, were produced by Him indirectly and mediately, that is, by the operation of secondary causes and what are commonly called the laws of nature.

Teachings of St. Augustine.

St. Augustine not only accepted the conclusions of his illustrious Greek predecessor, but he went much further than the Bishop of Nyssa. He was, likewise, much more explicit, especially in what concerned the development of the various forms of animal and vegetable life. According to the Doctor of Hippo, God did not create the world as it now appears, but only the primordial matter of which it is composed.

Not only the diverse forms of inorganic matter, rocks, minerals, crystals, were created by the operation of secondary causes, but plants and animals were also the products of such causes. For God, the saint insists, created the manifold forms of terrestrial life, not directly but in germ; potentially and causally—*potentialiter atque causaliter.* In commenting on the words of Genesis: "Let the earth bring forth the green herb," he declares that plants were created not directly and immediately, but causally and potentially, *in fieri, in causa;* that the earth received from God the power of producing herb and tree, *producendi accepisse virtutem.*

In his great work on the Trinity, the illustrious Doctor tells us that: "The hidden seeds of all things that are born corporeally and visibly, are concealed in the corporeal elements of the world." We are unable to see them with our eyes, "but we can conjecture their existence from our reason." They are quite different from "those seeds that are visible at once to our eyes, from fruits and living things." It is indeed from such hidden and invisible seeds that "The waters, at the bidding of the Creator, produced the first swimming creatures and fowl, and that the earth brought forth the first buds after their kind, and the first living creatures after their kind." They lay dormant, as it were, until long æons after the creation of matter, because "suitable combinations of circumstances were wanting, whereby they might be enabled to burst forth and complete their species."

"The world," he avers, "is pregnant with the causes of things that are coming to the birth;

which are not created in it, except from the highest essence, where nothing either springs up or dies, either begins to be or ceases." But the Creator of these seeds, the Cause of these causes, *Causa causarum*, is at the same time the Creator of all things that exist. He carefully distinguishes "God creating and forming within, from the works of the creature which are applied from without." "In the creation of visible things it is God," he affirms, "that works from within, but the exterior operations," that is, the operations of creatures or those of divers physical forces, "are applied by Him to that nature of things wherein He creates all things." "For," the Saint continues, "it is one thing to make and administer the creature from the innermost and highest turning point of causation, which He alone does who is God, the Creator; but quite another thing to apply some operation from without, in proportion to the strength and faculties assigned to each by Him, that that which is created may come forth into being at this time or at that, or in this way or that way. For all things, in the way of origin and beginning, have already been created in a kind of texture of the elements, *in quadam textura elementorum;* but they can come forth only when opportunity offers, *acceptis opportunitatibus.*" [1]

---

[1] "Aliud est enim ex intimo et summo causarum cardine condere atque administrare creaturam, quod qui facit, solus creator est Deus: aliud autem pro distributis ab illo viribus et facultatibus aliquam operationem foris secus admovere, ut tunc vel tunc, sic vel sic, exeat quod creatur. Ista quippe originaliter ac primordialiter in quadam textura elementorum cuncta jam creata sunt, sed acceptis opportunitatibus prodeunt." "De Trinitate," lib. III, cap. ix. In his great work, "De Genesi ad Litteram,"

THEISM AND EVOLUTION.

God, then, according to St. Augustine, created matter directly and immediately. On this primordial or elementary matter He impressed certain causal reasons, *causales rationes;* that is, He gave it certain powers, and imposed on it certain laws, in virtue of which it evolved into all the myriad forms which we now behold. The saint does not tell us by what laws or processes the Creator acted. He makes no attempt to determine what are the factors of organic development. He limits himself to a general statement of the fact of Evolution, of progress from the simple to the complex, from the homogeneous to the heterogeneous, from simple primordial elements to the countless, varied, complicated structures of animated nature.

Has any modern philosopher stated more clearly the salient facts of organic Evolution? Has anyone

---

lib. IV, cap. XXIII, the saint beautifully develops the evolutionary idea, when he exhibits the analogy between the growth of a tree from the seed and the Evolution of the world from its primordial elements. Speaking of the gradual growth of the tree—trunk, branches, leaves, fruit—from the seed, he declares : " In semine ergo illa omnia fuerunt primitus, non mole corporeæ magnitudinis sed vi potentiaque causali." After asking the question : " Quid enim ex arbore illa surgit aut pendet, quod non ex quodam occulto thesauro seminis illius extractum atque depromptum est ? " he continues with rare philosophical acumen : " sicut autem in ipso grano invisibiliter erant omnia simul quæ per tempora in arborem surgerent ; ita ipse mundus cogitandus est, cum Deus simul omnia creavit, habuisse simul omnia quæ in illo et cum illo facta sunt, quando factus est dies ; non solum cœlum cum sole et luna et sideribus, quorum species manet motu rotabili, et terram et abyssos, quæ velut inconstantes motus patiantur atque inferius adjuncta partem alteram mundo conferunt; sed etiam illa quæ aqua et terra produxit potentialiter atque causaliter, priusquam per temporum moras ita exorirentur, quo modo nobis jam nota sunt in eis operibus, quæ Deus usque nunc operatur."

insisted more strongly on the reign of law in nature, or discriminated more keenly between the operations of the Creator and those of the creature? Has anyone realized more fully the functions of a First Cause, as compared with those of causes which are but secondary or physical? If so, I am not aware of it. Modern scientists have, indeed, a far more detailed knowledge of the divers forms of terrestrial life than had the philosophical Bishop of Hippo; they have a more comprehensive view of nature than was possible in his day, but they have not, with all their knowledge and superior advantages, been able to formulate the general theory of Evolution a whit more clearly, than we find it expressed in the writings of the Doctor of Grace, who wrote nearly fifteen centuries ago.

Views of the Angelic Doctor.

The Angelic Doctor takes up the teachings of St. Augustine and makes them his own. He discusses them according to the scholastic method, and with a lucidity and a comprehensiveness that leave nothing to be desired. He carefully distinguishes between creation proper, and the production or generation of things from preëxisting material; between the operations of absolute Creative Energy, and those which may be performed by secondary causes. Indeed, so exhaustive and·so complete is his treatment of the origin and Evolution of the material universe and all it contains; so clear and so conclusive his argumentation, that his successors have·found but little to add to his brilliant propositions respecting the genesis of the world and its inhabitants.

The primordial Divine act of creation, according to St. Thomas, following St. Augustine, consisted in the creation, *ex nihilo*, of three classes of creatures; spiritual intelligences, the heavenly bodies and simple bodies, or elements. According to the physical theories of the time, the composition of the celestial bodies was supposed to be different from that of the earth. They were supposed to be incapable of generation or corruption;[1] to be constituted of elementary matter, indeed, but matter unlike that of sublunary bodies, in that it is incorruptible. We now know that mediæval philosophers were in error on this point. Spectrum analysis has demonstrated that all the celestial bodies have the same composition as our earth, and that the constitution of the material universe is identical throughout its vast expanse. Eliminating this error, which was one of physics, and not one of philosophy or theology, and one which in nowise impairs the teachings of

---

[1] The scholastic use of the words "generation" and "corruption" must carefully be distinguished from the ordinary meaning of these terms. "In its widest sense," as Father Harper tells us, "generation includes all new production even by the creative act. In a more restricted sense, it includes all transformations, accidental as well as substantial. In a still more restricted sense, substantial transformations only. Yet more specially, the natural production of living things; most specially, the natural production of man." Corruption, as understood by the Schoolmen, means, not "retrograde transformation, such as occurs, for instance, in the death of a living entity," but "the dissolution of a body by the expulsion of that substantial form by which it had been previously actuated. In the order of nature, it is the invariable accompaniment of generation." Cf. "Metaphysics of the School," vol. II, glossary, and pp. 273-279.

it being.[1] An element, accordingly, is a composite entity, a *compositum*, constituted of matter—which is the subject, potentiality or inferior part of the composite—and form, which is the act or superior part. And although there is but one matter, there are many forms.[2] And it is because this one matter is actuated by diverse forms, that we have the manifold elements which constitute the material universe.

Seminales Rationes.

But these elements, composed of matter and form, required something more, in order to be competent to enter into combinations and to give rise to higher and more complex substances.

---

[1] "Simpliciter loquendo, forma dat esse materiæ. . . . Sciendum etiam, quod licet materia prima non habeat in sua ratione aliquam formam, . . . materia tamen numquam denudatur a forma. . . . Per se autem numquam potest esse; quia cum in ratione sua non habeat aliquam formam, non potest esse in actu, cum esse actu non sit nisi a forma; sed est solum in potentia." Ibidem. The whole of this masterly and interesting treatise should be carefully pondered by those who desire to know the mind of the saintly Doctor respecting the nature of matter.

[2] The words "matter" and "form," it will be observed, are here employed in a strictly metaphysical or technical sense. Matter is that element in an entity which is indeterminate, passive, potential, "of all real entities the nearest to nothingness." It is one of the two essential constituents of all bodies. The other element or constituent of bodies is form. It is that which differentiates and actuates matter; which determines the specific nature of any composite. "The matter in which form adheres," according to Aristotle, "is not absolutely non-existent; it exists as possibility—$\delta\acute{v}\nu\alpha\mu\iota\varsigma$, *potentia*. Form, on the contrary, is the accomplishment, the realization—$\grave{\epsilon}\nu\tau\epsilon\lambda\acute{\epsilon}\chi\epsilon\iota\alpha$, $\grave{\epsilon}\nu\acute{\epsilon}\rho\gamma\epsilon\iota\alpha$, *actus*—of this possibility. For an elaborate explanation of these terms, see chaps. II and III, vol. II, of Harper's "Metaphysics of the School." Cf. also, § 48, vol. I, of Ueberweg's "History of Philosophy."

This something more, the Angelic Doctor designates seminal forces, or influences—*seminales rationes.* "The powers lodged in matter," he tells us, "by which natural effects result, are called *seminales rationes.* The complete active powers in nature, with the corresponding passive powers—as heat and cold, the form of fire, the power of the sun, and the like—are called *seminales rationes.* They are called seminal, not by reason of any imperfection of entity that they may be supposed to have, like the formative virtue in seed; but because on the individual things at first created, such powers were conferred by the operations of the six days, so that out of them, as though from certain seeds, natural entities might be produced and multiplied." The physical forces—heat, light, electricity and magnetism—would, doubtless, in modern scientific terminology, correspond to the *seminales rationes*[1] of the Angelic Doctor, as they are efficient in producing changes in matter and in disposing it for that gradual Evolution which has obtained in the material universe.

In the beginning, then, God created primordial matter, which was actuated by various substantial forms. With the elements thus created were associated certain *seminal influences*—certain physical forces, we now should say—and the various compounds which subsequently resulted from the action of these forces, on the diverse elements created, were

---

[1] For an elaborate explanation of the meaning of *seminales rationes*, according to the mind of the Angelic Doctor, see the "Metaphysics of the School," vol. II, appendix A, nn. III and IV, and vol. III, part I, glossary, sub vocibus.

the product of generation and not of creation. There was development, Evolution, under the action of second causes, from the simple elements to the highest inorganic and organic compounds; from the lowest kinds of brute matter to the highest bodily representatives of animated nature; but there was nothing requiring anew creative action or extraordinary interventions, except, of course, the human soul.

After this primordial creation, God continued and sustained His work by His Providence. Matter was then under the action of secondary causes, under what science calls the reign of law, and under the action of these secondary causes, under the influence of forces and laws imposed on it by God in the beginning, it still remains, and shall remain, until time is no more

Creation According to Scripture.

This teaching is in perfect harmony with the declarations of the opening chapter of Genesis, which speaks first of the creation of matter, then of the production from matter of plants and animals. It is consistent, too, with the teachings of science, which affirm that the material universe was once but a nebulous mass, which in the course of time condensed into solid bodies, the stars and planets, and which, after countless ages and by a gradual Evolution under the action of natural laws, generated those myriad objects of passing beauty and marvelous complexity which we now so much admire.

Matter alone, insists St. Thomas, in speaking of the visible universe, was created, in the strict sense of the term, and in this he but follows the indications of the Mosaic narrative of creation, and St. Augustine's interpretation of the work of the six days. Plants and animals were generated or produced from preëxisting material — "were gradually developed, by natural operations, under the Divine administration."

"In those first days," he tells us, "God created the creature in its origin and cause—*originaliter, vel causaliter*, and afterwards rested from this work. Nevertheless, He subsequently, until now, works according to the administration of created things by the work of propagation. Now, to produce plants from the earth belongs to the work of propagation; therefore, on the third day plants were not produced in act, but only in their cause—*Non ergo in tertia die productæ sunt plantæ in actu sed causaliter tantum*."[1]

Elsewhere, in defending the opinion of St. Augustine, he writes: "When it is said, 'Let the earth bring forth the green herb,' Gen. i, 11, it is not meant that plants were then produced actually in their proper nature, but that there was given to the earth a germinative power to produce plants by the work of propagation; so that the earth is then said to have brought forth the green herb and the tree yielding fruit in this wise, viz., that it received the power of producing them—*producendi accepisse virtutem*." And this he confirms by the authority of

---

[1] "Summa," Iæ, LXIX: 2.

Scripture, Gen. ii, 4—where it is said : " These are the generations of the heaven and the earth, when they were created, in the day that the Lord God made the heaven and the earth, and every plant of the field, *before it sprung up* in the earth, and every herb of the ground *before it grew*."

"From this passage," continues the Angelic Doctor, "two things are elicited: First, that all the works of the six days were created in the day that God made the heaven and earth and every plant of the field; and, accordingly, that plants, which are said to have been created on the third day, were produced at the same time that God created the heaven and the earth. Secondly, that plants were then produced, not in act, but according to causal virtues only; in that the power of producing them was given the earth—*fuerunt productæ non in actu, sed secundum rationes causales tantum, quia data fuit virtus terræ producendi illas.* This is meant, when it is said that it produced every plant of the field *before it actually sprang up in the earth* by the work of administration, and every herb of the earth *before it actually grew.* Prior, therefore, to their actually rising over the earth, they were made causally in the earth—*Ante ergo quam actu orirentur super terram, facta sunt causaliter in terra.* This view is likewise confirmed by reason. For in those first days God created the creature either in its cause or in its origin, or in act, in the work from which He afterwards rested. Nevertheless, He subsequently, until now, works according to the administration of created things by the work of propagation. But to

produce plants in act out of the earth, belongs to
the work of propagation; because it suffices for their
production that they have the power of the heavenly bodies, as it were, for their father, and the efficacy of the earth in place of a mother. Therefore,
plants were not actually produced on the third day,
but only causally.[1] After the six days, however,
they were actually produced according to their
proper species, and in their proper nature by the
work of administration." "In like manner fishes,
birds and animals were produced in those six days
causally and not actually—*Similiter pisces, aves et
animalia in illis sex diebus causaliter, et non actualiter producta sunt.*"[2]

Such, then, is the teaching of the illustrious
bishop of Hippo and of the Angel of the Schools, respecting creation and the genesis of the material
universe. To the striking passages just quoted, I
can do nothing better than add Father Harper's
beautiful and eloquent commentary as found in his
splendid work, "The Metaphysics of the School."

"In the creation," declares the learned Jesuit,
"represented by Moses in the manner best suited to
the intellectual calibre of the chosen people, under
the figure of six days—as St. Thomas, quoting from
St. Augustine, remarks—the elements alone, among
earthly things, were actually produced by the creative act; but simultaneously, in the primordial mat-

---

[1] It will be noted that a portion of this extract from "De Potentia," is verbally identical with a part of what is found in the preceding quotation from the "Summa."

[2] "Pot." q. iv, a 2, 28 m.

ter thus actuated by the elemental forms, a virtue was implanted, dispositive towards all the material forms conditionally necessary to the perfection of the earthly universe. But it was an ordered potentiality; so that in the after Evolution of the substantial forms, the lower should precede the higher; and that these latter should presuppose and virtually absorb the former. Thus were the figurative six days completed with the sowing of the seed of the future cosmos. There ensued thereupon a Sabbath of rest. The fresh, elemental world was sown with the germs of future beauty in diverse forms of life, in diversity of species, and possibly, varieties under the same species. But these, as yet, lay hidden in the womb of nature. No earthly substance existed in act save the simple bodies; primordial matter under its first and lowest forms. Such was the earthly creation when the first Sabbath closed in upon it. After this Sabbath followed the order of Divine administration, wherein, as it continues to the present hour, the Divine Wisdom and Omnipotence superintended the natural Evolution of visible things, according to a constant order of His own appointing, amid ceaseless cycles of alternate corruptions and generations.

"Compound inanimate substances were first evolved by means of the seminal forces bestowed on nature. Then, from the bosom of these compounds sprang into being the green life of herb, plant and tree, gradually unfolding into higher and more complex forms of loveliness as the ages rolled on, according to the virtual order imprinted at first upon the obedient matter. Thence onward marched the grand procession of life, marking epochs as it went along, till it culminated in man, the paragon of God's visible universe."

The Divine Administration.

But what, it may be inquired, does St. Thomas mean by the work of Divine administration? This phrase has been frequently employed, and it is of sufficient importance to demand an explanation.

No creature, as theology teaches, is competent to elicit a single act, even the smallest and most insignificant, without the coöperation of God. We cannot raise a foot, or move a finger, without Divine assistance. This is included in Divine administration, but it is far from being all that is so included. Over and above this the Divine administration embraces the order, or laws, by which the world is governed. It embraces, too, the Evolution of living

---

[1] "The Metaphysics of the School," vol. II, p. 741.

For one who wishes to master the doctrines and methods of Scholasticism, there is no work in English—if, indeed, there is in any language—that can be studied with more profit than this thorough and exhaustive treatise of Father Harper's. No one should attempt to discuss the teachings of the Schoolmen respecting derivative creation, who has not mastered Appendix A, in vol. II, on The Teaching of St. Thomas Touching the Genesis of the Material Universe, and the appendix in vol. III, part I, on The Teaching of the Angelic Doctor Touching the Efficient Causes of the Generation of Living Bodies in Its Bearings on Modern Physical Discoveries. Both these appendices are veritable magazines of fact and argumentation that cannot be duplicated elsewhere. I am indebted to the distinguished author, not only for the translation of many of the preceding quotations from the Angelic Doctor, but also for many valuable suggestions regarding the manner of treatment of theistic Evolution from the standpoint of patristic and scholastic philosophy.

things, without parentage, out of the potentiality of matter, or, what amounts to the same thing, it includes the proximate disposition of matter for the Evolution of organic from inorganic matter, and the higher from the lower forms of life. God, consequently, "must have been the sole efficient Cause of the organization requisite, and, therefore, in the strictest sense, He is said to have *formed* such living things, and, in particular, the human body, out of preexistent matter."

In the teachings of St. Augustine and St. Thomas respecting the creation and Evolution of the sum of all things, there is nothing uncertain, equivocal or vacillating. True to the declaration of the Inspired Record, and true to the faith of the Church from the earliest ages of her history, they teach that in the beginning God created all things, visible and invisible, and that He still continues to protect and govern by His Providence all things which He hath made, "reaching from end to end mightily, and ordering all things sweetly."[1] They tell us, not only that the Creator is "Lord of Heaven and earth, Almighty, Eternal, Immense, Incomprehensible, Infinite in intelligence, in will and in all perfections," not only that He is "absolutely simple and immutable spiritual substance, really and essentially distinct from the world," but also that he is omnipresent, omniscient; that for Him there is no past nor future; that all is present, and that "all things are bare and open to His eyes."[2]

---
[1] Wisdom, viii, 1.
[2] Heb. iv, 13.

According to the Fathers and the Schoolmen, therefore, as well as according to Catholic Dogma, God is the First Cause; finite beings are but secondary causes. God is the Primary Cause—*Causa Causarum;* while all finite causes are merely instrumental. God is preëminently the integral and efficient Cause of all things, for He, preëminently, is the Cause " whence," to use the words of Aristotle, "is the first beginning of change or of rest."

In the language of the Scholastics, He is the Form of forms; Absolute Form because Absolute Act. He is the Principiant of principiants, the first Beginning—'Ἀρχή, *Principium*—of all that exists or can exist.

Efficient Causality of Creatures.

But God, although the true, efficient Cause of all things, has willed, in order to manifest more clearly His wisdom and power and love, to receive the coöperation of His creatures, and to confer on them, as St. Thomas puts it, "the dignity of causality—*dignitatem causandi conferre voluit.*" It is not, however, as the Angelic Doctor declares, "from any indigence in God that He wants other causes for the act of production." He does not require the coöperation of secondary causes because He is unable to dispense with their aid. He is none the less omnipotent because He has chosen to act in conjunction with works of His own hand, for it is manifest that He who has created the causes, is able to produce the effects which proceed from such causes.

I have said that the efficient causality of creatures serves to disclose the wisdom and power and love of the Creator. It is true, but here again I shall quote from the eloquent and profound Father Harper, who so beautifully sums up all that may be said on the subject, that I need make no apology for quoting him in full.

The efficient causality of the creature serves to manifest God's wisdom, "for there is greater elaboration of design. To plan out a universe of finite entities, differing in essence and in grades of perfection, is doubtless a work of superhuman wisdom; but to include in the design the further idea, of conferring on these entities a complex variety of forces, qualities, active and passive, faculties by virtue of which nature should ever grow out of itself and develop from lower to higher forms of existence, and should multiply along definite lines of being; to conceive a world whose constituents should ceaselessly energize on one another, yet without confusion and in an admirable order; to allow to the creature its own proper causality, and yet, even spite of the manifold action of free will in a countless multiplicity of immortal intelligences, to elaborate a perfect unity; surely this is an incalculably higher manifestation of wisdom. It serves to manifest the power of the Creator; for every cause is proportioned to the effect. But the completion of a design such as has been described, is a more noble effect than if every production of natural operation were the result of immediate creation. The manufacture of a watch is a noble work of art; but if a watch should be made capable of constructing other watches in succession, and of winding up, regulating, cleaning, repairing its offspring, there is no one who would not be free to admit, that the inventor would possess a virtue of operation incomparably superior to his fellow-men. It serves to manifest the love and goodness of the Creator; since the Divine communication is more complete. Love shows itself in the desire of communicating its own perfection to the object of love; it is essentially self-diffusive. By bestowing on the creature existence which is a likeness to His own existence, the Creator communicates of His own, so to say, to the object of His charity; but by bestowing likewise an intrinsic activity proportioned in each case to the exigencies of the particular nature, he completes the similitude. By this consummation of the creature He causes it to partake, in its own proper measure, of the diffusiveness of His goodness. There is nothing of solitariness in nature. By the very constitution of things, being is impelled to impart to being of its own perfection. Not only does the substantial form bestow upon the matter a specific determination, and the matter sustain the form in being; not only does accident give its complement of perfection to substance, and substance give and preserve the being of accident; not only does part conspire with part towards the completeness of the whole, and the whole delight in the welfare of each part; but substance generates substance, accident, in its way, accident, and the whole visible universe is knit together in the solidarity of a common need and of mutual support. Passing upwards, the orders of spiritual being, both those that are included in the visible creation and those which are pure intelligences, bear in the activity of their will, which acts upon all that is around it, a yet nearer resemblance to the charity of the Creator. Assuredly, then, the causal activity of finite being is not superfluous; even though God can, by His sole omnipotence, do all that is effected by His creature."[1]

Such then, is the theistic conception of Evolution; such the Catholic idea as developed and taught by the Church's most eminent saints and Doctors. It were easy to add the testimony of other philosophers and theologians; but this is not necessary. It is not my purpose to write a treatise on the subject, but merely to indicate by the declarations of a few accredited witnesses, to show from the teachings of those "whose praise is in all the churches," that there is nothing in Evolution, properly understood, which is antagonistic either to revelation or Dogma; that, on the contrary, far from being opposed to faith, Evolution, as taught by St. Augustine and St. Thomas Aquinas, is the most reasonable view, and the one most in harmony with the explicit declarations of the Genesiac narrative of creation. This the Angelic Doctor admits in so many words. God could, indeed, have created all things directly; He could have dispensed with the coöperation of secondary causes; He could have remained in all things the sole immediate efficient Cause, but in His infinite wisdom He chose to order otherwise.

---

[1] "Metaphysics of the School," vol. III, part I, pp. 26 and 28.

Occasionalism.

The Evolution, however, of Augustine and Aquinas, I must here remark, excludes the Occasionalism of Geulincx and Malebranche as much as it does the specific creation of the older philosophers. In the opinion of the Cartesians, just mentioned, there are no second causes ; God is the sole Cause in the universe. The operations of nature, far from being the result of second causes, as the Angelic Doctor teaches, are due " exclusively to the action of God, who takes occasion of the due presence of what we should call secondary causes, with the subjects of operation, to produce, Himself, all natural effects;" Who, for instance, "takes an act of the will as the occasion of producing a corresponding movement of the body, and a state of the body as the occasion of producing a corresponding mental state." According to the doctrine of occasional causes, "body and mind are like two clocks which act together, because at each instant they are adjusted by God." Not only is God the cause of the concomitance of bodily and mental facts; He is the cause of their existence, their sequence and their coëxistence as well. The efficient causality is eliminated entirely from the scheme of creation and development, and God acts directly and immediately, not indirectly and mediately, in all the phenomena, and in all the countless and inconceivable minutiæ of the universe.[1] The refutation of this opinion

---

[1] A view similar to, if not identical with Occasionalism, is held by Mr. John Fiske. The doctrine of secondary causes, as above explained, he calls "the lower, or Augustinian Theism,"

Divine. In man they belong to the lower and created order; in God, to a higher and uncreated order. In man any moral perfection may be present or absent without the essential nature of man being thereby affected; in God, the absence of any perfection would thereby rob Him *ipso facto* of His Deity. Whatever the human attribute can perform, the Divine attribute can do in a far more perfect way, and the most exalted exhibition of human perfection is but a faint shadow of the Divine perfection that gave it birth. The most unbounded charity, mercy, gentleness, compassion, in man, is feeble indeed, and miserable, compared with the charity, mercy, gentleness, compassion of God. The Divine perfection is the ideal of human perfection, its model, its pattern, its origin, its efficient Cause, the source from which it came, the end for which it was created."[1]

Divine Interference.

Theistic Evolution, in the sense in which it is advocated by St. Augustine and St. Thomas, excludes also Divine interference, or constant unnecessary interventions on the part of the Deity, as effectually as it does a low and narrow Anthropomorphism. Both these illustrious Doctors declare explicitly, that "in the institution of nature we do not look for miracles, but for the laws of nature."[2]

---

[1] *The Month*, Sept., 1882, p. 20.
[2] Cf. "Gen. ad Lit.," lib. II, cap. 1, of St. Augustine and "Sum." I, LXVII, 4 ad 3ᵐ of St. Thomas. The Angelic Doctor's words are: "In prima autem institutione naturæ non quæritur miraculum, sed quid natura rerum habeat." Suarez expresses

Only the crudest conception of derivative creation would demand that the theist should necessarily, if consistent, have recourse to continued creative fiats to explain the multifold phenomena connected with inorganic or organic Evolution. For, as already explained, derivation or secondary creation is not, properly speaking, a supernatural act. It is merely the indirect action of Deity by and through natural causes. The action of God in the order of nature is concurrent and overruling, indeed, but is not miraculous in the sense in which the word "miraculous" is ordinarily understood. He operates by and through the laws which He instituted in the beginning, and which are still maintained by His Providence. Neither the doctrine of the Angel of the Schools nor that of the Bishop of Hippo, requires the perpetual manifestation of miraculous powers, interventions or catastrophes. They do not necessitate the interference with, or the dispensation from, the laws of nature, but admit and defend their existence and their continuous and regular and natural action. Only a misunderstanding of terms, only a gross misapprehension of the meaning of the word "creation," only, in fine, the "unconscious Anthropomorphisms" of the Agnostic and the Monist, would lead one to find anything irreconcilable between the legitimate inductions of science and the certain and explicit declarations of Dogma.

---

himself to the same effect when he tells us, in his tractate, "De Angelis," lib. I, no. 8, that we must not have recourse to the First Cause when the effects observed can be explained by the operations of secondary causes. "Non est ad Primam Causam recurrendam cum possunt effectus ad causas secundas reduci."

Science and Creation.

From what has already been learned, it is manifest that physical science is utterly incompetent to pronounce on primary or absolute creation. This, being by the very nature of the case, above and beyond observation and experiment, it is, for the same reason, necessarily above and beyond the sphere of science or Evolution. The Rev. Baden Powell clearly expresses this idea in his " Philosophy of Creation," when he affirms that " science demonstrates incessant past changes, and dimly points to yet earlier links in a more vast series of development of material existence ; but the idea of a *beginning*, or of *creation*, in the sense of the original operation of the Divine volition to constitute nature and matter, is beyond the province of physical philosophy." [1]

Again, belief in derivative creation is secure from attack, on the part of natural science, for the simple reason that it does not repose on physical phenomena at all, but on psychical reasons, or on our primary intuitions. Modern scientists are continually confounding primary with secondary creation, and speaking of the latter as if it were absolute creation, or as if it implied special supernatural action. This confusion of terms is at the bottom of many of the utterances of Darwin and Huxley, and is the cause of numerous erroneous views which they ascribe to their opponents. Thus, Darwin asks those who are not prepared to assent to his evolutionary notions, if "they really believe that at innumerable

---

[1] Essay III, sec. IV.

periods in the earth's history, certain elemental atoms have been commanded suddenly to flash into living tissues?"[1] And Huxley ridicules the notion that "a rhinoceros tichorhinus suddenly started from the ground like Milton's lion, 'pawing to get free its hinder parts,'"[2] and facetiously speaks of the improbability of "the sudden concurrence of half-a-ton of inorganic molecules into a live rhinoceros."

A grave objection, quotha! As if a belief in creation necessarily connoted the grotesque assumptions which he attributes to those who are not of his mind. Huxley and Darwin set up poor, impotent dummies, and forthwith proceed to knock them down, and then imagine they have proven the views of their adversaries to be untenable, if not absurd. A reference to what has already been said respecting absolute and derivative creation, and a recollection that creation by and through secondary causes is not a supernatural, but a natural act, will show how much ignorance of the elench there is in the difficulty suggested by the two naturalists just named.

Darwin's Objection.

Once more, Darwin speaks of a man building a house of certain stones found at the base of a precipice, and selecting those which, from their shape, happened to be most suitable. And in referring to this matter he writes: "The shape of the fragments of stone at the base of our precipice may be

---
[1] "The Origin of Species," vol. II, p. 297.
[2] "Life of Darwin," vol. I, p. 548.

called accidental, but this is not strictly correct, for the shape of each depends on a long sequence of events, all obeying natural laws, on the nature of the rock, on the lines of stratification or cleavage, on the form of the mountain, which depends upon its upheaval and subsequent denudation, and lastly on the storm and earthquake which threw down the fragments. But in regard to the use to which the fragments may be put, their shape may strictly be said to be accidental. And here we are led to face a great difficulty, in alluding to which I am aware that I am traveling beyond my proper province.

"An omniscient Creator must have foreseen every consequence which results from the laws imposed by Him; but can it be reasonably maintained that the Creator intentionally ordered, if we use the words in any ordinary sense, that certain fragments of rock should assume certain shapes so that the builder might erect his edifice?"[1]

The difficulty here raised is one of frequent occurrence in the writings of modern scientists. It reposes entirely on the crude and erroneous notions which they entertain respecting the nature and attributes of the Deity, and has its origin in that low and restricted Anthropomorphism, against which they are wont to inveigh so strongly, but into which they are continually lapsing, notwithstanding all their asseverations and protestations to the contrary. The objection, although urged in the name of natural and physical science, is in reality metaphysical in character and should be so treated. Those who urge

---

[1] "Animals and Plants under Domestication," vol. II, p. 432.

the objection seem to think, that in the boundless profusion and multitudinous forms of inorganic and organic nature, in the myriad worlds and systems of worlds which people the illimitable realms of space, there is more than God can provide for or superintend. They forget that He, by His very nature, is omniscient and omnipotent and omnipresent; that for Him there is neither past nor future, but that all is present and bare before His eyes; that far from being conditioned or limited in His actions, He is absolutely independent and free from all limitations; that He is infinite in all His perfections and can attend to a thousand million systems of worlds, and to each according to its proper needs, as well as to a single crystal or a solitary flower; and that He can do this during countless æons of time as easily as He can for a single moment. We have here, in a different guise, the old difficulty of time and space in their relations to God and His Divine operations. It is only necessary to form a proper, if not an adequate conception, of God and His attributes, to refer to the first principles of psychology, in order to realize how puerile is the objection, and what crass ignorance it betrays of the fundamental elements of metaphysics and theology on the part of the objector.

Limitations of Specialists.

In Darwin's case, one is not surprised that he should, in good faith, urge the objection included in the quotation just made from him, because he informs us himself that he was mentally disqualified for the discussion of abstract or metaphysical questions. "My power," he writes in his autobiography, "to follow a long and purely abstract train of thought, is very limited; and therefore I could never have succeeded with metaphysics or mathematics." But aside from his incompetence as a metaphysician, the very doctrine he championed so lustily seemed to render him nebulous and skeptical even about primary intuitions. Having occasion to give an opinion on the "Creed of Science," he wrote: "The horrid doubt always arises whether the convictions of man's mind, which has been developed from the mind of the lower animals, are of any value, or at all trustworthy. Would anyone trust in the convictions of a monkey's mind, if there are any convictions in such a mind?"[1]

One is not surprised, I repeat, to find metaphysical and theological errors in Darwin's works, for, in addition to his acknowledged incapacity in abstract subjects, his mind was so preoccupied with biology in its bearings on Evolution, that he was practically indifferent to, if not oblivious of, everything outside his immediate sphere of research. He is, indeed, a striking illustration of the truth of Cardinal Newman's observations when he declares, that "Any one study, of whatever kind, exclusively pursued, deadens in the mind the interest, nay, the perception, of any other. Thus, Cicero says, Plato and Demosthenes, Aristotle and Isocrates, might have respectively excelled in each other's province, but that each was absorbed in his own. Specimens of this pecul-

[1] "Life and Letters of Charles Darwin," vol. I, p. 285.

iarity occur every day. You can hardly persuade some men to talk about anything but their own pursuits; they refer the whole world to their own center, and measure all matters by their own rule, like the fisherman in the drama, whose eulogy on his deceased lord was, 'he was so fond of fish.'"[1]

But the observations of the learned cardinal are not more applicable to Darwin than to a host of contemporary scientists, who fancy there is an irreconcilable conflict between science on the one hand, and religion on the other. They fail to see that the conflict, so far as it exists, is due either to bias or ignorance, or to the fact that the very nature of their studies has imposed limitations on them, which utterly unfit them for pronouncing an opinion on the subjects which they are often in such haste to discuss.

In one of his thoughtful essays,[2] the Rev. James Martineau alludes to the injury which is done to sound philosophy by the undue cultivation of any one branch of knowledge. "Nothing is more common," he avers, "than to see maxims, which are unexceptionable as the assumptions of particular

---

[1] "Lectures on University Subjects," p. 322. Nearly forty years ago, in a lecture before the Royal Institution of Great Britain, the noted English writer, H. T. Buckle, adverting to this topic, declared that "an exclusive employment of the inductive philosophy was contracting the minds of physical inquirers, and gradually shutting out speculations respecting causes and entities; limiting the student to questions of distribution, and forbidding him questions of origin; making everything hang on two sets of laws, namely, those of coëxistence and of sequence; and declaring beforehand how far future knowledge can lead us." See vol. I, of "Miscellaneous and Posthumous Works."

[2] "A Plea for Philosophical Studies."

sciences, coerced into the service of a universal philosophy, and so turned into instruments of mischief and distortion. That 'we can know but phenomena;' that 'causation is simply constant priority;' that 'men are governed invariably by their interests;' are examples of rules allowable as dominant hypotheses in physics or political economy, but exercising a desolating tyranny when thrust onto the throne of universal empire. He who seizes upon these and similar maxims and carries them in triumph on his banner, may boast of his escape from the uncertainties of metaphysics, but is himself, all the while, the unconscious victim of their very vulgarest deception."

Evolution and Catholic Teaching.

From the foregoing pages, then, it is clear that far from being opposed to faith, theistic Evolution is, on the contrary, supported both by the declarations of Genesis and by the most venerable philosophical and theological authorities of the Church. I have mentioned specially St. Augustine and St. Thomas, because of their exalted position as saints and Doctors, but it were an easy matter to adduce the testimony of others scarcely less renowned for their philosophical acumen and for their proved and unquestioned orthodoxy; but this is unnecessary.[1] Of course no one would think of maintaining that any of the Fathers or Doctors of the Church taught Evolution in the sense in which it is now under-

---

[1] Cf., in this connection, chap. XII, of the "Genesis of Species;" and chap. XIV, of "Lessons from Nature," by St. George Mivart, where the subject, Theology and Evolution, is very cleverly treated.

stood. They did not do this for the simple reason that the subject had not even been broached in its present form, and because its formulation as a theory, under its present aspect, was impossible before men of science had in their possession the accumulated results of the observation and research of these latter times. But they did all that was necessary fully to justify my present contention; they laid down principles which are perfectly compatible with theistic Evolution. They asserted, in the most positive and explicit manner, the doctrine of derivative creation as against the theory of a perpetual direct creation of organisms, and turned the weight of their great authority in favor of the doctrine, that God administers the material universe by natural laws, and not by constant miraculous interventions. As far as the present argument is concerned, this distinct enunciation of principles makes for my thesis quite as much as would the promulgation of a more detailed theory of Evolution.

The Scholastic Doctrine of Species.

It may, however, be objected, that the authorities so far quoted favor development only in a vague or general way; that the Fathers and Scholastics distinctly maintained certain views which are absolutely incompatible with Evolution as now understood. It is said, for instance, that the scholastic doctrine of species, to which all the Schoolmen are irrevocably committed, completely negatives the view that their principles are compatible with

repeat, a matter not of *a priori* reasoning, but wholly and solely one of observation and experiment.

In his "Summa," the Angelic Doctor admits without hesitation the possibility of a new species, for he tells us that : " New species, if they make their appearance, preëxisted in certain active virtues, as animals are produced from carrion under the influence communicated in the beginning to the stars and the elements."[1]

More than this, he distinctly admits the mutability of species. To the objection that species must be immutable because they correspond with archetypes in the Divine intelligence, that they must be immutable because their forms are essentially immutable, he replies, that "immutability is proper to God only," and that "forms are subject to the variations of the reality."[2]

Again, it is erroneously supposed that St. Thomas always attaches to the terms genus and species, the same meaning as is given them by modern naturalists. This is a grave misapprehension. It will suffice to adduce a single instance in disproof of this notion. For example, the Angelic Doctor places man and animal in the same genus. But if, in the mind of St. Thomas, the word genus were in this

---

[1] " Species etiam novæ, si quæ apparent, præëxtiterunt in quibusdam activis virtutibus ; sicut et animalia ex putrefactione generata producuntur ex virtutibus stellarum et elementorum, quas a principio acceperunt ; etiamsi novæ species talium animalium producuntur." "Summa," pars I, quæst. 73, art. 1 ad 3.

[2] " Subjiciuntur tamen variationi in quantum subjectum secundum eas variatur." "Summa," pars I, quæst. 9, art. 2 et 3.

instance to be understood in its modern sense, it would, as Père Leroy puts it, be tantamount to admitting the "principle of materialism."[1] Obviously, therefore, the term genus is to be understood in a much more comprehensive sense. For a similar reason, species, the immediate subdivision of genus, must likewise have a much wider signification than it has in a strict technical sense. If we desire to have a measure of the relative amplitude of species as compared with genus, in the passage just quoted, in which genus is made to embrace man and animal, we must, as Père Leroy pertinently remarks, make species correspond to what naturalists now denominate a kingdom. Thus understood, species, in the instance referred to, would be immutable, but not otherwise.

It is a mistake, then, to suppose that the meaning of the term species, in its physiological sense, was fixed by the Angelic Doctor. Neither did it receive the signification afterwards ascribed to it from any of the other Schoolmen or mediæval theologians. Nor does such a meaning find any warrant in the teachings of the Fathers or in Scripture. Whence, then, the origin of the word in the sense so long attributed to it by special creationists? This is a question deserving of consideration, for an answer to it, if it does not remove wholly many difficulties, will at least clear the field for intelligent discussion.

---

[1] For an interesting discussion of Thomastic teaching respecting the nature of species, see chap. III of Père Leroy's "L'Évolution Restreinte aux Espèces Organiques."

CHAPTER V.

THE ORIGIN AND NATURE OF LIFE.

Spontaneous Generation.

OUR next inquiry is concerning the teachings of the Fathers and the Schoolmen in respect of the origin and nature of life, and what views one may, consistently with revealed truth and Catholic Dogma, entertain regarding this all-important topic. These are questions, as is well known, in which evolutionists of all classes, monistic, agnostic, and theistic, are specially interested, and questions, consequently, which cannot be passed over in silence.

The lower forms of life, as we learned in the beginning of this work, were supposed by Greek and mediæval philosophers to have originated spontaneously from the earth, or from putrefying organic matter. From the time of Aristotle to that of Redi, the doctrine of spontaneous generation was accepted without question, and it is scarcely yet a generation since the brilliant experiments of Pasteur drove abiogenesis from its last stronghold.

For over two thousand years the most extravagant notions were prevalent regarding certain of the smaller animals. Virgil, in his famous episode of Aristæus, tells us of the memorable discovery of the old Arcadian for the production of bees from the tainted gore of slain bullocks. But this is but an echo of what was universally believed and taught. Not only was it thought that putrefying flesh gave rise to insects, and other minute animals, but it was the current opinion that different kinds of carrion generated diverse forms of life. Thus, as bees were produced from decomposing beef, so beetles were generated from horseflesh, grass-hoppers from mules, scorpions from crabs, and toads from ducks. Diodorus Siculus speaks of multitudes of animals developed from the sun-warmed slime of the Nile valley. Plutarch assures us that the soil of Egypt spontaneously generates rats, and Pliny is ready to confirm the statement by an example of a rat, half metamorphosed, found in the Thebaid, of which the anterior half was that of a fully developed rodent, while the posterior half was entirely of stone! The Fathers and the Schoolmen, as we have seen, made no hesitation in accepting the doctrine of spontaneous generation. But while ready to admit abiogenesis as a fact, they gave it a different interpretation from what it had received from the philosophers and naturalists of Greece and Rome. According to Epicurus: "The earth is the mother of all living things, and from this simple origin not even man is excepted." Brute matter, said the Epicureans—as Hæckel and his school now proclaim—generates of its own power both vegetable and animal life ; that is, non-living gives rise to living matter. But Christian philosophy, contrariwise, teaches that it is impossible for inorganic to produce organic matter *motu proprio*, or by any natural inherent powers it may possess. "The waters, " declares St. Basil, in speaking of the work of creation, "were gifted with productive power, but this power was communicated to them by God." "From slime and muddy places, frogs, flies and gnats came into being," he was willing to admit, "but this was in virtue of a certain germinative force conferred on matter by the Author of nature." "Certain very small animals may not have been created on the fifth and sixth days," opines St. Augustine, "but may have originated later from putrefying matter," but still, even in this case, God it is who is their Creator.

Spontaneous generation, therefore, was never a stumbling block either to the Fathers or Scholastics, because the Creative act was always acknowledged, and because God was ever recognized as the Author, at least through second agents, of the divers forms of life which were supposed to originate from inorganized matter. Whether He created all things absolutely and directly, or mediately and indirectly, it mattered not, so long as it was understood that nothing could exist without His will and coöperation. Whether, then, the germ of life was specially created for each individual creature, or whether matter was endowed with the power of evolving what we call life, by the proper collocation of the atoms and molecules of which matter is constituted, was, from their point of view, immaterial, so far as dogma was concerned. The doctrine of spontaneous generation might be an error, scientifically, but, even if so, there was nothing in it contrary to the truths of revelation. It was always and fully recognized that God was the sole and absolute Creator of matter, and that He, by the action of powers conferred on matter, by certain seminal forces, as the Scholastics taught, disposed matter for the assumption of all the multitudinous forms into which it subsequently developed.

The Nature of Life.

Respecting the real nature, not the origin, of life, there have, indeed, been many and diverse opinions. Even now it is almost as much of an enigma as it was in the days of Aristotle, and we are at present, apparently, no better qualified to give a true definition of life than was the great Stagirite, twenty-five centuries ago. Living beings can, indeed, be distinguished from non-living beings by their structure, mode of genesis, and development, but this does not help us toward a clear and precise definition of life.

According to the philosophers of antiquity there was a certain independent entity, or vital principle, which, uniting with the body, gives life, and, separating from it, causes death. Plato and Aristotle, as is well known, admitted the existence of three souls, or animating spirits, the vegetative for plants, the vegetative and sensitive for animals; and for man, an intelligent and reasoning spirit in addition to those possessed by plants and animals.

Paracelsus and Van Helmont spoke of the principle of life under the name of *archæus*, and attempted to explain vital functions by chemical agencies. Others, still, " made the chyle effervesce in the heart, under the influence of salt and sulphur, which took fire together and produced the vital flame!"

Bichat defines life as "the sum total of the functions which resist death;" Herbert Spencer makes it "the continuous adjustment of internal relations to external relations," while Oliver Wendell Holmes tells us, that "Life is the state of an organized being in which it maintains, or is capable of maintaining, its structural integrity, by the constant interchange of elements with the surrounding media."[1]

Such definitions, however, are almost as vague and unsatisfactory as the notions implied in the "spirits" of Aristotle and Plato, and in the archæus of Van Helmont and Paracelsus. They afford us no clearer conception of what life really is in itself, of what it is that constitutes the essential difference between living and non-living matter, than we may derive from the idea of Hippocrates, who regarded "unintelligent nature as the mysterious agent in the vital processes."

But whatever views we may entertain respecting the actual nature of life; whether we regard it as a force entirely different in kind from the purely physical forces, or look upon it as a special coördination and integration of physical forces, acting in some mysterious way on inanimate matter, and in such wise as to cause it to exhibit what we call the phenomena of life, the fact still remains, that at some

---

[1] "La vie," writes a professor of physiology of the Faculty of Medicine, in Paris, "est une fonction chimique et la force dégagée par les êtres vivants est une force d'origine chimique." In contradistinction to this statement, Cardinal Zigliara declares: "Vita repeti non potest a materia." Again, life has been defined as "Une force qui tend à perfectionner et à reproduire, suivant une forme déterminée, l'être qu'elle anime par une impulsion spontanée."

period in the past history of our planet, the first germ of organic life made its appearance, and that, too, independent of any antecedent terrestrial germ.

The Germ of Life.

Whence this primordial germ, this first electric spark, which effected the combination of inorganic elements and transmuted non-living into living matter? Is it an "intellectual necessity" that we should, with Tyndall, "cross the boundary of the experimental evidence and discover in matter the promise and potency of all terrestrial life?"[1] Must we believe with Lucretius that nature "does all things spontaneously of herself, without the meddling of the gods;" and are we forced to regard matter and life as indissolubly joined, as entities which cannot be divorced from one another even in imagination? These are questions which are constantly recurring, and while in nowise sharing the materialistic views of Tyndall and Lucretius, we are, nevertheless, forced to admit that the problems involved are as difficult to solve as those concerning the nature of life itself.

In 1871, Sir William Thomson (Lord Kelvin), in an address at Edinburgh, discussed a theory which had been broached by a German speculator, Prof. Richter of Dresden, and involved the careering through space of "seed-bearing meteoric stones," and the possibility of "one such falling on the earth," and causing it, "by what we blindly call natural causes," to become "covered with vegetation." "The hy-

---

[1] "Fragments of Science," p. 524.

pothesis," the distinguished physicist tells us, "may seem wild and visionary; all I maintain is, it is not unscientific."

But even if it were proved that the first germ of life had been brought by some seed-bearing meteorite from the depths of space, or from some far distant world, it would, as is obvious, afford no explanation either of the real nature or of the ultimate origin of life. It would be but removing the difficulty farther away; not giving it a solution.

Still another question confronts us. Was there but one primordial germ, the origin and parent of all the multitudinous forms of life which now variegate and beautify the earth, or were there many germs independently implanted in the prepared soil of this globe of ours? And if many, did they make their appearance simultaneously, or at different and widely separated periods and localities?

Darwin inclines to the belief that "all animals and plants are descended from some one prototype." From this prototype, or primordial germ, as from a common root, is developed "the great tree of organic life," a tree which is conceived as having " two main trunks, one representing the vegetable and one the animal world," while each trunk is pictured as "dividing into a few main branches," the branches subdividing into a number of branchlets, and these, in turn, into "smaller groups of twigs." Prof. Weismann, on the other hand, is of the opinion that not one, but numerous organisms first arose "spontaneously, simultaneously, and independently one of the other."

Such considerations as the foregoing, and the diverse and contradictory opinions to which they have given rise, compel one, will-he nill-he, to recognize the fact that science, I mean experimental science, can tell us nothing more about the origin of life than it can regarding the origin of matter. These are questions which, by their very nature, are outside the sphere of inductive research, and their answers, so far as observation and experiment are concerned, must ever remain in inscrutable and insoluble mystery.

Abiogenesis.

So far as science can pronounce on the matter, spontaneous generation, as we have already learned, is, in the language of Pasteur, but a chimera. Even those whose theories imply, if they do not demand, the spontaneous origination of living from non-living matter, are forced to admit that there is, as yet, no warranty whatever for believing that abiogenesis obtains now, or ever has obtained, at any time in the past history of our globe.

"I should like," writes Darwin, "to see archebiosis"—Bastian's term for spontaneous generation—"proved true, for it would be a discovery of transcendent importance."[1] So much, indeed, does the theory of Evolution, as commonly held, imply the existence, at some time or other, of spontaneous generation, that Fiske avers: "However the question may eventually be decided, as to the possibility of archebiosis occurring at the present day amid the

---
[1] "Life and Letters," vol. II, p. 437.

artificial circumstances of the laboratory, it cannot be denied that archebiosis, or the origination of living matter in accordance with natural laws, must have occurred at some epoch in the past."[1]

With Huxley, as with Fiske, a belief in spontaneous generation is a necessary corollary to the theory of Evolution. "The fact is," he affirms, "that at the present moment there is not a shadow of trustworthy direct evidence that abiogenesis does take place, or has taken place, within the period during which the existence of life on the globe is recorded. But it need hardly be pointed out, that the fact does not in the slightest degree interfere with any conclusion that may be arrived at, deductively from other considerations, that, at some time or other, abiogenesis must have taken place."[2] Elsewhere he declares: "If it were given me to look beyond the abyss of geologically recorded time, to the still more remote period when the earth was passing through physical and chemical conditions, which it can no more see again than a man can recall his infancy, I should expect to be a witness of the Evolution of protoplasm from non-living matter. I should expect to see it appear under forms of great simplicity, endowed, like existing fungi, with the power of determining the formation of new protoplasm from such matter as ammonium carbonates, oxalates and tartrates, alkaline and earthy phosphates and water, without the aid of light. That is

---

[1] "Outlines of Cosmic Philosophy," vol. I, p. 430.
[2] See his article on Biology, "Encyclopædia Britannica," vol. III.

the expectation to which analogical reasoning leads me, but," he adds, "I beg you once more to recollect that I have no right to call my opinion anything but an act of philosophical faith."[1]

Hæckel, as we have seen, is far more positive in his assertions respecting spontaneous generation. His theory of Monism absolutely demands it as a *sine qua non*, and he is the first to announce that abiogenesis—he calls it autogeny—is a necessary and integral part of the hypothesis of universal Evolution, " a necessary event in the process of the development of the earth." " He who does not assume a spontaneous generation of monera . . . to explain the first origin of life upon our earth, has no other resource but to believe in a supernatural miracle; and this is the questionable standpoint still taken by many so-called exact naturalists, who thus renounce their own reason."[2]

But suppose that some time or other it should be proved, that spontaneous generation not only has taken place, but that it actually occurs, *hic et nunc?* The fact that we have as yet no evidence that it ever has taken place, or that it does not occur now, does not prove that it is impossible. We may not be prepared to affirm, with Huxley and Fiske, that it *must have* taken place at some period in past history, but may we not admit the possibility of the occurrence? We certainly do not agree with Hæckel that we renounce our reason if we believe in a special Divine intervention for the production

---
[1] " Lay Sermons, Addresses and Reviews," pp. 366 et seq.
[2] " The Evolution of Man," vol. I, p. 32.

gradually developed out of these, according to a fixed order of natural operation, under the supreme guidance of Divine administration." They teach that if spontaneous generation be, indeed, a reality, the matter which undergoes change, "having been proximately disposed, by the action of heat and of other causes, of itself evolves into act by Divine intervention, rather than that the causal action of an inanimate body should be efficacious towards the generation of life."

It is not, then, in the case of spontaneous generation, the principle of Evolution, but the misapplication of this principle, which has led to the grave philosophical errors into which so many modern evolutionists have fallen. None of the agnostic or monistic theories account for life. "They begin with organism, but organism connotes life. Whence then, this life? Take the first instance — and the first instance there must have been — of an inanimate chemical compound showing signs of life; say phenomena of cleavage and of subsequent gastræan inversion. How is it that this particular inanimate chemical compound has taken such a start? If matter evolved itself spontaneously into life, without aid of formal or efficient Cause, why have not the metamorphic rocks through all these æons of time shaken off the incubus of their primitive passivity, and wakened up into protoplasm, and thus secured to themselves the privilege of self-motion, internal growth, reproduction? Again, is it possible to imagine that brute matter, inert and purely passive, could by its own unaided exertion pass straight from the laboratory into the kingdom of life? And if one mass could do it, why not all? Why do those venerable metamorphic rocks remain at the root of the genealogical tree, unchanged? Perhaps this may prove another instance of the *survival of the fittest*. Here, then, is the flaw. These recent theorists accept life as a fact; and they start with it. They are superstitiously contented to begin and end with the mystery, because they are either afraid or unwilling to acknowledge the operation of a formal and efficient Cause in the Evolution of material substances."[1]

As to the artificial production of living from nonliving matter, of which sundry enthusiastic chemists have so fondly dreamed, it can be positively asserted that if ever effected it will be along lines quite different from those which certain over-sanguine speculators have indicated.

The great feat achieved by Wöhler, in 1828, in making urea—an organic compound, previously supposed to be the result of vital forces alone—from inorganic matter, was but the prelude of those brilliant triumphs of synthetic chemistry which since have so frequently astonished the world. During the past few decades, especially, organic compounds of the most marvelous complexity have been manufactured in the laboratory, until now there are not wanting chemists who affect to hope, that they will one day be able to rival nature herself in the number and complexity of her products. Their powers of analysis, we are willing to concede, are practically unlimited. They can tell us not only the composi-

---
[1] Harper's " Metaphysics of the School," vol. II, p. 747.

make even a microscopic speck of protoplasm than he can fashion a rose or a butterfly.

Another consequence follows from the recent discoveries regarding protoplasm, and that is, the impossibility of originating life. If protoplasm is the simplest form of matter in which life exists, and if it is impossible to manufacture even the smallest particle of inanimate protoplasm, much less living protoplasm, it is *a fortiori* impossible to produce an entity exhibiting the phenomena characteristic of a living being.

For a similar reason, all likelihood of discovering evidence in favor of spontaneous generation has vanished. One may not, indeed, assert that it is entirely impossible. So far, it is true, protoplasm is the simplest substance which exhibits the phenomena of life, and we know of no kind of protoplasm which is simpler than that above mentioned. This, however, does not imply that there are not simpler forms of living matter. It is possible that there are living beings so simple that their composition may be represented exactly by a chemical formula; that they have a fixed, definite, molecular arrangement, like some of our complex organic compounds. It is possible that ultimately the chemist may discover the proximate constituents of such a substance, and be able to indicate how it is produced by nature, or how it may be manufactured in an inanimate condition in the laboratory. All this is possible, all conceivable. The past triumphs of organic chemistry, as well as our increasing knowledge of the lower forms of life, permit such an assumption. Yet it is only an assumption. But so far as protoplasm is concerned, so far as there is question of the simplest unicellular moner which the microscopist has yet observed, we can unhesitatingly say that spontaneous generation is impossible. We may conceive how simple chemical forces can produce a chemical compound of even the greatest complexity. But we cannot picture to ourselves how such forces, unaided and alone, can produce an intricate organism, such as is even the lowest representative of animate nature. It were as easy to imagine a watch evolving itself spontaneously from the raw material which composes it; to picture a man-of-war arising spontaneously from the piles of wood and stores of iron and brass in a shipyard.

If, then, spontaneous generation is not a chimera, it is something which has far humbler beginnings than has ordinarily been supposed. If it ever took place at all, it must have occurred in some homogeneous chemical compound which was the product of known chemical forces. And if this be true, the time which elapsed from the formation of such a living compound, until its development into the highly organized protoplasm which we now know, must have embraced as many long æons as intervened between the advent of protoplasm and the first appearance of the higher orders of animal and plant life.

The mechanical theory of life, it is thus seen, is far from being borne out by the known facts of science. It assumed the homogeneity of protoplasm; and in this it was in error. It assumes the origin of life by the action on the elements of forces which are resident in matter, and teaches that living differs from brute matter only in the relative complexity of molecular structure, and of the higher integration of forces which is the natural result of complexity of structure. When such assumption denies, as it usually does deny, the existence of any force outside of matter; when it makes matter, as such, the sole cause of the countless evolutions which have occurred in the past development of the universe; when it attempts, as does Virchow, to resolve the production of the divers forms of life from inanimate matter into a question of mere mechanics; when, finally, it not only ignores, but positively denies, the ever present, unceasing action of the Divine administration; then we can as unhesitatingly pronounce it false, as it is demonstrably so in predicating homogeneity of protoplasm. Under such circumstances it is as difficult for the theist, without assuming the intervention of a miracle, to conceive of the formation of a single chemical compound from its constituent elements, not to speak of the spontaneous origination of living matter, as it was to Darwin to picture to his mind the production of an elephant by the sudden flashing of certain elemental atoms into living tissues. Given matter, however, and forces competent to transform matter—such forces, as well as the matter which they affect, being always under the guidance of the Divine administration—and there is nothing in the theory of the origination of living from not-living matter, that is contrary either to faith or philosophy. On the contrary, such a view is, as we have seen, quite in harmony with both the one and the other. Under such conditions the spontaneous generation, either in the laboratory of nature or in that of the chemist, presents no greater difficulties than does the conversion of a bar of steel into a magnet. In both cases it is God who is the author of the change, yet God acting not directly, but through the instrumentality of natural agencies; through the "seminal reasons" and the laws of nature which He conferred on matter in the beginning.

CHAPTER VI.

THE SIMIAN ORIGIN OF MAN.

The Missing Link.

ANOTHER question in connection with Evolution which has attracted even greater attention than spontaneous generation, is that respecting the animal origin of man. If it be true that living has evolved from not-living matter; if it be admitted that the higher are genetically related to the lower forms of life, then, we are told, the only logical inference is that man is descended from some form of animal. With the majority of contemporary non-Catholic evolutionists, the conviction of the truth of man's animal origin is so strong, that it is accepted as a fact which no longer admits of doubt. According to their view, all that remains is to trace man's relationship with his dumb predecessor, to discover the "missing link" which connects him with the beasts of the field, and the controversy is closed forever.

Here again, as in the case of spontaneous generation, we must carefully discriminate between fact and theory; between positive evidence for man's simian genealogy, and the various assumptions which so many evolutionists are ever too ready to ask us to accept.

I can do no better than reproduce here the testimony of one who will not be accused of bias towards Theism; who, far from being opposed to the theory of man's descent from the ape, most strongly favors it, but who insists on having evidence of such connection before giving his assent. I refer to the celebrated anatomist and anthropologist, Dr. Rudolph Virchow, than whom no one is more competent to give an opinion on this much-vexed question.

In an address delivered before the twentieth general meeting of the German Anthropological Association, at Vienna, August, 1889, he gave a review of the progress of anthropology during the preceding two decades. In the course of his discourse he asserted, what he has more recently affirmed at Moscow and elsewhere, that there is as yet not a scintilla of evidence for the ape-origin of man, and that even the hope of discovering the missing link is something that does not find any warranty in the known facts of anthropology.

"At the time of our coming together twenty years ago," he says, "Darwinism had just made its first triumphal march through the world. My friend, Carl Vogt, with his usual vigor entered the contest, and through his personal advocacy secured for this theory a great adherence. At that time it was hoped that the theory of descent would conquer, not in the form promulgated by Darwin, but in that advanced by his followers; for we have to deal now not with Darwin but with Darwinians. No one doubted that the proof would be forthcoming, demonstrating that man descended from the monkey and that this descent from a monkey, or at least from some kind of an animal, would soon be established. This was a challenge which was made and successfully defended in the first battle. Everybody knew all about it and was interested in it. Some spoke for it; others against it. It was considered the greatest question of anthropology.

"Let me remind you, however, at this point, that natural science, so long as it remains such, works only with real, existing objects. A hypothesis may be discussed, but its significance can only be established by producing actual proofs in its favor, either by experiments or direct observations. This, Darwinism has not succeeded in doing. In vain have its adherents sought for connecting links which should connect man with the monkey. Not a single one has been found. The so-called *pro-anthropos*, which is supposed to represent this connecting link, has not as yet appeared. No real scientist claims to have seen him. Hence the *pro-anthropos* is not at present an object of discussion for an anthropologist. Some may be able to see him in their dreams, but when awake they will not be able to say they have met him. Even the hope of a future discovery of this *pro-anthropos* is highly improbable; for we are not living in a dream, or in an ideal world, but in a real one."[1]

---

[1] See Smithsonian Report for 1889, pp. 563, et seq. In his address before the International Archæological Congress at Moscow, in 1892, Prof. Virchow made the following declaration:

"C'est en vain qu'on cherche le chaînon, *the missing link*, qui aurait uni l'homme au singe ou à quelque autre espèce animale.

"Il existe une limite tranchée qui sépare l'homme de l'animal et qu'on n'a pu jusqu' ici effacer; c'est *l'hérédité* qui transmet aux enfants les facultés des parents. Nous n'avons jamais

But although there is no tangible evidence of the existence of the missing link, connecting man with the monkey or with lower forms of life, some people have, nevertheless, to use Virchow's ironical words, "seen him in their dreams." They have seen him in the gorilla and in the orang-outang, in the lemur and in the kangaroo. They have observed him in the Neanderthal man, and in the men of Naulette, Denise, of Canstadt and of Eguisheim. De Mortillet has scrutinized him in the imaginary being that fashioned the flint-flakes of Thenay, Puy-Courny and Portugal. And so sure is he that he has discovered our immediate ancestor, that he has dubbed him with the name, *anthropopithecus*, the man-ape, or the apeman.[1] Darwin has described him as a hairy pithecoid animal, arboreal in habits and a denizen of "some warm forest-clad land." According to Cope, man is

---

vu qu'un singe mette au monde un homme, ou que l'homme produise un singe. Tous les hommes à l'aspect simiesque ne sont que de produits pathologiques.

"À première vue, il est très facile de supposer qu'un crâne dolicocephale se transforme en un crâne brachycephale, et cependant personne n'a encore observé la transformation d'une race dolicocephale en une race brachycephale, et *vice versa*, ou celle d'une race nègre en une race aryenne.

"Ainsi, dans la question de l'homme, nous sommes repoussés sur toute la ligne. Toutes les recherches entreprises dans le but de trouver la continuité dans le développement progressif, ont été sans résultat; il n'existe pas de *pro-anthropos;* il n'existe pas d'homme-singe; le chaînon intermédiaire demeure un fantôme." *Revue Scientifique*, Nov. 5, 1892.

[1] In striking contrast with the fanciful theories of De Mortillet, are the clearly expressed views of De Quatrefages, one of the most eminent of modern anthropologists. Referring to the subject under consideration he asserts "Dolichocephalic or brachycephalic, large or small, orthognathous or prognathous, Quaternary man is always man in the full acceptance of the word." "The Human Species," p. 294.

but "a pentadactylic, plantigrade bunadont," and is genetically connected with the lemuroid, *phenacodus* and the *anaptomorphus homunculus*, both of which flourished in the early Tertiary Period. Hæckel goes further back and discerns in the skull-less, brainless and memberless amphioxus, an animal which we should regard with special veneration "as being of our own flesh and blood," and as being the only one of all extant animals which "can enable us to form an approximate conception of our earliest vertebrate ancestors."

All these imaginings, however, are, as Virchow truly observes, but dreams, hypotheses more or less extravagant, which have secured for their originators a certain amount of temporary notoriety, but which have no foundation whatsoever in any fact or legitimate induction of science.[1]

But if the fact of the animal origin of man has not been established, if there is no likelihood that it will be established, at least in the immediate future, even according to the testimony of those who are most desirous of seeing the pithecoid ancestry of man demonstrated, what is to be said of the opinions of those who, nevertheless, maintain the animal origin of man, if not as a fact, at least as a tenable opinion? Is such an opinion compatible with Dogma, and can a consistent Catholic assent to any of the

---

[1] In his admirable study, "Apes and Man," St. George Mivart, a pronounced evolutionist, gives, in a few words, the verdict of comparative anatomy respecting the simian origin of man. He says, p. 172: "It is manifest that man, the apes and half-apes, cannot be arranged in a single ascending series of which man is the term and culmination."

theories now in vogue which claim that man is genetically related to the inferior animals? This is a question which is often put, and one which, far from being treated with derision, as is so often the case, should receive a serious and a deliberate answer.

We have seen that a belief in spontaneous generation, and in the development of the higher forms of animal and plant life from the lower forms, is quite compatible with both revelation and faith; but can this likewise be said of the development of man from a monkey or from any other inferior animal?

The Human Soul.

As to the soul of man we can at once emphatically declare, that it is in nowise evolved from the souls of animals, but is, on the contrary, and in the case of each individual, directly and immediately created by God Himself. I do not say that this is a *dogma* of faith, because the question has never been formally defined by the Church. It is, however, Catholic doctrine, and has been taught almost universally from the time of the apostles.

I say "almost universally," because other opinions regarding the origin of the soul have been held and defended even by some of the most eminent of the Church's Doctors and Fathers. Origen, for instance, misled by a conception of Plato, imagined that God, in the beginning, created a large number of spirits, all equally endowed with natural and supernatural gifts. Many of these spirits having sinned, God, to punish them, created the corporeal world and imprisoned them in various kinds of

This is, not, however, the place to discuss in detail the divers theories above referred to respecting the origin of the human soul, nor to refute the errors which these theories contain. It will suffice for our present purpose to state, that corporeal Traducianism, as well as the opinion of Origen, have been condemned as contrary to faith. As to spiritual Traducianism, as favored by Rosmini, Klee and Ubaghs, it will be sufficient to say that while it is not heresy, no one can now defend it without justly being regarded as temerarious.

I have said that Creationism has never been formally defined as a dogma of faith, but it can most probably be regarded as implicitly defined, and possessing all the conditions necessary to its being considered as one of those truths which constitute a part of revealed doctrine, and a portion, therefore, of the original deposit of the Christian faith. During the time of St. Augustine, owing to the Pelagian

---

que les ames qui seront un jour ames humaines, ont été dans les semences et dans les ancêtres jusqu'à Adam, et ont existé par conséquent, depuis le commencement des choses, toujours dans une manière de corps organisé." In his "Anthropologia," lib. IV, cap. v, Rosmini writes : " Unde in generatione individui speciei humanæ concurrunt duæ causæ simul operantes, homo generatione et Deus manifestatione suæ lucis ; homo ponit animal, Deus creat animam intelligentem in eodem instanti quo animal humanum ponitur, creat animam eam illuminando splendore vultus sui, ipsi participando aliquid sui, ens ideale, quod est lumen creaturarum intelligentium." Froschammer, in his "Defensio Generationis Anime," attributes to parents the power of creating the souls of their children, for says he : "Generatione parentum homo secundum corpus et animam oritur vi potestatis creandi secundariæ, quæ naturæ humanæ immanens et in prima rerum origine a Deo collata est. . . . Itaque generatio est actus creationis naturæ humanæ, est creatio ex nihilo, per potentiam secundariam a Deo humanitati collatam."

heresy and the discussions which arose concerning the transmission of original sin, the dogmatic tradition respecting the origin of the soul was not so strongly affirmed as it was subsequently, and hence the vacillations of the great Bishop of Hippo, and others, between Creationism and Traducianism.[1] Since the time, however, of St. Thomas Aquinas and St. Bonaventure, the doctrine of Creationism has been regarded as practically beyond controversy, among all well-accredited theologians, and we can now look upon Melchior Cano as accurately expressing the mind of the Church, when he declares that it "without doubt pertains to faith, that the soul exists not through generation, but by creation."[2]

Creation of Man's Body.

So far, then, as the soul of man is concerned, it is manifest from the foregoing paragraphs that according to Catholic teaching, each individual soul is created directly and immediately by Almighty God. Man, however, is not a pure spirit, but a creature composed of a rational soul and a corruptible body. The question now arises: Was the body of the first man, the progenitor of our race, created directly and immediately by God, or was it created indirectly and through the operation of secondary

---

[1] "Tempore Augustini nondum erat per Ecclesiam declaratum, quod anima non esset ex traduce," writes the Angelic Doctor.

[2] "Nunc autem, cum post ea tempora theologorum fideliumque omnium firmatum sit, animam non per generationem, sed per creationem existere, sine dubio ad fidem illa quæstio pertinet." "De Loc. Theol.," lib. XII, cap. xiv.

existence as little probable, as it was thirty years ago, if indeed it is not less probable.

But granting that the search for the link connecting man with the ape has so far been futile; admitting, with Virchow, that "the future discovery of this pro-anthropos is highly improbable;" may we not, nevertheless, believe, as a matter of theory, that there has been such a link, and that, corporeally, man is genetically descended from some unknown species of ape or monkey? Analogy and scientific consistency, we are told, require us to admit that man's bodily frame has been subject to the same law of Evolution, if an Evolution there has been, as has obtained for the inferior animals. There is nothing in biological science that would necessarily exempt man's corporeal structure from the action of this law. Is there, then, anything in Dogma or sound metaphysics, which would make it impossible for us, *salva fide*, to hold a view which has found such favor with the great majority of contemporary evolutionists?

Mivart's Theory.

It was the distinguished biologist and philosopher, St. George Mivart, who first gave a categorical answer to these questions in his interesting little work, "The Genesis of Species," published nearly a quarter of a century ago. He contended that it is not "absolutely necessary to suppose that any action different in kind took place in the production of man's body, from that which took place in the production of the bodies of other animals, and of the whole material universe."¹ To judge from his subsequent writings, time has but confirmed him in this view and afforded him opportunities of developing and corroborating his argument.

When Mivart's book first appeared it was severely criticised by the Catholic press, both of the Old and the New World, and its author was in many instances denounced as a downright heretic. Indeed, he was almost as roundly and as generally berated, by a certain class of theologians, as was Charles Darwin after the publication of his "Origin of Species." In England, France and Germany the denunciation of the daring biologist was particularly vehement, and strenuous efforts were made to have his work put on the Index. It was almost the universal opinion among theologians, that the proposition defended was heretical, and it was considered only a matter of a short time until it would be formally condemned. The book was forwarded to Rome, but, contrary to the expectations of all who were eagerly watching the course events would take, the book was not condemned. Neither was its author called upon to retract or modify the proposition which had been such an occasion of scandal. Far from censuring the learned scientist, the pope, Pius IX, made him a doctor of philosophy, and the doctor's hat was conferred on him by no less a personage than Cardinal Manning himself.²

---

¹ Page 282.

² " My 'Genesis of Species,'" writes Mivart, "was published in 1870, and therein I did not hesitate to promulgate the idea that Adam's body might have arisen from a non-human animal,

Since 1871, when Mivart's book was given to the world, a great change of sentiment has been effected among those who were at first so opposed to his opinions, and who imagined they discerned lurking in them not only rank heresy but also bald and unmitigated Materialism. Men have had time to examine dispassionately the suspected propositions, and to compare them with both the formal definitions of the Church and the teachings of the Fathers. The result of unimpassioned investigation and mature reflection has been, not indeed a vindication of the truth of the position of the English scientist, but a feeling that his theory may be tolerated, and that because it deals rather with a question of science than with one of theology. It has been shown that his propositions do not positively contravene any of the formal definitions of the Church, and that both St. Augustine and the Angelic Doctor, to mention no others, have laid down principles, which may be regarded as reconcilable with the thesis defended with so much ingenuity by the brilliant author of "The Genesis of Species."

Angelic Doctor on Creation of Adam.

The Angelic Doctor, in accord with the traditional teaching of the Fathers, holds that the body of the first man was immediately and directly formed by God Himself, but he admits the possibility of

---

the rational soul being subsequently infused. Great was the outcry against such a view, but I forwarded my little book to the Supreme Pontiff, and thereupon Pius IX benignantly granted me a doctor's hat, which the late Cardinal Archbishop of Westminster bestowed on me at a public function." *The Nineteenth Century*, Feb., 1893, p. 327.

angelic intervention in its formation and preparation for the reception of its informing principle, the rational soul.[1] According to this view God created absolutely, *ex nihilo*, the human soul, but delegated to His creatures, the angels, the formation, or at least the formation in part, *aliquod ministerium*, of man's body. It is manifest, however, that if God could have formed the body of Adam through the agency of angels, He could have communicated the same power to other agencies, if He had so willed. Instead, for instance, of delegating angels to form the body of the common father of mankind, He could, we may believe, have given to matter the power of evolving itself, under the action of the Divine administration, into all the forms of life which we now behold, including the body of man. The product of such an Evolution would not be a rational animal, as man is, but an irrational one; the highest and noblest representative of the brute creation, but, nevertheless, only a brute.

Such an irrational animal, the result of long years of development, and the product of the play, during untold æons, of evolutionary forces on lower forms of life, such a *substratum* it was, according to Mivart's theory, into which the Creator breathed the breath of life and man forthwith "became a living soul." According to this theory, then, God created

---

[1] "Quia igitur corpus humanum numquam formatum fuerat, cujus virtute per viam generationis aliud simile in specie formaretur, necesse fuit, quod primum corpus hominis immediate formaretur a Deo. . . . Potuit tamen fieri ut aliquod ministerium in formatione corporis primi hominis angeli exhiberent, sicut exhibebunt in ultima resurrectione, pulveres colligendo." "Sum. Theol.," pars 1ma, quæst. 91, art. 2.

the soul of man directly, and his body indirectly or by the operation of secondary causes. In both cases, however, He is really and truly the Creator, and there is nothing in the theory which is in any wise derogatory to His power or wisdom. We simply admit for the body of man what we have seen may readily be admitted for the rest of the animate world—creation through the agency of secondary causes, instead of direct and immediate creation without the concurrence of any of God's creatures.

This view of the derivative origin of Adam's body, is also quite in harmony with other principles laid down both by the great Bishop of Hippo and the Angel of the Schools. For they both taught, that in the beginning God created, in the absolute and primary sense of creation, only corporeal elements and spiritual substances. Plants, animals and even man, did not exist as we know them—*in natura propria;* but only potentially, receiving their full development afterwards — *per volumina sæculorum.* They existed only in what the saint calls seminal reasons—*in rationibus seminalibus;*[1] and the production of the manifold forms of life, man included, which now adorn our planet, was the work of Evolution, viz., secondary causes acting under the con-

---

[1] "Et ideo concedo," says St. Thomas . . . "quod rationes seminales dicuntur virtutes activæ completæ in natura cum propriis passivis, ut calor et frigus, et forma ignis, et virtus solis, et hujusmodi ; et dicuntur seminales non propter esse imperfectum quod habeant, sicut virtus formativa in semine, sed quia rerum individuis primo creatis, hujusmodi virtutes collatæ sunt per opera sex dierum, ut ex eis quasi ex quibusdam seminibus producerentur et multiplicarentur res naturales." "Sentent.," lib. II, dist. 18, quæst. 1ma, art. 2.

tinued and uninterrupted guidance of the Divine administration.¹

Again, this view of the origin of man's body may be regarded as conformable with the teachings of the Angelic Doctor from another standpoint. As all who are familiar with the scholastic philosophy are aware, St. Thomas, in common with the School generally, teaches that there is a true development in animated nature, a veritable ascent of life from lower to higher forms. There is, he tells us, a succession of vital principles in the organic world, superior principles superseding those which are inferior. In the development of man, as in that of the lower animals, there is an ascending succession of substantial forms, by means of which that which is destined to become a human body, acquires a proper structure and receives the necessary disposition for becoming the receptacle of a rational soul. First the embryo is animated by the vegetable soul; subsequently it is informed by a more perfect soul, which is both nutritive and sensitive. This is what is known as the animal soul. In man this is succeeded by the rational soul—*ab extrinseco immissa*, says the Angelic Doctor—a soul specially created and infused into the human body by God Himself.²

---

¹ "Augustinus enim vult," writes the Angelic Doctor, " in ipso creationis principio, quasdam res per species suas distinctas fuisse in natura propria, ut elementa, corpora cœlestia et substantias spirituales; alia vero in rationibus seminalibus tantum, ut animalia, plantas et *homines*, quæ omnia postmodum in naturis propriis producta sunt." "Sentent.," lib. II, dist. 12ª, quæst. Iᵐᵃ, art. 11.

² The following passage is sufficient to exhibit the Angelic Doctor's teaching in this matter: " Quanto igitur aliqua forma

From what precedes, it is evinced that the Evolution of the body of man, according to Mivart's view, and the subsequent infusion into this body, by God, of a rational soul, is not necessarily antagonistic to the teachings of St. Thomas. The theory may, indeed, encounter certain grave difficulties in the domains of metaphysics and Biblical exegesis, but I do not think it can absolutely be asserted that such difficulties are insuperable.[1]

At all events, whatever one may be disposed to think of the theory, it is well always to bear in mind that it has never been condemned by the Church, although it has been publicly discussed and defended for full five-and-twenty years. If it were as dangerous as some have imagined, and, still more, if it were heretical, as others have thought, it is most probable that the "Genesis of Species" would have been put on the Index long ago.

---

est nobilior et magis distans a forma elementi, tanto oportet esse pluras formas intermedias, quibus gradatim ad formam ultimam veniatur et, per consequens, plures generationes medias; et ideo in generatione animalis et hominis, in quibus est forma perfectissima, sunt plurimæ formæ et generationes intermediæ, et per consequens corruptiones, quia generatio unius est corruptio alterius. Anima igitur vegetabilis, quæ primo inest, cum embryo vivit vita plantæ, corrumpitur, et succedit anima perfectior, quæ est nutritiva et sensitiva simul, et tunc embryo vivit vita animalis; hæc autem corrupta, succedit anima rationalis ab extrinseco immissa, licet precedentes fuerint virtute seminis." "Contra Gentiles," Lib. II, cap. LXXXIX.

[1] For a consideration of some of the difficulties alluded to, consult Padre Mir's "La Creacion," cap. XL, Dierck's "L'Homme-Singe," pp. 91 et seq., and Cardinal Gonzales' "La Biblia y la Ciencia," tom. I, cap. XI, art. III, IV and V.

Views of Cardinal Gonzales.

The late Cardinal Gonzales, that profound Thomist and man of science, whose untimely death the Catholic world will mourn for a long time to come, who has treated so luminously the question of Evolution from the point of view of Scripture, patristic theology and scholastic philosophy, has suggested a modification of Mivart's theory, which, he thinks, would make it more acceptable to theologians than it is as it now stands. If, he says, without however committing himself to the opinion expressed — if instead of affirming, as the English biologist does, that the body of Adam was nothing more than a fully-developed ape, into which God infused a rational soul, we admit that the body of the first man was *partly* the product of Evolution from some lower animal form, and partly the direct work of God Himself, we may thereby, he opines, eliminate many of the objections urged against the theory as formulated by its author. According to this modified view, the body of man was developed from the inferior forms of life only until a certain point, but in this condition it was not prepared to be endowed by an intelligent soul. This imperfect body, however, this unfinished product of evolutionary forces, is taken in hand by the Almighty, who perfects what was begun, gives it the finishing touches, as it were, and renders it a fit habitation, which it was not previously, for a soul which was to be made to His own image and likeness, a soul which was to be dowered with the noble attributes of reason, liberty and immortality.

Speaking for myself, I must confess that such a modification appears unnecessary, and, in the light of the teachings of St. Augustine and St. Thomas, it seems that one may as readily accept the theory as proposed by Mivart, as the restricted form of it which the distinguished cardinal suggests. If we are to admit the action of Evolution at all, in the production of Adam's body, it appears more consistent to admit that it was competent to complete the work which it began, than to be forced to acknowledge that it was obliged to leave off its task when only partially completed. For, whether we assert that the body of the first man was entirely, or only partially, the result of evolutionary action, it was, in both cases, according to the principles we have adopted, the work, and ultimately the sole work, of Almighty God. According to Mivart's view, the body of Adam was formed by God solely through the agency of secondary causes; according to Gonzales it was formed by God partly through the concurrence of secondary causes, and partly by His direct and immediate action. If we are to admit that Evolution had anything whatever to do with man's corporeal frame, it seems more logical to admit that it finished the work which it began, always, of course, under the guidance of the Divine administration, than to suppose that God gave to His secondary agents a work which they might commence, indeed, but which, by reason of limitations imposed on them, they were unable to complete.

One cannot help thinking, when one seriously reflects on the matter, that the learned Cardinal — and what is said of him may be predicated of creationists generally — unconsciously favors the very notion he wishes to oppose. He wishes, above all things, to safeguard the creative act and bring out in bold relief the Divine attributes of wisdom and omnipotence, but he unwittingly, it would seem, makes greater demands than his case requires. Indeed, it strikes me that those who hold the special creation theory as to the body of the father of our race, and the same may be said of believers in the special creation of the forms of life below man, constitute themselves defenders of the very theory which the great St. Athanasius, full fifteen centuries ago, felt called upon to criticise adversely. Arguing against the anthropomorphic views which the heathen entertained of the Almighty, he contended that the God of the Christians is a Creator, not a carpenter — κτίστης οὐ τεχνίτης. In accord with the illustrious Alexandrian Doctor's view, it has been truthfully observed that: "The Great Architect theory in theology is the analogue of the *emboitement* theory in science. Both were invented when mechanism dominated thought, and we have outgrown both."

In commenting on Mivart's theory, the erudite Cardinal Archbishop of Seville manifests his characteristic liberality and breadth of view, strikingly resembling in this respect his immortal master, the Angel of the School. "As the question stands at present," he says, "we have no right to reprobate or

writes: "One may not be of your opinion, because there is question of but an opinion only, but I do not see in what anyone can find fault with your orthodoxy. Science progresses and its discoveries permit us to see better every day the grandiose unity of creation. Whatever be its progress, it will never efface from the first pages of the Bible these two truths: all creation is the work of God; and there are in this creation acts of such transcendence that they can be attributed only to the immediate and effective intervention of an Infinite Power."

From the foregoing it is evident, that whatever may be the final proved verdict of science in respect of man's body, it cannot be at variance with Catholic Dogma. Granting that future researches in paleontology, anthropology and biology, shall demonstrate beyond doubt that man is genetically related to the inferior animals, and we have seen how far scientists are from such a demonstration, there will not be, even in such an improbable event, the slightest ground for imagining that then, at last, the conclusions of science are hopelessly at variance with the declarations of the sacred text, or the authorized teachings of the Church of Christ. All that would logically follow from the demonstration of the animal origin of man, would be a modification of the traditional view regarding the origin of the body of our first ancestor. We should be obliged to revise the interpretation that has usually been given to the words of Scripture which refer to the formation of Adam's body, and read these words in the sense which Evolution demands, a sense which, as we have seen, may be attributed to the words of the inspired record, without either distorting the meaning of terms or in any way doing violence to the text.[1]

---

[1] As illustrations of the extravagant notions, which even eminent men have entertained respecting the origin of our first ancestors, the following paragraphs are pertinent.

Many of the mediæval rabbins, following the teachings of the cosmogonies of India, Persia, Chaldea, Phœnicia, and the account of primitive man as given by Plato in his "Symposium," were believers in the androgynous character of the common father of humanity. The philosopher, Maimonides, expressly declares: "Adam et Eva creati sunt sicut unus, et tergis vel dorso conjuncti. Postea vero a Deo divisi sunt, qui dimidiam partem accepit, et fuit Eva, et adducta est ad ipsum."

The eminent French naturalist, Isidore Geoffroy Saint-Hilaire, was not unfavorable to this view. "On a cherché," he writes, "à expliquer l'hermaphrodisme dans l'espèce humaine, par la réunion de deux sexes chez notre premier père; réunion formellement énoncé dans ce verset de la Genèse, cap. i, ver. 27. 'Et creavit Deus ad imaginem suam, ad imaginem Dei creavit illum, masculum et feminam creavit eos.' On pourrait sans doute trouver dans ce verset, à plusieurs égards remarquable, un emblème de l'état primitivement indecis, ou, si l'on veut, hermaphroditique, de l'appareil sexuel, comme on a trouvé dans l'œuvre des six jours celui du développement progressif de la vie végétale et animale, et de l'apparition tardive de l'homme à la surface du globe." "Histoire Générale et Particulière des Anomalies de l'Organization chez l'Homme," vol. II, p. 53.

Among modern scholars who have inclined to the primitive androgynous condition of Adam, and the subsequent formation of Eve by separation or division, is the distinguished orientalist, François Lenormant. In his "Origines de l'Histoire d'après la Bible," pp. 54 and 55, he expresses himself as follows: " D'après notre version vulgate, d'accord en ceci avec la version grècque des Septante, nous avons l'habitude d'admettre que, selon la Bible, la première femme fut formée d'une côte arrachée au flanc d'Adam. Cependant, on doit sérieusement douter de l'exactitude de cette interprétation. Le mot employé ici, signifie dans tous les autres passages bibliques où on le rencontre, 'côté' et non côte. La traduction philologiquement la plus probable du texte de la Genèse est donc celle que nous avons adoptée plus haut. 'Yaveh Elohim fit tomber un profond sommeil sur l'homme, et celui-ci s'endormit; il prit un de ses côtés et il en ferma la place avec la chair. Et Yaveh Elohim forma le côté qu'il avait pris à l'homme en femme. Et l'homme

have seen, those who study it most deeply and philosophically are driven to go behind it in the search after a true cause. . . . For clearly the development under fixed laws and gradual process of the organic world, no more prevents the original creative and directive Idea from being the true Cause of all, than the passing of the individual being through all stages of embryonic existence from the simple cell, makes it less the creature of the Supreme Hand. That the archetypal idea of the Creative Mind may fulfill itself equally, whether it act directly or through intermediate gradations, we can see clearly not only by abstract theory but by experience of our own 'creations.'"[1]

---

[1] "Some Lights of Science on the Faith," by Alfred Barry, D.D., D.C.L., pp. 111 and 112.

CHAPTER VII.

TELEOLOGY, OLD AND NEW.

The Doctrine of Final Causes.

FROM what precedes it is evident, that the most that Evolution can do is to substitute derivative for special creation, a substitution which, as we have learned, can be admitted without any derogation whatever to either faith or Dogma. But there is yet another objection against Evolution, which, by some minds, is regarded as more serious than any of the difficulties, heretofore considered, of either philosophy or theology. This objection, briefly stated, is that Evolution destroys entirely the argument from design in nature, and abolishes teleology, or the doctrine of final causes. In the case of Darwin, for instance, as we learn from his "Life and Letters," he had no difficulty in accepting derivative in lieu of special creation, but when it came to reconciling natural selection and Evolution with teleology, as taught by Paley, he felt that his chief argument for believing in God had been wrested from him entirely.

So persuaded, indeed, have many naturalists and philosophers been, if we are to believe their own words, that Darwinism and Evolution have given the deathblow to teleology, that they forthwith dismiss all arguments based on design and final causes as utterly worthless. And, of those who are not in sympathy with Christianity, we find not a few who are unable to conceal their exultation over what they regard as the inglorious and complete discomfiture of the theologians. Thus Hæckel, in his "History of Creation," writes: "I maintain with regard to the much-talked-of 'purpose in nature,' that it really has no existence but for those persons who observe phenomena in animals and plants in the most superficial manner."[1] Büchner boasts that "modern investigation and natural philosophy have shaken themselves tolerably free from these empty and superficial conceptions of design, and leave such childish views to those who are incapable of liberating themselves from such anthropomorphic ideas, which unfortunately still obtain in school and church to the detriment of truth and science."[2]

It were easy to multiply similar quotations, but the two just given are quite sufficient for our present purpose. Judging from their public utterances, as well as from their well-known private opinions, there is no mistaking the animus of these soi-disant exponents of modern thought. If we are to take them at their own words, they seem to be as eager, if not more eager, for the extirpation of Dogma and all forms of religious belief, as they are for the advancement of what they denominate "science."

---

[1] Vol. I, p. 19, Eng. trans. In his "Generelle Morphologie," vol. I, p. 160, he asserts: "Wir erblicken darin (in the Darwinian theory) den definitiven Tod aller teleologischen und vitalistischen Beurtheilung der Organismen."

[2] "Force and Matter," p. 218.

A Newer Teleology.

It would be a grave mistake, however, to think that Hæckel and Büchner truthfully reflect the opinions of scientists generally, or that the large body of naturalists are at one with them in proclaiming that the argument from design in nature is no longer tenable, or that Evolution and teleology are wholly incompatible. So far, indeed, is this from being the case, that the most philosophical of contemporary naturalists, those who are most competent to interpret the facts and phenomena of nature and to draw legitimate conclusions from the facts observed, are almost unanimous in declaring that the teleological argument, not only is not weakened, much less destroyed, but that it is, on the contrary, illustrated and corroborated in the most remarkable and unexpected manner. And strange as it may appear, the very one who, according to Hæckel, Büchner, Vogt, G. H. Lewes and others whose anti-theological animus is so marked as to require no comment, was supposed to have banished forever from science and theology, not only design and purpose but all final causes whatsoever, is the very one who, above all others, has put teleology on a firmer and a nobler basis than it ever occupied before. We have no longer, it is true, the argument as it was presented by Paley, and developed by Chalmers and the authors of the Bridgewater Treatises, but we have in its stead one that is grander, more comprehensive, more effective and more conclusive.

Professor Asa Gray, admittedly one of the ablest botanists of the century, and to the day of his death a strenuous and consistent advocate of the theory of Evolution, thus expresses himself when speaking of the work of Charles Darwin: "Let us recognize Darwin's great service to natural science in bringing back to it teleology; so that instead of morphology *versus* teleology, we shall have morphology wedded to teleology."[1] In another place he speaks of "the great gain to science from his [Darwin's] having brought back teleology to natural history. In Darwinism, usefulness and purpose come to the front again as working principles of the first order; upon them, indeed, the whole system rests."[2] "In this system," he continues, "the forms and species in all their variety are not mere ends in themselves, but the whole a series of means and ends, in the contemplation of which we may obtain higher and more comprehensive, and perhaps worthier, as well as more consistent views, of design in nature, than heretofore." In it we have "a theory that accords with, if it does not explain, the principal facts, and a teleology that is free from the common objections," for, "the most puzzling things of all to the old school teleologists are the *principia* of the Darwinian."[3]

Evolution and Teleology.

In the "Life and Letters of Charles Darwin,"[4] edited by his son, we read: "One of the greatest

---
[1] "Darwiniana," p. 288.
[2] Ibid., p. 357.
[3] Ibid., p. 378.
[4] Vol. II, p. 430.

services rendered by my father to the study of natural history is the revival of teleology. The evolutionist studies the purpose or meaning of organs with the zeal of the older teleology, but with far wider and more coherent purpose. He has the invigorating knowledge that he is gaining, not isolated conceptions of the economy of the present, but a coherent view of both past and present. And even where he fails to discover the use of any part, he may, by a knowledge of its structure, unravel the history of the past vicissitudes in the life of the species. In this way a vigor and unity is given to the study of the forms of organized beings, which before it lacked."[1]

---
[1] According to the Duke of Argyll: "The theory of development is not only consistent with teleological explanations, but it is founded on teleology and on nothing else. It sees in everything the results of a system which is ever acting for the best, always producing something more perfect or more beautiful than before, and incessantly eliminating whatever is less faulty or less perfectly adapted to every new condition. Prof. Tyndall himself cannot describe this system without using the most intensely anthropopsychic language. 'The continued effort of animated nature,' he says in his Belfast address, 'is to improve its conditions and raise itself to a loftier level.'" "The Unity of Nature," p. 171.

Mr. Alfred Wallace, who shares with Darwin the honor of having introduced to the world the theory of natural selection, asks, when speaking of the bearing of Evolution on the doctrine of design: "Why should we suppose the machine, too complicated to have been designed by the Creator, so complete that it would necessarily work out harmonious results? The theory of 'continual interference' is a limitation of the Creator's power. It assumes that He could not work by pure law in the organic as he has done in the inorganic world." "Natural Selection," p. 280.

Similar language is employed by the late Prof. Richard Owen, one of the greatest comparative anatomists of the age. He was a firm believer not only in the "ordained becoming" of new species, but was also a zealous and consistent teleologist.

Prof. Huxley, who loves to pose as an agnostic, but who is endowed with a critical acumen that is possessed by neither Büchner nor Hæckel, affirms that: "The most remarkable service to the philosophy of biology rendered by Mr. Darwin, is the reconciliation of teleology and morphology, and the explanation of the facts of both, which his views offer. The teleology which supposes that the eye, such as we see it in man or one of the higher vertebrates, was made with the precise structure it exhibits, for the purpose of enabling the animal which possesses it to see, has undoubtedly received its death-blow. Nevertheless, it is necessary to remember that there is a wider teleology which is not touched by the doctrine of Evolution, but is actually based upon the fundamental principle of Evolution."[1]

To the foregoing testimonies, and others of like import which could easily be adduced in any number desired, I will add the matured opinion of the distinguished naturalist and keen metaphysician, whose name has already figured so frequently in these pages, St. George Mivart. A biologist of marked eminence, an evolutionist of pronounced convictions, a theologian of recognized ability, no one is better qualified to express a judgment regarding the bearings of the Evolution theory on the argument from design and the doctrine of final causes. "A careful study," he tells us, "of the inter-relation and interdependencies which exist between the various orders of creatures inhabiting this planet, shows us a yet more noteworthy teleology—the existence of whole

---

[1] "Darwiniana," p. 110.

orders of such creatures being directed to the service of other orders, in various degrees of subordination and augmentation, respectively. This study reveals to us, as a fact, the enchainment of all the various orders of creatures in a hierarchy of activities, in harmony with what we might expect to find in a world, the outcome of a First Cause possessed of intelligence and will, since it exhibits, at the same time, both 'continuity' and 'purpose.' It shows us, indeed, that a successively increasing fulfillment of 'purpose' runs through the irrational creation up to man. And thus the study of final causes reveals to us how great is our dignity, and, consequently, our responsibility."[1]

Design and Purpose in Nature.

The quotations just made from some of the most eminent and most philosophical of modern naturalists, and they are in perfect accord with the sentiments of the great majority of contemporary evolutionists, prove that true votaries of science, far from denying design and purpose in nature, affirm, on the contrary, their existence, and profess themselves unable to account for the facts and phenomena of the visible universe without postulating a First Cause, the Creator and Ordainer of all the beauty and harmony we so much admire, both in organic and in inorganic nature. From these quotations, too, we see how erroneously the teachings of true science are interpreted by a blatant and anti-religious minority, and

---

[1] "On Truth," pp. 483-484; cf., also, his "Lessons from Nature," pp. 358 et seq., and "Genesis of Species," pp. 273 et seq.

what a grievous injustice is done to the real representatives of science, by those whose chief object seems to be to foment discord between science and religion, and to intensify an *odium theologicum* on one hand, and provoke an *odium scientificum* on the other, which are both as silly as they are unwarranted. In spite of all that may be said to the contrary, the unbiased and reverent student must see in nature the evidence of a Power which is originative, directive, immanent; a Power which is intelligent, wise, supreme. And, notwithstanding the asseverations of the noisy and supercilious few, who are notorious rather for their fanciful theories than prominent for genuine contributions to science, no serious investigator can fail to discern, in the world of beauty and usefulness with which we are surrounded, the most conclusive evidence that what we denominate the laws of nature must have existed in idea before they existed in fact; must have existed in the mind of a supreme, creative Intelligence, as the realities which we now observe and coördinate.[1] Evolution, therefore, far from weakening the argument from design, strengthens and ennobles it; and far from banishing teleology from science and theology, illustrates and corroborates it in the most admirable manner. And despite all attempts to connect teleology with Pan-

---

[1] Paley, in referring to those who speak of law as if it were a cause, very pertinently remarks: "It is a perversion of language to assign any law as the efficient, operative cause of anything. A law presupposes an agent, for it is only the mode according to which the agent proceeds; it implies a power, for it is the order according to which that power acts. Without this agent, without this power, which are both distinct from itself, *the law* does nothing, is nothing." "Natural Theology," p. 12.

theism or Materialism, or to make Evolution subserve the cause of Atheism or Agnosticism, the result has been that we have now a higher, a subtler, a more comprehensive teleology than the world has ever before known. We have a teleology which is indissolubly linked with the teachings of revealed truth ; a teleology which, while receiving light from Evolution, illumines, in turn, this grand generalization, and shows us that Evolution, when properly understood, is a noble witness to a God who, unlike the God of the older Deism, that "simply sets the machine of the universe in motion, and leaves it to work by itself," is, on the contrary, One who, in the language of Holy Scripture, is not only "above all, but through all, and in all."

the teachings of Greek philosophy and modern science respecting the theory of Evolution. According to Thales, Anaximander and Anaximenes, the world and all it contains were generated from simple primordial matter. From the simple proceeds the complex, from the indeterminate, τὸ ἄπειρον, arise all the manifold differentiated forms of the cosmos. Living originates from non-living matter, because all life had its origin in pristine mud. Heraclitus anticipates Darwin's notion of "the struggle for existence," in his view of conflict, πόλεμος, as the originator of all things, and also in his conception of the endeavor made by individuals to insure their existence against the processes of destruction with which they are surrounded. Empedocles, like our modern scientists, taught not only that all terrestrial things arise from certain primitive elements, but also, like Darwin, recognized a development in animal and vegetable forms. He likewise attempted to explain the origin of the various organic beings, species, genera, etc., by the existence of certain adaptations which tend to perpetuate themselves.

Teleological Ideas of Anaxagoras and Aristotle.

The first one of the Greek philosophers to take a teleological view of nature, to perceive in the wonderful adaptations everywhere manifested an evidence of intelligent design, was Anaxagoras. His predecessors and contemporaries were, for the most part, believers in the doctrine that all things were originated by chance, or the fortuitous concourse of atoms, and were, consequently, adherents of what is now known as the monistic or mechanical theory of the universe. This can be predicated especially of Democritus, the founder of Atomism and the forerunner of Materialism.

But it was reserved for "the wisest of wise Greeks, the Stagirite," to develop the teleological ideas of Anaxagoras, and to show that the succession of the myriad forms of terrestrial life was due, not to simple fortuity but to the continued, or at least to the preordaining action, of an intelligent, efficient Cause or Prime Mover. Whether Aristotle believed that God is immanent in nature, and continually working through the agency of natural causes, or conceived Him as preordaining from the beginning all the harmony we now observe, is open to question, but it is quite clear that he was a firm believer in Evolution in its modern sense, as opposed to the theory of special creations. His theistic views are, indeed, in marked contrast with the agnostic and materialistic teachings of the Ionians, and of the earlier and later materialistic schools, especially of those represented by Empedocles, Democritus, Epicurus and Lucretius.

In the Stagirite's doctrines, too, we find the germs of those views on creation which were developed later on with such wonderful fullness, and in such marvelous perfection, by those great Doctors of the Church, Gregory of Nyssa, Augustine and Thomas Aquinas. According to Aristotle it was necessary, that is, in compliance with natural law, that germs, and not animals, should have been first

Darwinism Not Evolution.

Darwinism, as has already been remarked, is not Evolution; neither is Lamarckism nor Neo-Lamarckism. The theories which go by these names, as well as sundry others, are but tentative explanations of the methods by which Evolution has acted, and of the processes which have obtained in the growth and development of the organic world. They may be true or false, although all of them undoubtedly contain at least an element of truth, but whether true or false, the great central conception of Evolution remains unaffected. Whether natural selection has been the chief agent in the Evolution of plants and animals, as Darwin and Wallace contend, or whether the influence of activity and environment has been a more potent factor, as Lamarck and Cope maintain, is as yet uncertain. But be this as it may, it matters not. It is still far from certain that we have discovered the leading factor or factors of Evolution. All theories so far advanced, to account for the phenomena of change and development, are at best but guesses and provisional hypotheses; and no serious man of science claims that they are anything more. They have unquestionably contributed much towards the advancement of the science of biology, and have enabled naturalists to group together facts which were formerly considered as disparate and irreconcilable. They have suggested explanations of phenomena that were shrouded in mystery, and enabled us to perceive in nature a unity of plan and purpose, which, without such theories, would either be obscured or entirely elude our view.

Much, undoubtedly, remains yet to be done, but no one who is familiar with the history of science in the past half century, can deny that marvels have been accomplished during this time, and that a flood of light has been thrown on some of the most puzzling problems of natural science. Whatever value, then, we may attach to the theories of Lamarck and Saint-Hilaire, of Darwin and Wallace and Mivart, no one can deny that they are entitled to a lasting debt of gratitude for their brilliant researches, and for their untiring zeal and signal success in collecting and coördinating facts in a way that has never before been accomplished. Whether their theories be all that has been claimed for them or not, they have certainly popularized an idea which prior to their promulgation interested but a few, and given to the study of science an impetus which it had never before experienced. They have given to the evolutionary idea a relief, and endowed it with a fascination, which have captivated the world. They have inspired among the masses a love of nature which did not previously exist, and have stimulated investigation and spurred on progress in a manner to win the admiration and extort the plaudits of the most indifferent and phlegmatic. As to the authors of these theories they have ushered in a new era, and are the kings and prophets of the most active and most prolific period of research that the world has yet witnessed. Others will come after them who will correct their errors and improve on their theories, but the triumphs of these pioneers of the renaissance of science will endure with undiminished lustre as long as there shall remain an annalist to record the achievements of human progress.

Evolution in the Future.

What shall ultimately be the fate of the arguments now so confidently advanced in favor of Evolution by its friends, and against it by its enemies, only the future can decide. The grounds of defense and attack will, no doubt, witness many and important changes. Future research and discovery will reveal the weakness of arguments that are now considered unassailable, and expose the fallacies of others which, as at present viewed, are thoroughly logical. But new reasons in favor of Evolution will be forthcoming in proportion as the older ones shall be modified or shown to be untenable. And, as the evolutionary idea shall be more studied and developed, the objections which are now urged against it will, I doubt not, disappear or lose much of their cogency. New theories will be promulgated, new explanations of present difficulties will be suggested, and a clearer knowledge will be vouchsafed of what are the real, if not the chief factors, of the vast evolutionary processes which are at the bottom of all forms of organic development. As in physics so also in biology; continued investigation of facts and phenomena is sure to issue in a clearer and truer view of nature, and of the agencies which have been instrumental in bringing animated nature from its primordial to its present condition. And every new discovery, every new fact brought to light and correlated with facts already known, will mean a step forward; will betoken progress, knowledge and enlightenment.

As the old emission theory of light, originated by Descartes and Newton, was followed by the undulatory theory formulated by Huygens, Young and Fresnel; and as the latter has been succeeded by the electro-magnetic theory of Maxwell and Hertz, so likewise will the various theories which are now offered in explanation of the facts of Evolution, be replaced by others which shall be a closer approximation to the truth, or which shall eventually exhibit the truth in all its beauty and grandeur. The hypotheses of Darwin, Wallace, Spencer, Mivart and Weismann will, no doubt, give way in greater or less degree to other theories which, while being more in conformity with the facts observed, shall afford a truer view of nature and supply a more accurate knowledge of those of her operations that are now so mysterious and so ill-understood. The work to be accomplished will, of course, be slow and require time. For, unlike the theory of light, Evolution deals not merely with one form of energy, or forms of energy which are reducible to one. It is not confined to the discussion of only a narrow and limited range of phenomena, but is, on the contrary, a theory which is universal in its application, embracing all forms of energy and dealing with all kinds of matter, from simple elementary atoms to that highest and most complex of organisms, man.

That the task will be accomplished sooner or later; that we shall ultimately have a satisfactory explanation of evolutionary processes; and that the theory of Evolution will at length be established on a firm and logical basis, no reasonable man can doubt. Numerous and great difficulties have been removed during the past few decades, and one need not be a seer to foretell, that even more effective work will be accomplished during the same period of time in the years to come. The world has proceeded too far to admit of retrogression. Advance is the order of the hour, and final triumph is inevitable.

Evolution Not Antagonistic to Religion.

Yet more. In proportion as Evolution shall be placed on a solider foundation, and the objections which are now urged against it shall disappear, so also will it be evinced, that far from being an enemy of religion, it is, on the contrary, its strongest and most natural ally. Even those who have no sympathy with the traditional forms of belief, who are, in principle, if not personally, opposed to the Church and her dogmas, perceive that there is no necessary antagonism between Evolution and faith, between the conclusions of science and the declarations of revelation. Indeed, so avowed an opponent of Church and Dogma as Huxley informs us that: " The doctrine of Evolution does not even come into contact with Theism, considered as a philosophical doctrine. That with which it does collide, and with which it is absolutely inconsistent, is the conception of creation which theological speculators have based upon the history narrated in the opening book of Genesis."[1]

In other words, Evolution is not opposed to revelation, but to certain interpretations of what some have imagined to be revealed truths. It is not opposed to the dogmas of the Church, but to the opinions of certain individual exponents of Dogma, who would have us believe that their views of the Inspired Record are the veritable expressions of Divine truth.[2]

To say that Evolution is agnostic or atheistic in tendency, if not in fact, is to betray a lamentable ignorance of what it actually teaches, and to display a singular incapacity for comprehending the relation of a scientific induction to a philosophical—or, more truthfully, an anti-philosophical—system. The simple assertion of Hæckel and his school, that Evolution implies the monistic or mechanical theory of the universe, proves nothing, for assertion is not proof. Rather should it be affirmed that Evolution, in so far as it is true, makes for religion and Dogma; because it must needs be that a true theory of the origin and development of things must, when properly understood and applied, both strengthen and illustrate the teachings of faith. "When from the

---

[1] " Life and Letters of Charles Darwin," vol. I, p. 556.

[2] Lamarck, with keen philosophic insight, thus expresses himself in his " Philosophie Zoölogique," tom. I, p. 56 : " Sans doute rien n'existe que par la volonté du sublime Auteur de toutes choses, mais pouvons-nous lui assigner des règles dans l'exécution de sa volonté et fixer la mode qu'il a suivi à cet égard ? Assurément, quelle qu'ait été sa volonté, l'immensité de sa puissance est toujours la même, et de quelque manière que se soit exécutée cette volonté suprême, rien n'en peut diminuer la grandeur."

dawn of life," says Prof. Fiske, who is an ardent evolutionist, "we see all things working together towards the Evolution of the highest spiritual attributes or man, we know, however the words may stumble in which we try to say it, that God is in the deepest sense a moral being."[1] Elsewhere the same writer truly observes: "The doctrine of Evolution destroys the conception of the world as a machine. It makes God our constant refuge and support, and nature His true revelation." And again he declares: "Though science must destroy mythology, it can never destroy religion; and to the astronomer of the future, as well as to the Psalmist of old, the heavens will declare the glory of God."[2]

Evolution does, indeed, to employ the words of Carlyle, destroy the conception of "an absentee God, sitting idle, ever since the first Sabbath, at the outside of His universe and seeing it go."[3] But it compels us to recognize that "this fair universe, were it in the meanest province thereof, is, in very deed, the star-domed city of God; that through every star, through every grass-blade, and most, through every living soul, the glory of a present God still beams."[4]

Objections Against New Theories.

It is true, indeed, as we have already learned, that Evolution has been decried, even by men of

---

[1] "The Idea of God," p. 167.
[2] "Outlines of Cosmic Philosophy," vol. II, p. 416.
[3] "Sartor Resartus," book II, chap. VII.
[4] Ibid., book III, chap. VIII.

marked ability, as leading to Atheism or Materialism. But similar charges have also been made against other theories and generalizations which are now universally acknowledged as true.

Anaxagoras, it will be remembered, was condemned as a heretic for asserting that the sun, the great god Helios, was but a mass of molten matter. Spectroscopy has vindicated him, and shown that his accusers were in error. Aristarchus was accused of impiety for having taught that the earth revolves round the sun, and for having anticipated a theory independently discovered and developed eighteen centuries later by Copernicus. The Samian astronomer was charged with having "disturbed the repose of Vesta," and the worshippers of the offended goddess accordingly suppressed or destroyed his sacrilegious works.

Newton's great laws of universal gravitation, when first promulgated, were looked upon with suspicion, and, in some instances, denounced as atheistic. Even so great a mathematician and philosopher as Leibnitz, did not hesitate to condemn Newton's grand discovery, "not only as physically false, but as injurious to the interests of religion."

All are familiar with the absurd objections urged against the heliocentric theory as advocated by Galileo. Lord Bacon rejected it with contempt, and even the distinguished astronomer, Tycho Brahe, notwithstanding all the evidence offered in favor of the Copernican system, invented one of his own which was but a modification of Ptolemy's and no less complex and cumbersome.

Galileo and the Copernican Theory.

It is often said, even by those who should be better informed, that the greatest obstacle in the way of the general acceptance of the Copernican theory was the Church, and that the cause of all of Galileo's woes was the ignorant officials of the Inquisition. The fact is, however, that it was not churchmen, as such, who were opposed to the views which Galileo so ardently and so successfully championed. It was rather the old peripatetic system of philosophy, which, after dominating the world of thought for two thousand years, saw itself finally face to face with what, it was felt on all sides, was destined to prove the most formidable adversary it had yet encountered. For the Ptolemaic system was so closely bound up with the philosophy of Aristotle, and this in turn was so intimately connected with theology, especially since the time of St. Thomas Aquinas, that any attack on the geocentric system was at once regarded as an onslaught on both philosophy and theology. So great, indeed, was the authority of the "Master," as Aristotle was called, and so long had his *dicta* been accepted without question, that in the minds of many it was almost as impious to assail his opinions as it was to attack the dogmas of faith.

One of the fundamental teachings of the Stagirite was, for instance, that concerning the incorruptibility and immutability of the heavens. Galileo's telescopic discoveries showed that this opinion was not based on fact. He proved that "the heavens can change and lay aside their former aspects, and assume others entirely new;" and in doing this, he gave a death blow to one of the leading tenets on which peripatetics generally had so long set such store. Learned professors at Pisa, Padua and Bologna, tried to silence the illustrious Florentine by the profuse use of syllogisms and to disprove the truth of his observations by *a priori* reasonings. He was declared by others to be the victim of strange optical illusions, and, accordingly, it was asserted that the spots on the sun, and the satellites of Jupiter and the variable stars had no existence outside of the observer's diseased imagination. Aristotelians indignantly denied the existence of sun-spots, because, said they: " It is impossible that the eye of the universe could suffer from ophthalmia." For an equally trivial reason they rejected Kepler's great discovery of the accelerated and retarded motions of the planets in different parts of their orbits. "It is undignified," they declared, "for heavenly bodies to hurry and slacken their pace in accordance with the law of the German astronomer." Aristotelianism, it was almost universally agreed, was to be safeguarded at all hazards, and Galileo, Kepler and other innovators, who thus ruthlessly trampled under foot the philosophy of the master—" *Si calpesta tutta la filosofia d'Aristotele*"—were to be vanquished at whatever cost, for if they were allowed to continue their sacrilegious work, they would eventually undermine, not only philosophy and theology, but also sacred Scripture as well.

as science. In like manner those who impeded the advance of science were not the representatives of the Church, as such, but the advocates of some theory or the adherents of some school or system of thought. For generally, if not always, those who are accused of opposing the advancement of science, and who may actually be in error in matters scientific, are as zealously laboring, so far as their lights go, in the interests of science, as those who have the truth on their side. The enemies of Galileo, for instance, imagined that they were doing the greatest possible service to science in battling as they did for Peripateticism and Ptolemaism. But if they had had before them the same evidences of the truth which we at present possess, they would have made no hesitation in acknowledging their mistakes, or rather, they would never have fallen into the errors for which they are now condemned.

Conflict of Opinions Beneficial.

In the long run, however, the conflict of opinions in questions of science, far from having a pernicious, has a beneficial influence on the advancement of knowledge. It stimulates investigation and discovery, and serves to place the truth in such a light as no longer to admit of contradiction.

The long-fought battle on the subject of spontaneous generation is a case in point. Pasteur and Van Beneden have proven by their epoch-making researches, that so far as experiment can give any in-information on the subject, abiogenesis is a chimera.

But while we cheerfully accord to these great savants all the encomiums to which they are entitled, we should not withhold from their great antagonists, Pouchet and Bastian, the meed of praise which their researches have earned for them. The latter were mistaken in their views, it is true; they were vanquished in the controversy which they carried on so ably; but, by the very force and originality of their objections, they contributed materially, though indeed indirectly, towards putting the truth in a bolder relief than it would otherwise have received. Had not Pasteur met with the contradictions he did, had he not been obliged to confute objections of all kinds, objections presented in the name of chemistry, objections urged in the name of biology, objections advanced in the name of metaphysics, he would undoubtedly have discontinued his investigations much sooner than he did, and would have rested satisfied with his earlier and simpler proofs of the untenableness of spontaneous generation.

All glory, therefore, to Galileo and Pasteur for their brilliant achievements! But while sounding the praises of the victors, let us not forget the honors due to those who battled long and gallantly only to suffer defeat in the end. By the very persistence and stubbornness of their contest, they enhanced not only the splendor of the results obtained by their conquerors, but they also labored effectually, albeit indirectly, for the attainment of the same object which was had in view by their antagonists— the truth, the advancement of science, and the placing of it on a surer and firmer foundation.

Kircher and their collaborators lived in the infancy of science; that they had to blaze the way for their successors, and that, notwithstanding their best efforts to arrive at the truth, error was inevitable. Ignorant of countless facts now known to every schoolboy, and unacquainted with the theories and laws which are now the common possession of all who read and think, it was but natural that they should have had recourse to explanations and hypotheses which we should at present regard as fanciful and absurd.

Thus, Kepler taught that the heavenly bodies were guided in their orbits by angels. Water, it was universally believed, would not rise in a pump above a certain height because nature abhors a vacuum. Fossils, it was thought, were but outlines of future creations which the great Artificer had cast aside, or objects placed in the tilted and contorted strata of the earth "to bring to naught human curiosity."

The statements regarding animals found in the "Physiologus" and in the "Bestiaries," allegorical works much esteemed during the Middle Ages, were accepted as veritable facts, and believed as firmly as were the ludicrous stories of Pliny, the naturalist. For a thousand years and more, even those who professed to teach natural history saw in the fables regarding the dragon and the unicorn, the phœnix and the basilisk, the hippogriff and the centaur, nothing to stagger their faith and nothing that was inconsistent with the science of the times. They believed without question that the phœnix rose from its ashes, that the pelican nourished its young with its blood, that the salamander could quench fire, that the basilisk killed serpents by its breath and men by its glance, and many similar things equally preposterous.[1]

The frame of mind, even of the most intelligent men, was such, that the extraordinary tales of Marco Polo and Sir John Mandeville were credited as readily as the most ordinary facts of history or biography. It was indeed difficult to exaggerate the powers or marvels of animated nature to such an extent that they would be pronounced unworthy of credence. But the world has moved since the times of Polo and Mandeville. Science has made wondrous strides forward since the days of Kepler and Kircher. Men are now more familiar with the laws and processes of the organic world, and have learned to recognize the value and necessity of careful observation on the part of the votaries of science.

And in proportion as our knowledge has widened, and become more precise, so likewise have our conceptions of nature and of the Deity's methods of work been modified and exalted. We no longer look upon God as an architect, a carpenter, an artificer; one who must plan and labor in a human fashion, as He was contemplated in the infancy of

---

[1] In the "Physiologus" we read the following about the ant-lion, or myrmekoleon: "His father hath the shape of a lion, his mother that of an ant; the father liveth upon flesh and the mother upon herbs. And these bring forth the ant-lion, a compound of both and in part like to either, for his forepart is that of a lion and his hind part like that of an ant. Being thus composed he is neither able to eat flesh like his father, nor herbs like his mother, therefore he perishes from inanition." See "Encyclopædia Britannica," art., Physiologus.

our race, when the knowledge of the universe was much more circumscribed than it is at present. We now regard Him as a Creator in the highest and truest sense of the term; as one who "protects and governs by His Providence all things which He hath made," and who "reacheth from end to end mightily and ordereth all things sweetly."[1]

Science Not Omnipotent.

But although science has made marvelous advances during recent times, especially during the present century, and although Evolution has contributed in a wonderful manner towards unifying what was before a heterogeneous mass of almost unintelligible facts, science is not omnipotent, nor is Evolution competent to furnish a key to all the mysteries of nature. To judge from the declarations of some of the best known representatives of modern thought, science was to replace religion and the Church, and to do far more for the welfare and elevation of humanity than the Gospel and its ministers are capable of effecting. Renan declares, that it is "science which will ever furnish man with the sole means of bettering his condition." Again he assures us, that "*to organize humanity scientifically* is the last word of modern science, its daring but legitimate aim."[2]

---

[1] "Wisdom," viii, 1, and "Council of the Vatican," chap. 1.

[2] "La science restera toujours la satisfaction du plus haut désir de notre nature, la curiosité; elle fournira toujours à l'homme le seul moyen qu'il ait pour améliorer son sort."
"Organiser scientifiquement l'humanité, tel est donc le dernier mot de la science moderne, telle est son audacieuse, mais légitime prétension." "L'Avenir de la Science," p. 37.

Science, we were told but a few decades ago, would suppress the supernatural, remove mysteries and explain miracles. It would tell us all about the origin of things; the world, life, sensation, rational thought. It would inform us about the origin of society, language, morality, religion. It would throw light not only on the origin of man's body and soul, but also on his ultimate destiny. It would, in a word, frame for us a complete cosmology, a complete code of ethics, and introduce a new religion, which would be as superior to Christianity as science is superior to superstition. It promised that we should one day be able to "express consciousness in foot-pounds;" that we should be able to trace the connection between "the sentiment of love and the play of molecules;" that we should be in a position to discern " human genius and moral aspiration in a ring of cosmical vapor." Thanks to science and to its grand generalization, Evolution, old systems of thought were to be wiped out of existence, and we were to be ushered into an era of general enlightenment and universal progress.

But has science, as represented by Renan, Hæckel and others of their way of thinking, made good its promises? Has it been able to dispense with a personal God, and to relegate the supernatural to the limbo "where entities and quiddities, the ghosts of unknown bodies lie"? Has it, in the words of Virchow, succeeded in referring the origin of life to "a special system of mechanics," or in proving Renan's view that "the harmony of nature is but a resultant," and that "the existence of things is but an affair of equilibrium"?[1] Has the religion which makes a God of humanity regarded in the abstract, or which evolves a Deity from the universe considered as a whole, rendered men better or happier? These are questions which press for an answer, but which, fortunately, can be answered as readily as they are asked.

The response to all these questions, collectively and severally, is a peremptory negative. It is the response which true philosophers and true men of science the world over have given all along. For it would be a mistake to imagine that the utterances of Renan, Hæckel, and their followers, have the indorsement of the worthier representatives of science, or that true science has ever made the pretensions claimed for it by some of its self-constituted exponents and protagonists. There are soi-disant scientists and true scientists, as well as there is a sham science and a science deserving the name.

Bankruptcy of Science.

It was in speaking of such soi-disant scientists and their unfulfilled promises, of such sham science and its boastful pretensions, that a brilliant member of the French Academy, M. Brunetière, did not hesitate to declare recently that "science had become bankrupt." Science has promised to tell us whence we come, what we are, whither we are going; but it

---

[1] "Ceux qui s'obstinent à reconnaître les traces d'une intelligence créatrice dans le développement de l'univers, sont encore dans les liens des vieilles illusions, car l'harmonie de la nature n'est qu'une résultant, et l'existence des choses une affaire d'équilibre." Renan, "L'Avenir de la Science."

has signally and totally failed to give an answer to any of these questions.

Hellenists had engaged themselves to exhibit the whole of Christianity in the philosophy of Greece and Rome, and to pick out for us in the "Thoughts" of Marcus Aurelius, and the "Manual" of Epictetus, all the "scattered members" of the Sermon on the Mount. But they did not succeed in this, and still less did they succeed in explaining why the Sermon on the Mount has conquered the world, and why the "Manual," and the "Thoughts" of Epictetus and Marcus Aurelius have always remained completely sterile.

Hebraists undertook to dissipate the "irrational" and "the marvelous," in the Bible; to exhibit it as a book like the "Iliad" or the "Mahabahrata," but the sum total of their researches has issued in the very opposite of what they anticipated, and their labors have had the effect of reintegrating what they had hoped to destroy.

Orientalists, in their turn, promised to deduce Christianity from Buddhism, and to prove that the teachings of Christ were drawn wholly, or in great part, from the doctrines of Buddha. Like the Hellenists and Hebraists, however, these orientalists failed completely to establish their thesis, and, far from throwing light on the subjects which they set out to clear up, they but plunged them into greater obscurity and introduced new hypotheses instead of reaching positive and incontestable conclusions.

All along the line, the science of which we are speaking—the phyiscal, natural, historical, and philological sciences—has shown itself incapable of giving an answer to the very questions which most interest us. And still more has it forfeited the claim, which it has made during the past hundred years, to frame laws for the government of mankind in lieu of those given by Christ and His Church. The consequence is that all thoughtful men are beginning to realize the fact, if they did not realize it before, that questions of free-will and moral responsibility are not to be settled by physiology, nor are rules of conduct to be sought for in Evolution. Hence, if we are to live anything more than an animal life, we must have something higher than science is able to afford; we must be guided by the teachings of the Founder of Christianity, by the saving influence of that Church which, for well-nigh two thousand years, has shown herself the sole power capable of lifting man from a lower to a higher moral and spiritual plane.

The net result, therefore, of a hundred years of aggressive warfare against the Church and religion, the outcome of all the flattering but misleading promises of science in the matters which we have been considering, have been the very opposite of those intended. M. Brunetière resumes the result in two words—and no well-informed person will, I think, be disposed to contradict his conclusions— these are: "Science has lost its prestige, and religion has recovered a portion of hers."[1]

---

[1] "La Science a perdu son prestige; et la Religion a reconquis une partie du sien." See his interesting article, "Après une Visite au Vatican," in the *Revue des Deux Mondes*, for Jan. 1, 1895.

M. Brunetière's study is pretty much in the same strain as Lord Salisbury's much-discussed address at Oxford, before the British Association for the Advancement of Science. And has not Huxley, one of the most applauded representatives of science, and one of the staunchest defenders of Evolution, been forced to admit, in his celebrated Romanes Lecture, that science and Evolution have limitations which he would have been loath to acknowledge but a few years before he made the confession that so startled many of his scientific friends? The conclusion of this studied effort of the noted evolutionist is, briefly stated, that the cosmic process, or Evolution, is utterly incompatible with ethical progress, or rather, the two are ever and essentially antagonistic.[1]

And Herbert Spencer, too, the great philosopher of Evolution, who sees the working of Evolution in everything; in the development of society, language, government, of worlds and systems of worlds, was obliged not long since to admit, not without reluctance we may be sure, that Evolution is not operating so rapidly as he expected it would, and is not fulfilling all the fond hopes he entertained regarding it as a factor of human progress. "My faith in free institutions," says he, "originally strong, though always formed with the belief that the maintenance and success of them is a question of popular charac-

---

[1] "Social progress," he tells us, "means a checking of the cosmic process at every step and the substitution for it of another, which may be called the ethical process; the end of which is not the survival of who may happen to be the *fittest*, in respect of the whole of the conditions which obtain, but of those who are ethically the *best*."

ter, has, in these later years, been greatly decreased by the conviction that the fit character is not possessed by any people, nor is likely to be possessed for ages to come."[1]

Conquests of Science.

It would be a grave mistake, however, to imagine that, because science has become bankrupt in some things, she has lost her prestige entirely. Nothing could be farther from the truth. No one who is acquainted with the brilliant conquests of science during the present century, could entertain such an opinion for a moment. What M. Brunetière means, and what all those who indorse his statements mean, is that she has failed by attempting what was beyond her competence; by essaying to solve problems and effect reforms that lie entirely within the domain of religion and philosophy. She has erred by confounding empiricism with metaphysics, and become insolvent only by assuming liabilities that were manifestly outside of her sphere of action. But so long as she was content with her own methods, and confined her investigations to her own province, she made good all her promises, if she did not accomplish even more. A glance at the annals of science during the past few decades, to go back no further, should satisfy the most skeptical on this point. She has given to the arts of life an impetus they never felt before. The forces of steam and electricity have received a development and been given applications that have been the marvel of the world.

---

[1] See *McClure's Magazine*, for March, 1894.

Nor has theoretical science in anywise failed to keep pace with the practical. Chemistry, biology, astronomy, physics, geology, aside from their practical applications, have wonderfully extended our views of the universe and given us far nobler conceptions both of nature and nature's God.

And, paradoxical as it may appear, not the least noble of these conceptions comes to us from that very theory which, only a few years ago, was supposed to have banished forever the Creator from the world of reality; a theory which was at once the scandal of the pious and the incubus of the orthodox. Evolution, it was asserted, had disproved the declarations of Scripture, and shown the inutility of a religion based on Dogma. It had dethroned the Almighty, had demonstrated that the universe is eternal, and that the order and beauty which we everywhere behold is the result of a fortuitous concourse of atoms. There is, therefore, we were told, neither design nor purpose in nature, and the doctrine of final causes, on which theologians were wont to lay so much stress, is completely and forever discredited.

More mature reflection, however, shows that all these assertions are as rash as they are unwarranted. Never in the history of science have thoughtful students of nature felt more deeply the necessity of recognizing a personal Creator, a spiritual, intelligent First Cause, than at present. Never have men seen more clearly the necessity of religion, as the sole agency which is capable of elevating and saving human society from the countless dangers with

of design has been greatly too much lost sight of in recent zoölogical speculations. Overpoweringly strong proofs of intelligent and benevolent design lie around us, and if ever perplexities, whether metaphysical or scientific, turn us away from them for a time, they come back upon us with irresistible force, showing to us, through nature, the influence of a free will, and teaching us that all living things depend on one everlasting Creator and Ruler."

No, the argument from design has not been invalidated; it has been modified. It has not been weakened; it has been strengthened and expanded. Teleology to-day is not, indeed, the same as it was in Paley's time, nor as it was when the authors of the Bridgewater Treatises lived and labored. It is now a more comprehensive, a more beautiful, and a more stimulating science. To Paley, a watch found on the heath by a passing traveler, was evidence of design and of a designer. To the evolutionist, the evidence of design is not merely a watch, but a watch which is capable of producing other and better watches. To Paley, God was an Artificer who fashioned things directly from the materials at hand; to the evolutionist, as to St. Athanasius, St. Gregory of Nyssa and St. Augustine, God is a Creator who makes things make themselves. To Paley, as to the older school of natural theologians, God was the direct cause of all that exists; to the evolutionist he is the Cause of causes—*Causa causarum*, of the world and all it contains. According to the older view, God created everything directly and in the condition in which it now exists; according to Evolution, creation, or development rather, has been a slow and gradual process, demanding untold æons for converting chaos into a cosmos, and for giving to the visible universe all the beauty and harmony which it now exhibits. It seems, indeed, more consonant with our ideas of God, to Whom a thousand years are as one day and one day as a thousand years, to conceive Him as creating all things in the beginning, and in ordering and administering them afterwards through the agency of secondary causes, rather than to represent Him as perpetually taking up a work which He had left unfinished, and bringing it to a state of perfection only by a long series of interferences and special creations. Understood in this, its true sense, Evolution teaches, as Temple phrases it, that the execution of God's " purpose belongs more to the original act of creation, less to acts of government. There is more Divine foresight, there is less Divine interposition; and whatever has been taken from the latter has been added to the former."[1]

Rudimentary Organs.

For a long time naturalists were sorely puzzled as to how to account for the existence of nascent and rudimentary organs, which are manifestly of no use to their possessors. On the theory of special creations, the only explanation that could be offered for their existence was, that the Creator added them for the sake of symmetry, or because they were a part of His plan. Evolution, however, which contemplates not only the history of the individual but

---

[1] "The Relations Between Religion and Science," p. 123.

the idea of separation or differentiation, and the idea of progressive development or perfecting. Although Moses looks upon the results of the great laws of organic development, which we shall later point out as the necessary conclusions of the doctrine of descent, as the direct action of a constructing Creator, yet in this theory there lies hidden the ruling idea of a progressive development and differentiation of the originally simple matter. We can, therefore, bestow our just and sincere admiration of the Jewish law-giver's grand insight into nature, and his simple and natural hypothesis of creation."[1]

Evolution has been condemned as anti-Patristic and anti-Scholastic, although Saints Gregory of Nyssa, Augustine and Thomas Aquinas, are most explicit in their assertion of principles that are in perfect accord with all the legitimate demands of theistic Evolution. It suffices to recall the admirable passage of the Bishop of Hippo, in his "De Genesi ad Litteram," in which he proleptically announced all the fundamental principles of modern Evolution. He recognized Evolution not only in individuals, but he also discerned its workings in the sum of all things. God did not create the world, as it now exists, actually, *actualiter*, but potentially and causally, *potentialiter et causaliter*. Plants and animals were created virtually, *vi potentiaque causali*, before they received their subsequent development, *priusquam per temporum moras exorirentur*.[2]

---

[1] "History of Creation," vol. I, p. 38.

[2] Vid. sup., part II, chap. iv, for St. Augustine's views on Evolution.

Evolution and Special Creation.

In reference to the popular objections against Evolution that it reposes on no positive demonstration; that none of the arguments advanced in its behalf are conclusive; that all of them, whether taken severally or collectively are vitiated by some flaw, and that, consequently, they are not of such a character as to command the assent of reasonable men, it may be observed that all of them can be urged with equal, and even with greater force against the rival of the Evolution theory, to wit, the theory of special creation.[1] Contrary to what its supporters would be disposed to admit, it has no foundation but assumption, and can claim no more substantial basis than certain postulates which are entirely gratuitous, or certain views regarding the Genesiac account of creation, the truth of which views may as readily and with as much reason be denied as it can be affirmed. For as the learned Abbé Guillemet declared before a sympathetic audience, composed of distinguished ecclesiastics and scholarly laymen, at the International Catholic Scientific Congress at Brussels, the theory of special creation, or fixism as he prefers to call it, explains nothing whatever in science. Not only this, "it closes the door to all explanations of nature, and notably so in the domain of paleontology,

---

[1] According to the theory of special creation as formerly held, everything in the inorganic, as well as in the organic world, was created by God directly and essentially as it now appears. But as at present understood, special creation means rather that the Deity created immediately all the species and higher groups, of animals and plants, as they now exist.

comparative anatomy, embryology and teratology. It affords no clue to the significance of rudimentary organs, and tends inevitably to force science into a veritable cul-de-sac."[1]

Again, it may be observed that the objections referred to are based not only on a misapprehension of the significance of the theory of Evolution, as well as of that of the theory of special creation, but also on a misconception of the character of the arguments which are urged in favor of both theories. The misapprehension arises from the fact, that Evolution is regarded as being at best but a flimsy hypothesis, while special creation is represented as a positive dogma, which admits neither of doubt nor of controversy. The truth is, however, that both Evolution and special creation are theories, and no one who is exact in the use of language can truthfully assert that either of them is anything more. Evolution, I know, is oftentimes called a proved doctrine; but no evolutionist who has any regard for accuracy of terminology would pretend that the theory has passed all the requirements of a rigid demonstration, because he knows better than anyone else, that anything approaching a mathematical demonstration of Evolution is an impossibility. The most that the evolutionist can hope for, or that he has hitherto attained, or is likely to attain, at least for a long time to come, is a certain degree of probability; but such a degree of probability as shall give his

---

[1] See Compte Rendu du Troisième Congrès Scientifique des Catholiques, Section d'Anthropologie, p. 20.

theory sufficient weight to command the assent of anyone who is competent to estimate the value of the evidence offered in its support. The degree of probability which already attaches to the theory of Evolution is very great, as all who have taken the trouble to investigate its claims must admit; and every new discovery in the realms of animate nature but contributes towards placing the theory on a firmer and more impregnable basis.

Such being the case the question now is: Which of the two theories is the more probable, Evolution or special creation? Both of them, it must be admitted, rest upon a certain number of postulates; both of them have much to be said in their favor, as both of them may be assailed with numerous and serious objections. For our present purpose it will here suffice to repeat the answer of the Abbé Guillemet, who tells us that Evolution, as against special creation, has this in its favor, that it explains and coördinates the facts and phenomena of nature in a most beautiful and simple manner; whereas the theory of special creation not only explains nothing and is incapable of explaining anything, but, by its very nature, tends to impede research, to bar progress, or, as he phrases it, "it forces science into a blind alley—*met la science dans une impasse.*"

Genesiac Days, Flood, Fossils and Antiquity of Man.

As matters now stand, the case of special creation versus Evolution is analogous to several other questions which have supplied materials for long and acrimonious controversy. Thus, until the last century it was the almost universally accepted belief that the days of Genesis were real solar days of twenty-four hours each. It was likewise the general opinion that the Noachian Deluge was universal, not only as to the earth's surface but also as to the destruction "of all flesh, wherein is the breath of life, under heaven." And until a few decades ago it was the current belief, that the advent of our race on earth did not date back much farther than four thousand years B. C., and that the only reliable evidence we had for the solution of the problem involved, was to be found in certain statements of the Sacred Text. So, too, from the time of Aristotle until that of Palissy, the potter, we might say even until the time of Cuvier, it was believed that fossils were but "sports of nature," "results of seminal air acting upon rocks," or "rejected models" of the Creator's work.

Now it would probably be difficult, if not impossible, to give an absolute proof of the unsoundness of these views, and that for the simple reason that anything like a mathematical demonstration is, by the very nature of the case, out of question. Rigorously speaking, the theories involved in the above beliefs, with the exception, perhaps, of that regarding the antiquity of man, are susceptible neither of proof nor of disproof. The most we can have, at least for the present, is a greater or less degree of probability, for it is manifest that the Almighty, had He so willed, could have created the world as it now is in six ordinary days. He could have created it just as it exists at present in a single instant, for He is above and independent of time. The teachings, however, of geology and paleontology are diametrically opposed to the supposition that He did fashion this globe of ours, as we now see it, in six ordinary days, while it is found that there is nothing in Scripture which precludes the view that the days of Genesis were indefinite periods of time. God could have caused the flood to cover the entire earth to the height of the highest mountain, and He could thus have destroyed every living thing except what was preserved in the ark; but did He? Ethnology, linguistics, prehistoric archæology, and even Scripture, supply us with practically conclusive reasons for believing that He did not. It is within the range of possibility, that the four thousand and four years allowed by Usher for the interval which elapsed between the creation of Adam and the birth of Christ, are ample to meet the demands of the case, but it is in the highest degree improbable. If the evidence of history, archæology, and cognate branches of science have any value at all, it is almost demonstrably certain that the time granted by Usher and his followers is entirely inadequate to meet the many difficulties which modern science has raised against the acceptance of such a limited period since man's advent on earth. And so, too, regarding fossils. God could, undoubtedly, have created them just as they are found in the earth's crust, but there is no reason for believing that He did so, while there are many and grave reasons for thinking that He did not. In the first place all *prima facie* evidence is against it. It is contrary to the known analogy of the Creator's methods of work in other instances; contrary to what is a rational conception of the Divine economy in the plan of creation. It is contrary also to our ideas of God's wisdom and goodness; for to suppose that fossils are not the remains of forms of life now extinct, to suppose that they were created as we now find them, would be to suppose that the Creator would have done something which was specially designed to mislead and deceive us. Against such a view we can assert what Suarez affirms in another connection, that God would not have designedly led us into error—*Incredibile est, Deum . . . illis verbis ad populum fuisse locutum quibus deciperetur.* We see fossils now forming, and from what we know of the uniformity of nature's operations we conclude that in the past, and during the lapse of long geologic eras, fossils have been produced through the agency of natural causes as they are produced at present, and that, consequently, they were not created directly and immediately during any of the Genesiac days, days of twenty-four hours each, as was so long and so universally believed even by the wisest theologians and philosophers.

What has been said of the traditional views respecting the six days of creation, the Noachian Deluge, the antiquity of the human race and the nature and age of the fossil remains entombed in the earth's crust, may, in a great measure, be iterated regarding the long-accepted view of special creation. It is possible, for there is nothing in it intrinsically absurd; but in the light afforded by the researches and discoveries of these latter days, it is the conviction of the great majority of those who have studied the question with the greatest care, and who are the most competent to interpret the facts involved, that as between the two rival theories, special creation and Evolution, the preponderance of probability is overwhelming in favor of Evolution of some kind, but of just what kind only the future can determine.

Evolution, then, I repeat it, is contrary neither to reason nor to Scripture. And the same may be said of the divers theories of Evolution which, during these latter times, have had such a vogue. Whether, therefore, we accept the theory of extraordinary births, the saltatory Evolution of Saint-Hilaire and St. George Mivart; or Darwin's theory of natural selection, which takes account of only infinitesimal increments; or Weismann's theory of heredity, which traces specific changes to the germ-plasm, we are forced to admit that the ultimate efficient Cause of all the changes produced, be they slow or sudden, small or great, is the Creator Himself, acting through the agency of second causes, through the forces and virtues which He, Himself, communicated to matter in the beginning. Such being the case, it is obvious that Evolution does not exclude creation, and that creation is not incompatible with Evolution.

Strictly speaking, Evolution, whether it progress by saltation or by minute and fortuitous increments, as we are wont to regard them, is, in the last resort, a kind of special creation, and, reason as we may, we can view it in no other light. The same may be said of spontaneous generation, or the Evolution of organic from inorganic matter. For secondary or derivative creation implies Evolution of some kind, as Evolution, whether rapid or operating through untold æons, demands, in the last analysis, the action of intelligence and will, and presupposes what is termed creation in a restricted sense, that is, formation from preëxisting material. Our primary intuitions, especially our ideas of causation, preclude us from taking any other view in the premises. As reason and revelation teach, it was God who created the materials and forces which made Evolution possible. "It was Mind," as Anaxagoras saw, "that set all things in order" — πάντα διεκόσμησε νόος; that from chaos educed a cosmos and gave to the earth all that infinitude of variety and beauty and harmony which we so much admire.

But not only is Evolution a theory which is in perfect accordance with science and Scripture, with Patristic and Scholastic theology; it is likewise a theory which promises soon to be the generally accepted view; the view which will specially commend itself not only to Christian philosophy, but also to Christian apologetics as well. We have seen some indications of this in the already quoted opinions of such eminent Catholic authorities as Monsabré, D'Hulst, Leroy, De Lapparent and St. George Mivart.

Eminent Catholics on Evolution.

Geoffroy Saint-Hilaire, Cuvier's great rival, and a man of profound religious sentiments, looked upon the succession of species, as disclosed by Evolution, as "one of the most glorious manifestations of creative power, and a fresh motive for admiration and love." The noted Belgian geologist, D'Omalius d'Halloy, as distinguished for his loyalty to the Church as for his eminence in science, declares: "It appears to me much more probable and more conformable to the eminent wisdom of the Creator, to admit that, just as He has given to living beings the faculty of reproducing themselves, so, likewise, has He endowed them with the power of modifying themselves according to circumstances, a phenomenon of which nature affords us examples even at present."[1]

---

[1] "Sur Le Transformisme," Bulletin de l'Académie Royale de Belgique, 1873, tiré à part, p. 5.

The illustrious paleontologist, M. Albert Gaudry, a member of the French Institute and a devoted son of the Church, in speaking of the plan of creation, "où l'Être Infini a mis l'empreinte de son unité," expresses himself as follows: "Les paléontologistes ne sont pas d'accord sur la manière dont ce plan a été réalisé; plusieurs, considérant les nombreuses lacunes qui existent encore dans la série des êtres, croient à l'indépendance des espèces, et admettent que l'Auteur du monde a fait apparaître tour à tour les plantes et les animaux des temps géologiques de manière à simuler la filiation qui est dans sa pensée; d'autres savants, frappés, au contraire, de la rapidité avec laquelle les lacunes diminuent, supposent que la filiation a été réalisé matériellement, et que Dieu a produit les êtres des diverses époques en les tirant de ceux qui les avaient précédés. *Cette dernière hypothèse est celle que je préfère; mais qu'on l'adopte, ou qu'on ne l'adopte pas, ce qui me paraît bien certain c'est qu'il y a eu un plan.* Un jour viendra sans doute où les paléontologistes pourront saisir le plan qui a présidé au développement de la vie. Ce sera là un beau jour pour eux, car, s'il y a tant de magnificence dans les détails de la nature, il ne doit pas y en avoir

Commenting on this question, the learned Belgian Jesuit, Father Bellinck, asks: "What matters it if there have been creations prior to that which Moses describes: what matters it whether the periods required for the genesis of the universe were days or epochs; whether the apparition of man on the earth was at an earlier or later date; whether animals have preserved their primitive forms, or whether they have undergone gradual transformations; whether even the body of man has experienced modifications, and, finally, what matters it whether, in virtue of the Creative Will, inorganic matter be able or not to produce plants and animals spontaneously?

"All these questions are given over to the disputes of men, and it is for science to distinguish truth from error."[1]

These are pertinent questions. What matters it, indeed, from the standpoint of Catholic Dogma, if they are all answered in the affirmative? If science should eventually demonstrate that spontaneous generation is probable, or has actually occurred, or is occurring in our own day, what matters it? The Fathers and Schoolmen found no difficulty in believing in abiogenesis, and most of them, if not all of them, believed in it so far as it concerned the lower forms of life. More than this. As we learned in the beginning of our work, spontaneous generation was almost universally accepted until about a cen-

---

moins dans leur agencement générale." "Les Enchaînements du Monde Animal dans les Temps Géologiques," introduction, p. 3.

[1] Vid. "Revue des Études Historiques et Littéraires," 1864.

tury ago. Materialists then bethought themselves that abiogenesis might be urged as an argument in favor of Materialism. Theologians, in their eagerness to answer the objection, denied the fact instead of denying the inference. Later on, men of science discovered that so far as evidence goes abiogenesis is not a fact, and, still later, it dawned upon a few theologians that whether a fact or not, it is quite immaterial so far as theology is concerned. Whether non-living matter may ever give rise to living matter, science is unable to state with absolute certainty, but should it ultimately be shown that spontaneous generation is a fact, we should simply say with the Fathers and Doctors of the Church: The Creator gave to inorganic matter the power, under suitable conditions, of evolving itself into organic matter, and thus science and Dogma would be in harmony.[1]

---

[1] The illustrious Gladstone referring to this subject in his admirable introduction to the "People's Bible History," writes as follows: "Suppose for a moment that it were found, or could be granted in the augmentation of science that the first and lowest forms of life had been evolved from lifeless matter as their immediate antecedent. What statement of Holy Scripture would be shaken by the discovery? What would it prove to us, except that there had been given to certain inanimate substances the power, when they were brought into certain combinations, of reappearing in some of the low forms which live, but live without any of the worthier prerogatives of life? No conclusion would follow for reasonable men, except the perfectly rational conclusion that the Almighty had seen fit to endow with certain powers in particular circumstances, and to withhold from them in other circumstances, the material elements which He had created, and of which it was surely for Him to determine the conditions of existence and productive power, and the sphere and manner of their operation."

In his "Psychology," Rosmini has a couple of chapters on spontaneous generation and the animation of the elements of matter, which the reader will find curious and interesting. Referring to spontaneous generation as an argument in favor of

Faith Has Nothing to Apprehend from Evolution.

Suppose, then, that a demonstrative proof of the theory of Evolution should eventually be given, a proof such as would satisfy the most exacting and the most skeptical, it is evident, from what has already been stated, that Catholic Dogma would remain absolutely intact and unchanged. Individual theorists would be obliged to accommodate their views to the facts of nature, but the doctrines of the Church would not be affected in the slightest. The hypothesis of St. Augustine and St. Thomas Aquinas would then become a thesis, and all reasonable and consistent men would yield ready, unconditional and unequivocal assent.

And suppose, further, that in the course of time science shall demonstrate—a most highly improbable event—the animal origin of man as to his body. There need, even then, be no anxiety so far as the

---

Materialism, he says: "If the fact of spontaneous generation does really occur in nature, it does not follow, as Cabanis maintained, that pure matter of itself passes into life. On the contrary, we must say that the matter itself was animate, and that the principle of life which was in it, operating in its matter, produced organism. In this way this great fact would be the most manifest proof of an immaterial principle." Again: "Spontaneous generations would never prove that matter was dead; on the contrary, they would prove that it was alive." Further on he declares that "if there should suddenly leap forth from the ground a full-grown mastodon, or a rhinoceros, all that would legitimately follow from the fact would be, that there was a vital principle in the ground, and that this was the secret organizer of these huge bodies." Book IV, chap. XIV.

As for Pantheism, he asserts in Book IV, chap. XV: "It is altogether indifferent whether we admit that the animate substances in the universe are more or fewer, some or all, so long as we admit that they are created, and, therefore, altogether distinct from the Creator, Pantheism is excluded."

REFLECTIONS AND CONCLUSION. 429

truths of faith are concerned. Proving that the body of the common ancestor of humanity is descended from some higher form of ape, or from some extinct anthropopithecus, would not necessarily contravene either the declarations of Genesis, or the principles regarding derivative creation which found acceptance with the greatest of the Church's Fathers and Doctors.

Mr. Gladstone, in the work just quoted from, expresses the same idea with characteristic force and lucidity. " If," he says, "while Genesis asserts a separate creation of man, science should eventually prove that man sprang, by a countless multitude of indefinitely small variations, from a lower, and even from the lowest ancestry, the statement of the great chapter would still remain undisturbed. For every one of those variations, however minute, is absolutely separate, in the points wherein it varies, from what followed and also from what preceded it; is in fact and in effect a distinct or separate creation. And the fact that the variation is so small that, taken singly, our use may not be to reckon it, is nothing whatever to the purpose. For it is the finiteness of our faculties which shuts us off by a barrier downward, beyond a certain limit, from the small, as it shuts us off by a barrier upward from the great; whereas for Him whose faculties are infinite, the small and the great are, like the light and the darkness, 'both alike,' and if man came up by innumerable stages from a low origin to the image of God, it is God only who can say, as He has said in other cases, which of those stages may be worthy to be noted with the distinctive name of creation, and at what point of the ascent man could first be justly said to exhibit the image of God."

But the derivation of man from the ape, we are told, degrades man. Not at all. It would be truer to say that such derivation ennobles the ape. Sentiment aside, it is quite unimportant to the Christian "whether he is to trace back his pedigree directly or indirectly to the dust." St. Francis of Assisi, as we learn from his life, "called the birds his brothers." Whether he was correct, either theologically or zoölogically, he was plainly free from that fear of being mistaken for an ape which haunts so many in these modern times. Perfectly sure that he, himself, was a spiritual being, he thought it at least possible that birds might be spiritual beings, likewise incarnate like himself in mortal flesh; and saw no degradation to the dignity of human nature in claiming kindred lovingly with creatures so beautiful, so wonderful, who, as he fancied, "praised God in the forest, even as angels did in heaven."[1]

---

[1] Kingsley, "Prose Idylls," pp. 24 et seq. Ruskin in referring to the matter in his "Aratra Pentelici," expresses himself with characteristic force and originality. "Whether," he says, "your Creator shaped you with fingers or tools, as a sculptor would a lump of clay, or gradually raised you to manhood through a series of inferior forms, is only of moment to you in this respect, that, in the one case, you cannot expect your children to be nobler creatures than yourselves; in the other, every act and thought of your present life may be hastening the advent of a race which will look back to you, their fathers—and you ought, at least, to have retained the dignity of desiring that it may be so—with incredulous disdain."

Misapprehensions Regarding Evolution.

Many, it may here be observed, look on the theory of Evolution with suspicion, because they fail to understand its true significance. They seem to think that it is an attempt to account for the origin of things when, in reality, it deals only with their historical development. It deals not with creation, with the origin of things, but with the *modus creandi*, or, rather, with the *modus formandi*, after the universe was called into existence by Divine Omnipotence. Evolution, then, postulates creation as an intellectual necessity, for if there had not been a creation there would have been nothing to evolve, and Evolution would, therefore, have been an impossibility.

And for the same reason, Evolution postulates and must postulate, a Creator, the sovereign Lord of all things, the Cause of causes, the *terminus a quo* as well as the *terminus ad quem* of all that exists or can exist. But Evolution postulates still more. In order that Evolution might be at all possible it was necessary that there should have been not only an antecedent creation *ex nihilo*, but also that there should have been an antecedent involution, or a creation *in potentia*. To suppose that simple brute matter could, by its own motion or by any power inherent in matter as such, have been the sole efficient cause of the Evolution of organic from inorganic matter, of the higher from the lower forms of life, of the rational from the irrational creature, is to suppose that a thing can give what it does not possess, that the greater is contained in the less, the superior in the inferior, the whole in a part.

No mere mechanical theory, therefore, however ingenious, is competent to explain the simplest fact of development. Not only is such a theory unable to account for the origin of a speck of protoplasm, or the germination of a seed, but it is equally incompetent to assign a reason for the formation of the smallest crystal or the simplest chemical compound. Hence, to be philosophically valid, Evolution must postulate a Creator not only for the material which is evolved, but it must also postulate a Creator, *Causa causarum*, for the power or agency which makes any development possible. God, then, not only created matter in the beginning, but He gave it the power of evolving into all forms it has since assumed or ever shall assume.

But this is not all. In order to have an intelligible theory of Evolution, a theory that can meet the exacting demands of a sound philosophy as well as of a true theology, still another postulate is necessary. We must hold not only that there was an actual creation of matter in the beginning, that there was a potential creation which rendered matter capable of Evolution, in accordance with the laws impressed by God on matter, but we must also believe that creative action and influence still persist, that they always have persisted from the dawn of creation, that they, and they alone, have been efficient in all the countless stages of evolutionary progress from atoms to monads, from monads to man.

This ever-present action of the Deity, this immanence of His in the work of His hands, this continuing in existence and developing of the creatures He has made, is what St. Thomas calls the "Divine administration," and what is ordinarily known as Providence. It connotes the active and constant coöperation of the Creator with the creature, and implies that if the multitudinous forms of terrestrial life have been evolved from the potentiality of matter, they have been so evolved because matter was in the first instance proximately disposed for Evolution by God Himself, and has ever remained so disposed. To say that God created the universe in the beginning, and that He gave matter the power of developing into all the myriad forms it subsequently exhibited, but that after doing this He had no further care for what He had brought into existence, would be equivalent to indorsing the Deism of Hume, or to affirming the old pagan notion according to which God, after creating the world, withdrew from it and left it to itself.

Well, then, can we say of Evolution what Dr. Martineau says of science, that it "discloses the method of the world, not its cause; religion, its cause and not its method."[1] Evolution is the grand and stately march of creative energy, the sublime manifestation of what Claude Bernard calls "the first, creative, legislative and directing Cause."[2] In it we have constantly before our eyes the daily miracles,

---

[1] See Essay on Science, Nescience, Faith.

[2] "En résumé, il y a dans un phénomène vital, comme dans tout autre phénomène naturel, deux ordres de causes : d'abord

quotidiana Dei miracula, of which St. Augustine speaks, and through it we are vouchsafed a glimpse, as it were, of the operation of Providence in the government of the world.

Evolution, therefore, is neither a " philosophy of mud," nor " a gospel of dirt," as it has been denominated. So far, indeed, is this from being the case that, when properly understood, it is found to be a strong and useful ally of Catholic Dogma. For if Evolution be true, the existence of God and an original creation follow as necessary inferences. "A true development," as has truthfully been asserted, " implies a *terminus a quo* as well as a *terminus ad quem.* If, then, Evolution is true, an absolute beginning, however unthinkable, is probable ;"— I should say certain—"the eternity of matter is inconsistent with scientific Evolution." [1]

"Nature," Pascal somewhere says, "confounds the Pyrrhonist, and reason, the dogmatist." Evolution, we can declare with equal truth, confounds the agnostic, and science, the atheist. For, as an English positivist has observed : " You cannot make the slightest concession to metaphysics without ending in a theology," a statement which is tantamount to the

---

une cause première, créatrice, législative et directrice de la vie, et inaccessible à nos connaissances ; ensuite une cause prochaine, ou *exécutive*, du phénomène vital, qui est toujours de nature physico-chimique et tombe dans le domaine de l'expérimentation. La cause première de la vie donne l'évolution ou la *création de la machine organisée;* mais la machine, une fois créée, fonctionne en vertu des propriétés de ses élements constituants et sous l'influence des conditions physico-chimiques qui agissent sur eux." " La Science Expérimentale," p. 53.

[1] Vid. Moore's " Science and the Faith," p. 229.

admission that "If once you allow yourself to think of the origin and end of things, you will have to believe in a God." And the God you will have to believe in is not an abstract God, an unknowable x^n, a mere metaphysical deity, "defecated to a pure transparency," but a personal God, a merciful and loving Father.

As to man, Evolution, far from depriving him of his high estate, confirms him in it, and that, too, by the strongest and noblest of titles. It recognizes that although descended from humble lineage, he is "the beauty of the world, and the paragon of animals;" that although from dust—tracing his lineage back to its first beginnings—he is of the "quintessence of dust." It teaches, and in the most eloquent language, that he is the highest term of a long and majestic development, and replaces him "in his old position of headship in the universe, even as in the days of Dante and Aquinas."

Evolution an Ennobling Conception.

And as Evolution ennobles our conceptions of God and of man, so also does it permit us to detect new beauties, and discover new lessons, in a world that, according to the agnostic and monistic views, is so dark and hopeless. To the one who says there is no God, "the immeasurable universe," in the language of Jean Paul, "has become but a cold mass of iron, which hides an eternity without form and void."

To the theistic evolutionist, however, all is instinct with invitations to a higher life and a happier existence in the future; all is vocal with hymns of praise and benediction. Everything is a part of a grand unity betokening an omnipotent Creator. All is foresight, purpose, wisdom. We have the entire history of the world and of all systems of worlds, "gathered, as it were, into one original, creative act, from which the infinite variety of the universe has come, and more is coming yet."[1] And God's hand is seen in the least as in the greatest. His power and goodness are disclosed in the beauteous crystalline form of the snow-flake, in the delicate texture, fragrance and color of the rose, in the marvelous pencilings of the butterfly's wing, in the gladsome and melodious notes of the lark and the thrush, in the tiniest morning dew-drop with all its gorgeous prismatic hues and wondrous hidden mysteries. All are pregnant with truths of the highest order, and calculated to inspire courage, and to strengthen our hope in faith's promise of a blissful immortality.

The Divine it is which holds all things together: περιέχει τό θεῖον τὴν ὅλην φύσιν.[2] So taught the old Greek philosophy as reported by the most gifted of her votaries. And this teaching of the sages of days long past, is extended and illuminated by the far-reaching generalization of Evolution, in a manner

---

[1] Vid. Bishop Temple's "The Relations Between Religion and Science," p. 116.

[2] Παραδέδοται δέ ὑπό τῶν ἀρχαίων καί παμπαλαίων ἐν μίθου σχήματι καταλελείμμενα τοις ὑστερον, ὅτι περιέχει τό θεῖον τήν ὅλην φύσιν. Aristotle, "Metaphysics," XI, VIII.

that is daily becoming more evident and remarkable. But what Greek philosophy faintly discerned, and what Evolution distinctly enunciates, is rendered gloriously manifest by the declaration of revealed truth, and by the doctrines of Him who is the Light of the World.

Science and Evolution tell us of the transcendence and immanence of the First Cause, of the Cause of causes, the Author of all the order and beauty in the world, but it is revelation which furnishes us with the strongest evidence of the relations between the natural and supernatural orders, and brings out in the boldest relief the absolute dependence of the creature on its Maker. It is faith which teaches us how God "binds all together into Himself;" how He quickens and sustains "each thing separately, and all as collected in one."

I can, indeed, no better express the ideas which Evolution so beautifully shadows forth, nor can I more happily conclude this long discussion than by appropriating the words used long ago by that noble champion of the faith, St. Athanasius. "As the musician," says the great Alexandrine Doctor, in his "Oratio Contra Gentiles," "having tuned his lyre, and harmonized together the high with the low notes, and the middle notes with the extremes, makes the resulting music one; so the Wisdom of God, grasping the universe like a lyre, blending the things of air with those of earth, and the things of heaven with those of air, binding together the whole and the parts, and ordering all by His counsel and His will, makes the world itself and its appointed order one in fair and harmonious perfection; yet He, Himself, moving all things, remains unmoved with the Father."[1]

---

[1] Οἶον γὰρ τί τις λύραν μουσικὸς ἁρμοσάμενος καὶ τὰ βαρέα τοῖς ὀξέσι, καὶ τὰ μέσα τοῖς ἄκροις, τῇ τέχνῃ συναγαγών ἓν τὸ σημαινόμενον μέλος ἀποτελοίη. οὕτως καὶ ἡ τοῦ Θεοῦ Σοφία, τὸ ὅλον ὡς λύραν ἐπέχων, καὶ τὰ ἐν ἀέρι τοῖς ἐπὶ γῆς συναγαγών, καὶ τὰ ἐν οὐρανῷ τοῖς ἐν ἀέρι, καὶ τα ὅλα τοῖς κατὰ μέρος συνάπτων, καὶ περιάγων τῷ ἑαυτοῦ νοήματι καὶ θελήματι, ἕνα τὸν κόσμον καὶ μίαν την τοίτου τάξιν ἀποτελεῖ, καλῶς καὶ ἡρμοσμένως, αὐτὸς μὲν ἀκινήτως μενων παρὰ τῷ Πατρί. Sec. XLII.

AUTHORS AND WORKS

CITED IN

"EVOLUTION AND DOGMA."

ABUBACER, Arabian scientist, "The Nature-Man."
AGASSIZ, Prof. LOUIS, "Essay on Classification;" "Lake Superior;" "Methods of Study in Natural History."
ALLEN, GRANT, Canadian littérateur and scientist.
ANAXAGORAS, Greek philosopher.
ANAXIMANDER, Greek mathematician.
ANAXIMENES, Greek historian.
ARGYLL, DUKE OF (8th), "The Unity of Nature."
ARISTOTLE, "Physics;" "History of Animals;" "Metaphysics."
ATHANASIUS, ST., "Oratio Contra Gentiles."
AUGUSTINE, ST., "De Trinitate;" "De Genesi ad Litteram;" "De Libero Arbitrio;" "De Anima et ejus Origine;" "Retractationes."
AURELIUS, MARCUS, "Meditations."
AVEMPACE, Arabian philosopher.
AVICENNA, Arabian physician.

BABINGTON, CHAS. C., British botanist.
BACON, FRANCIS, Lord, "Novum Organum."

BAER, KARL E. VON, Russian naturalist.
BAIRD, SPENCER F., American naturalist.
BALFOUR, ARTHUR J., "Foundations of Belief."
BARRANDE, JOACHIM, "Système Silurien de la Bohème;" "Defense des Colonies."
BARRY, ALFRED, "Some Lights of Science on the Faith."
BASTIAN, HENRY C., English scientist.
BATESON, WILLIAM, British naturalist.
BELLINCK, FATHER, S. J., art. in "Études Historiques et Littéraires."
BENEDEN, P. J. VAN, "Animal Parasites and Messmates."
BENTHAM, JEREMY, English philosopher.
BERKELEY, Bishop GEORGE, British philosopher.
BERNARD, CLAUDE, "La Science Expérimentale."
BERZELIUS, Baron JOHAN J., Swedish chemist.
BLAINVILLE, H. M. DE, French naturalist.
BLANCHARD, ÉMILE, "La Vie des Êtres Animés."
BONNET, CHARLES, Swiss naturalist.
BROCA, PAUL, French surgeon.
BRUNETIÈRE, FERDINAND, art. in *Revue des Deux Mondes.*
BRUNO, GIORDANO, Italian philosopher.
BRYANT, WM. CULLEN.
BÜCHNER, F. KARL, "Force and Matter;" "Man in the Past, Present and Future."
BUCKLE, H. T., "Miscellaneous and Posthumous Works."
BUFFON, Comte GEORGES DE, "Théorie de la Terre."
BURMEISTER, HERMANN, German naturalist.
BUTLER, Bishop JOSEPH, British prelate.

AUTHORS AND WORKS.

CABANIS, PIERRE J., French physicist.
CALMET, DOM A., French Benedictine.
CAMPER, PIETER, Dutch anatomist.
CANDOLLE, ALPHONSE DE, Swiss botanist.
CANO, MELCHIOR, "Locorum Theolog. Libri."
CARLYLE, THOMAS, "Sartor Resartus."
CARRUTHERS, WILLIAM, Scotch naturalist.
CARUS, PAUL, "The Religion of Science."
CHAMBERS, ROBT., Scotch littérateur, "Vestiges of Creation."
CHRYSOSTOM, ST. JOHN.
CLARKE, FATHER, S. J., arts. in *The Month.*
CLEMENT, ST., OF ALEXANDRIA, "Stromata."
COMTE, AUGUSTE, French philosopher.
COPE, EDWARD D., American biologist, "Origin of the Fittest."
CORLUY, Rev. J., S. J., "Specilegium Dogmatico-Biblicum."
CUVIER, Baron GEORGES, "Règne Animal;" "Leçons sur l'Anatomie Comparée;" "Ossements Fossiles;" "Révolutions de la Surface du Globe."
CUVIER, FRÉDÉRIC, French naturalist.

DARWIN, CHARLES, "The Origin of Species;" "Animals and Plants Under Domestication."
DARWIN, ERASMUS, "Temple of Nature;" "Zoönomia;" "Botanic Garden."
DAVIDSON, Prof., English scientist.
DAWSON, Sir J. W., "Story of the Earth and Man."
DEMOCRITUS OF ABDERA, Greek philosopher.
DESCARTES, RENÉ.
DIERCKS, FATHER, S. J., Flemish naturalist, "L'Homme-Singe."

Diogenes of Appolonia, Greek philosopher.
Duilhe, de St. Projet, French apologist.

Ehrenberg, Chr. G., German naturalist.
Empedocles, Greek philosopher.
Epictetus, Stoic philosopher, "Manual."

Fabricius, Hieronymus, Italian anatomist.
Falloppio, G., of Padua, Italian anatomist.
Faye, H. A., French astronomer.
Fichte, J. G., German metaphysician.
Fiske, Prof. John, "Outlines of Cosmic Philosophy;" "The Idea of God."
Flourens, M. J. P., French physiologist.
Fontenelle, B. de, French philosopher.
Fracostorio, Italian physician.

Galen, Greek physician.
Gaudry, Albert, "Les Animaux Fossiles de Pikermi;" "Les Enchaînements du Monde Animal dans les Temps Géologiques."
Gladstone, W. E., Introduction to "People's Bible History."
Goethe, J. W. von.
Gonzales, Cardinal, "La Biblia y la Ciencia."
Gore, Canon Charles.
Gray, Prof. Asa, "Darwiniana."
Gregory of Nyssa, St.
Guillemet, Abbé, "Pour la Théorie des Ancêtres Communs;" various "Comptes Rendus."
Güttler, Prof., "Lorenz Oken und sein Verhältniss zur modernen Entwickelungslehre."

HÆCKEL, ERNST, "The Evolution of Man;" "Confessions of a Man of Science;" "Universal Morphology."

HALLOY, D'OMALIUS D', "Sur le Transformisme."

HAMARD, Canon, French savant and apologist.

HAMILTON, Sir W., "The Philosophy of the Unconditioned."

HARPER, Father T. N., S. J., "Metaphysics of the School."

HARRISON, FREDERICK, British essayist.

HARTMANN, CARL R. VON, German philosopher.

HARVEY, Dr. WILLIAM.

HEGEL, GEORG, German philosopher.

HERACLITUS, Greek philosopher.

HERDER, JOHAN G. VON, German critic.

HERSCHEL, Sir WILLIAM, British astronomer.

HEWIT, V. Rev. A. F., "The Christian Agnostic and the Christian Gnostic."

HOBBES, THOMAS, English philosopher.

HOLBACH, Baron PAUL D', French philosopher.

HOLY BIBLE.

HOMER, "Iliad."

HOOKER, Sir JOSEPH, English botanist.

HOWORTH, Sir HENRY H., "The Mammoth and the Flood."

HUGGINS, WILLIAM, English astronomer.

HUGO, VICTOR, "Les Contemplations."

HULST, Mgr. MAURICE D'.

HUME, DAVID, Scotch philosopher.

HUXLEY, Prof. T. H., "Lectures on Evolution;" "Science and Hebrew Tradition;" "Classification;" "Life and Letters of Ch. Darwin;"

"Science and Christian Tradition;" "Collected Essays;" art. "Biology" in Encyclopædia Britannica.

JÄGER, Prof., German critic.
JAUGEY, ABBÉ J. B., "Dictionnaire Apologétique de la Foi Catholique."
JUSSIEU, ANTOINE L. DE, "Genera Plantarum."

KANT, IMMANUEL, "Kritik der reinen Vernunft."
KELVIN, Lord (Sir WILLIAM THOMSON), Scotch physicist, Address at Edinburgh.
KINGSLEY, CHARLES, "Prose Idylls."
KIRWAN, M. DE, "Le Transformisme et la Discussion Libre."
KÖLLIKER, RUDOLF A., Swiss histologist.

LACÉPÈDE, Comte B. DE, French naturalist.
LACTANTIUS, "De Ira Dei."
LAMARCK, J. B. DE, "Histoire Naturelle;" "Philosophie Zoölogique."
LAND, Prof. J. P. N., art. "Physiologus" in Encyclopædia Britannica.
LANESSAN, French naturalist.
LANKESTER, RAY, English zoölogist.
LAPLACE, Marquis PIERRE DE, French astronomer.
LAVOISIER, A. L., French chemist.
LAYARD, Sir AUSTEN, "Nineveh and Babylon."
LE CONTE, Prof. J., "Evolution and Its Relations to Religious Thought."
LEEUWENHOEK, ANTONIUS VON, Dutch microscopist.
LEIBNITZ, Baron GOTTFRIED VON, German philosopher.

LENORMANT, FRANÇOIS, "Origines de l'Histoire d'après la Bible."
LEO XIII, Pope, Encyclicals " Æterni Patris;" and " Providentissimus Deus."
LEROY, Père, " L'Évolution Restreinte aux Espèces Organiques."
LEUCIPPUS, Greek philosopher.
LEUCKART, KARL, German zoölogist.
LEWES, GEORGE HENRY, English littérateur.
LIEBIG, Baron JUSTUS VON, German chemist.
LILLY, W. S., English Littérateur, " The Great Enigma."
LINNÆUS, CAROLUS, "Amænitates Academicæ," " Philosophia Botanica;" "Systema Naturæ."
LOCKE, JOHN, English philosopher.
LOCKYER, JOSEPH, British astronomer.
LONGFELLOW, HENRY W.
LUCAS, Rev. GEO. J., "Agnosticism and Religion."
LUCRETIUS, " De Rerum Natura."
LYELL, Sir CHARLES, " Principles of Geology;" " Manual of Geology."

McCOSH, Dr. JAMES, " Religious Aspect of Evolution."
MAIMONIDES, rabbinical philosopher.
MAISONNEUVE, Dr., "Création et Évolution."
MALPIGHI, MARCELLO, Italian anatomist.
MANSEL, Dean, " The Limits of Religious Thought."
MARSH, Prof. O. C., American paleontologist.
MARSHALL, ARTHUR M.," Lectures on the Darwinian Theory."
MARTINEAU, Rev. JAS., D.D., "A Plea for Philosophical Studies;" "Science, Nescience and Faith."

MAUPERTUIS, PIERRE DE, French philosopher.
MILL, J. STUART, British philosopher.
MILNE-EDWARDS, H., French naturalist.
MILTON, JOHN, "Paradise Lost."
MIR, Padre, S. J.
MIVART, ST. GEORGE, "Genesis of Species;" "On Truth;" "Lessons from Nature."
MOLESCHOTT, JACOB, Dutch physiologist.
MONSABRÉ, Père P. J., O. S. D., French theologian.
MOORE, AUBREY L., "Science and Faith."
MÜLLER, F. MAX, German English philologist.
MÜLLER, FRITZ, German ethnologist.
MÜLLER, JOHANN, German physicist.

NADAILLAC, MARQUIS DE, "Le Problème de la Vie;" "Progrès de l'Anthropologie," etc., in Comptes Rendus.
NÄGELI, Prof. KARL VON, German botanist.
NAUDIN, CHARLES, French botanist.
NEWMAN, Cardinal HENRY, "Lectures on University Subjects."
NOTT, JOSIAH C., American ethnologist.

OKEN, LORENZ, German naturalist.
OLIVI, of Cremona.
OMAR "THE LEARNED," Arabian scholar.
ORIGEN.
OSBORN, H., "From the Greeks to Darwin."
OVID, "Metamorphoses."
OWEN, Prof. RICHARD, "Anatomy of Vertebrates;" "Chimpanzees and Orangs."

PALEY, "Natural Theology."
PALISSY, BERNARD.

PASCAL, BLAISE, "Pensées."
PASTEUR, LOUIS, French bacteriologist.
PLATO.
PLINY, the elder.
POUCHET, HENRI C., French naturalist.
POUSSIN, C. DE LA VALLÉE, "Paléontologie et Darwinisme."
POWELL, BADEN, English apologist and scientist.
PYTHAGORAS.

QUATREFAGES, J. L. DE, "Darwin et ses Précurseurs Français;" "The Human Species," in *Journal des Savants*.

RAY, JOHN, "Historia Plantarum."
RÉAUMUR, RENÉ DE, French physicist.
REDI, FRANCESCO, "Esperienze intorno alla Generazione degl' Insetti."
RENAN, ERNEST, "L'Avenir de la Science."
ROBIN, Dr. CHARLES P., French anatomist.
ROBINET, J. F., French physician.
ROMANES, Prof. GEORGE, "Darwin and After Darwin;" "Scientific Evidence of Organic Evolution;" "Thoughts on Religion."
ROSMINI, Prof., "Psychology."
RUSKIN, JOHN, "Aratra Pentelici."
RÜTIMEYER, LOUIS, Swiss naturalist.

SAINT-HILAIRE, E. GEOFFROY, "Histoire Générale et Particulière des Anomalies de l'Organization chez l'Hommes."
SAYCE, A. H., "The Higher Criticism;" "The Verdict of the Monuments;" "People's Bible History."

SCHELLING, FRIEDRICH VON, German philosopher.
SCHMANKEWITSCH, Russian naturalist.
SCHOPENHAUER.
SCHOUW, J. F., Danish naturalist.
SCHULTZE, MAX, German biologist.
SCHWANN, THEODOR, German physiologist.
SCHWEINFURTH, GEORG A., German botanist.
SCOTUS, ERIGENA, "De Divisione Naturæ."
SECCHI, PADRE ANGELO, Italian astronomer.
SENECA, "De Beneficiis;" "Naturales Quæstiones."
SHAKESPEARE.
SIEBOLD, K. VON, German zoölogist.
SPALDING, Rt. Rev. J. L., "Agnosticism."
SPENCER, HERBERT,
    "First Principles;" "Principles of Biology."
SPINOZA.
STENO, NICOLAUS, Danish anatomist.

TEMPLE, FREDERICK, "Bampton Lectures."
TERTULLIAN.
THEOPHRASTUS.
THOMAS, ST., of Aquin, "Summa;" "Opusculi."

UEBERWEG, FRIEDRICH, "History of Philosophy."

VARRO.
VATICAN COUNCIL, "Dogmatic Constitution of the Catholic Church."
VESALIUS, A., Belgian anatomist.
VINCI, LEONARDO DA, Italian artist and scholar.
VIRCHOW, Prof. RUDOLF, Address before International Archæological Congress, at Moscow.

WAGNER, MORITZ, German naturalist.
WALLACE, ALFRED R., "Darwinism;" "Natural Selection."
WHEWELL, WILLIAM, "History of the Inductive Sciences."
WOLF, CHR. VON, German philosopher.
WOOD, Prof., "Giants and Dwarfs."
WOODWARD, HENRY, British geologist.

ZAHM, J. A., "Bible, Science and Faith."
ZAHN, ADOLPH, German Biblicist.
ZELLER, EDWARD, "Philosophy of the Greeks."
ZIGLIARA, Cardinal.

GENERAL INDEX.

Abiogenesis, believed in by Anaxagoras, 26; as a theory of the ancients, 33; import of its discussion, 41; early prevalence of the theory, 42; Roman philosophers believed in, 43; Fathers and Schoolmen accept, 44; Father Kircher's curious recipe in, 45; disproof of by Redi's experiments, 46; theory loses standing, 48; fruits of the controversy on, 50; notions of affecting science, 320; some ancient ideas on, 321; Darwin's wish in regard to, 327; as a corollary to Evolution, 328; Hæckel positively believes in, 329; discovery of still possible, 330; if true not against Dogma, 331; scholastic and other views of, 332; proof unlikely to offer, 336; review of the long battle in, 396; Rosmini's speculations on, 427.
Abubacer, curious philosophical romance by, 29.
Accad, science questions studied in, 13.
Administration, Divine, views of St. Thomas on, 295.
Africa, pygmies of as the "missing link," 351.
Agassiz, Prof. Louis, critique on Darwin's theory by, 65; as an adversary of Evolution, 74; on the origin of species, 79; views on classification by, 90; definition of species by, 96; on creation and species, 101; argument from coral reefs, 152; denunciation of Darwinism by, 207.
Agates, argument from the figures in, 33.
Agnosticism, as an outcome of Evolution, 229; scope and nature of, 254; term devised by Huxley, 255; late developments of, 256; views of Romanes on, 260; discussed by Duke of Argyll, 262; cannot be a via media, 264; Max Müller's views on, 268; the Christian form of, 273.
Agricola, strange theory on fossils by, 32.
Albertus Magnus, the Evolution idea discussed by, 29.
Allen, Grant, survey of transitional types by, 131.
Amœbæ, theory of the, 247.
Amphioxus, curious life history of, 117; Hæckel's exalted notion of, 344.

Analogous, compared with homologous, 110.
Analogy, Hæckel's quibbling with, 249.
Anarchists, Evolution kindly received by, 209.
Anatomy, period of development of, 56; Kant's brilliant suggestion on, 57.
Anaxagoras, theory of life germs by, 26; teleological views of nature by, 380.
Anaximander, views on origin of life by, 25.
Anaximenes, on the Cause of all things, 26.
Ancients, their part in the Evolution idea, 23; abiogenesis a common belief with, 43. *See also* Antiquity.
Anthropomorphism, excluded from Christian Evolution, 302.
Anthropopithecus, views of Darwin on the, 343.
Antiquity, species seen in the monuments of, 147; scientific errors and follies of, 400.
Ant-Lion, remarkable pedigree of, 401.
Apes, Hæckel's genealogy of the, 247; question of man's descent from, 340; Mivart on their human relationship, 344; possible human kinship with, 430.
Apis, its identity with living species, 146.
Archæology, objections to Evolution from, 143; value of Asiatic research in, 179.
Archæopteryx, as a transitional type, 131; its discovery predicted, 137.
Archæus, Paracelsus and the theory of, 324.
Archebiosis, as a term for abiogenesis, 327.
Arctic Region, Darwin on species of, 160.
Argyll, Duke of, saltatory Evolution favored by, 198; views on Agnosticism, 262; on the accord of teleology and Evolution, 373.
Aristotle, conceptions of Evolution by, 27; comparison of Empedocles with, 28; as a yoke on early science, 34; abiogenesis one of his teachings, 42; describes continuity of species, 144; doctrine of the four elements by, 286; on classification of species, 323; scientific achievements of, 379; his influence on scholasticism, 382.
Artemia, valuable experiments with, 192.
Assassination, Evolution held responsible for, 210.

Assurbanipal, tablets from Nineveh library of, 13.
Assyria, cosmology as a study in, 13.
Assyriology, proofs of paleontology helped by, 179.
Astronomy, questions of antiquity in, 14; new discoveries suggested in, 25; advanced by Secchi and others, 53; some pioneer ideas on, 391.
Atavism, facts of known to Aristotle, 27.
Athanasius, St., view of the Creator by, 361; on the order of creation, 437.
Atheism, an outgrowth of science speculations, 15; Evolution receives welcome from, 209; agnosticism only a disguise for, 264.
Atomic Theory, its revival in monism, 236.
Atoms, chemically and philosophically viewed, 236; the chemist's jugglery with, 334.
Augustine, St., Kant revises teachings of, 57; on potential creation, 71; on the natural forces, 220; the theistic Evolution of, 280; strictures on anthropomorphism, 302; on the generation of life, 322; on the soul's origin, 347.
Authorities, the author's gratitude to, xxiii; list of books and, 439.
Avempace, Arabian ideas on Evolution, 28.

Babylonia, study of cosmology in, 13; species as shown in monuments of, 148.
Bacon, Francis, a believer in organic Evolution, 56; satire on natural history by, 383; on relations of science to the Deity, 410.
Bacteria, Pasteur's valuable studies in, 50; evidence from further research in, 52; difficulty in noting species of, 100. *See also* Infusoria.
Baer, Karl E. von, wonders found in embryology by, 115.
Baird, Spencer F., on species in American birds, 104.
Balfour, Arthur, J., on science and faith, xxi; work on foundations of belief by, 278.
Barrande, Joachim, as an anti-evolutionist, 74; studies in Silurian strata by, 154.
Barry, Dr. Alfred, views on creation by, 368.
Basil, St., views on generation by, 321.
Basilisk, as creature of science-fable, 400.
Bastian, H. C., opposition to Pasteur's views by, 52; term used for abiogenesis by, 327.
Bateson, Prof., theory of discontinuous variations by, 198.
Bathybius, Huxley and Haeckel on, 246.
Bees, a native variety crowded out, 164; Virgil on the generation of, 320.
Bellinck, Father, on faith and Evolution, 426.

Beneden. P. J. van, as student of the animalculæ, 49; standing against Evolution, 74.
Berzelius, conclusions on infusoria by, 49.
Bible, The Holy, fanciful interpretations of, 35; quoted to sustain abiogenesis, 47; Darwinism scored by friends of, 207; Dr. McCosh on Evolution and, 212; is not opposed by true Evolution, 388; its cosmogony agrees with Evolution. *See also* Genesis.
Bichat, M. F. X., definition of life by, 324.
Biology, powerful help to Evolution by, 54; the question of species in, 315. *See also* Life.
Birds, differences and blendings of species in, 104.
Births, the theory of extraordinary, 197.
Blanchard, Émile, challenge to evolutionists by, 141.
Bohemia, valuable geological facts from, 154.
Botany, outcome of recent progress in, 51; difficulties regarding species in, 97.
Brazil, evidence from the cave-birds of, 126.
Brongniart, Adolphe, T., geological investigations by, 38.
Brunetière, Ferdinand, on the "bankruptcy of science," 404; verdict on science and religion, 407.
Bruno, Giordano, Hæckel as an imitator of, 236.
Büchner, Ludwig, the doctrine of materialism by, 217; some atheistic notions of, 221; on design in nature, 370.
Buckle, H. T., on effects of exclusive studies, 311.
Buffon, Georges L., wrong views on animalcules by, 48; notions on environment held by, 194.
Burnouf, E. H., value of oriental research by, 179.

Cabanis, Pierre J., views on thought by, 238.
Cairo, plant specimens of at, 150.
Calmet, Dom, discussion of Noah's ark by, 60.
Candolle, A, de, position on the species problem, 79; a definition of species by, 95; study of the oak by, 103.
Caro, Prof., on attitude of Evolution to faith, 210; views on materialism, 216; résumé of Hæckelism by, 238.
Carruthers, William, as an anti-evolutionist, 74; lessons from Egyptian botany by, 149.
Catholicity, its attitude to atheism and materialism, 223; question of the missing link in, 344; Evolution among noted adherents of, 425. *See also* Church, Dogma, Religion.

Catholic Congresses, scientific discussions of, 367.
Causa Causarum, St. Augustine's statement of, 282.
Cereals, as raised in prehistoric times, 151.
Chaldea, cosmology as a study in, 13; species identified by monuments, 148.
Chambers, Robert, a famous science treatise by, 63.
Champollion, value of researches by, 179.
Chemistry, its phenomena sustain Evolution, 53.
Church, The, its teachings on creation and Providence, 296; Evolution and the doctrines of, 312; never inimical to true science, 396. *See also* Dogma, Religion, etc.
Cicero, on the transitory value of opinion, xv.
Civil War, American, the myriad writings on, 20.
Clarke, Father, S. J., analysis of term agnostic by, 256.
Classification, various systems of, 84; Aristotle's ideas on, 85; elements of study in, 89; is it real or a myth, 90; ancient and mediæval views on, 91; a leading evidence for Evolution, 105; the tree-like system of, 107; blunders in, 108.
Clement of Alexandria, St., cause of error stated by, 204.
Climate, relations to permanence of species, 158.
Cockroach, victory of Asiatic species, 164.
Coleridge, Samuel T., on errors in nomenclature, 319.
Compsognathus, an intermediate fossil type, 132.
Comte, an erroneous prediction by, 53; the philosophic creed of, 276.
Concordistic theory, Cuvier as father of, 93.
Contents, table of, 7.
Cope, Edward D., as adherent of the Evolution idea, 68; researches in fossils by, 174; as champion of neo-Lamarckism.
Coral, Agassiz on the reefs of, 153.
Corluy, Rev. J., on effects of Darwinism, 213.
Corruption, as understood by scholastics, 285.
Cosmology, antiquity of speculations in, 13.
Creation, questions of antiquity concerning, 14; fanciful views on, 35; the Miltonic view of, 76; Agassiz on the plan of, 101; the more noble conception of, 122; derivative as against special, 135; misunderstandings of the term, 215; definition in Catholic theology, 220; various meanings of, 221; relation of agnosticism to, 255; St. Augustine on the order of, 281; the Genesiac narrative of, 290; God as the first cause in, 297; summing up of views, 302; science fails to explain, 306; various Catholic teachers on, 360.
Creationism, choice between Evolution and, 75; the soul's relation to theory of, 348; its attitude toward Evolution, 398.
Creatures, as endowed with causality, 297.
Crustacea, curious experiments on species with, 192.
Cuttle-fish, development of the eye in, 120.
Cuvier, Baron Georges, as founder of paleontology, 37; effect of his discoveries, 38; discussion with Saint-Hilaire, 39; system of classification by, 85; Agassiz' estimate of, 86; great scientific work of, 87; views on species by, 92; on evidence from Egyptian mummies, 146; on animal figures of antiquity, 147.
Cuvier, Frederick, views on hybrids by, 182.

Darwin, Charles, Evolution not founded by, 23; antiquity of pet theory of, 26; forestalled by Buffon, 60; publishes "The Origin of Species," 66; his chief disciples, 68; difficulty of noting species by, 98; on rudimentary organs, 113; on distribution of species, 123; on succession of types, 126; on predictions in Evolution, 137; on species of Arctic regions, 160; on paucity of transitional forms, 162, 163; on gradation of fossil deposits 165; on fossil bird forms, 172; views on geological research by, 181; on the problem of hybrids, 190; natural selection defended by, 194; admits a weak point, 195; the theory and critics of, 207; Asa Gray makes defense of, 211; nature as personified by, 226; out-Heroded by Hæckel, 231; estimate of Herbert Spencer by, 257; his confused ideas on creation, 306; unfitness for abstract studies, 309; theory of primordial germ by, 326; in conflict with teleology, 369; Prof. Gray's tribute to his work, 372.
Darwin, Erasmus, services to the Evolution idea, 384.
Darwinism, as distinguished from Evolution, 206; various opinions on, 207; a great problem evaded by, 342; man's origin viewed by, 350; not to be held as Evolution, 384.
Davidson, Prof., as an anti-evolutionist, 74; researches in British fossils by, 156.
Dawson, Sir J. W., as an anti-evolutionist, 74; pronounces Evolution atheistic, 209.
Deity, Hæckel's concept of, 236; relations of time and space to, 270; as the

primary cause, 297; attributes of, 304; errors of scientists on, 308; science promotes just views of, 401; a necessary postulate of Evolution, 432.
De Lapparent, Prof. A., attitude on creationism, 363.
Deluge, Noah's, supposed relation to fossils, 35; controversy on duration and extent of, 420.
Denudation, fossil deposits affected by, 170.
Descartes, René, tendencies toward Evolution, 56; on relations of science to God, 410.
Deslongchamps, dictum on species by, 98.
Diercks, S. J., Father, discussion of creationism, 362.
Diogenes of Appolonia, theory of animal life by, 26.
Discussions, counsel of Leo XIII. regarding, xxii; by the ancients on creation, 15; those of antiquity still fresh, 16; between Cuvier and Saint-Hilaire, 39.
Divine Administration, meaning of the term, 295.
Doctors, Evolution and teachings of the, 312.
Dog, long identity of the species, 147; the numerous varieties of, 186.
Dogma, science can never contradict, xv; how affected by Evolution, 206; not antagonized by this science, 300; abiogenesis not opposed to, 331; standing as to the missing link, 344; zeal of certain scientists against, 370; not contradicted by Evolution, 388, 426.
Dragons, a myth of ancient science, 400.
Dredging, contributions to science from, 52.
Dryopithecus, as the supposed missing link, 351.
Dualism, contrast of materialism with, 215.
Dufrénoy, Pierre A., on the mating of species, 182.

Earth's age, review of controversy on, 420.
Egypt, testimony from monuments of, 144; the ancient vegetation of, 149.
Egyptology, paleontology sustained by, 179.
Elements, Simple, argument from relationship of, 53; scholastic and scientific views on, 286.
Emanation, an unsound theory, 76.
Emanationism, outgrowth of science speculations, 15.
Embryology, facts of noted by antiquity, 28; Evolution theory sustained by, 54; a leading evidence for Evolution, 105; its argument set forth, 115; status in Evolution, 250.
Empedocles, as father of Evolution, 26; a guess at Evolution by, 28; as precursor of Darwin, 380.
Environment, Buffon a teacher of, 60; noted adherents of theory, 72; permanence of species affected by, 158; as a factor of Evolution, 193; curious changes from, 195.
Epicurus, on the generation of life, 321.
Epigenesis, as foreshadowed by Aristotle, 27.
Evolution, can Christians accept theory, xiv; the odium cast upon, xviii; its discussion opportune, xxv; a resource of baffled science, 16; wide-spread use of term, 17; Spencer's definition of, 18; discussion and vast literature of, 20; bitterness aroused by, 21; used by foes of religion, 22; not begun by Darwin, 23; discerned among the Greeks, 25; Aristotle's conception of, 27; among mediæval schoolmen, 29; Saint-Hilaire's championship of, 40; relation of abiogenesis to, 41; sustained by advancing science, 51; astronomy and chemistry sustain, 53; biology a supreme aid, 54; its later champions, 55; Goethe as a herald of, 61; Robert Chambers' argument for, 63; Darwin's first book on, 65; the high-water mark of, 67; two ways of regarding, 69; the pervading idea of, 72; its noted antagonists, 73; no middle course in, 75; Darwin's changes on, 82; atheistic disciples of, 83; bearings of classification on, 91; solves the mystery of species, 102; leading evidences for, 105; the whale in support of, 111; explains rudimentary organs, 114; solves embryological problems, 122; the demonstrative evidence of, 127; proof from gradation of fossils, 133; summing up of proofs, 134; special creation and, 135; prediction of discoveries in, 136; objections made against, 140; challenge from opponents of, 141; what history offers against, 140; nature of misapprehended, 157; Lamarck to objectors against, 158; sterility of hybrids against, 182; standing of species in, 191; the array of factors in, 193; some difficult theories of, 196; rôle of extraordinary births in, 197; friends of saltatory theory, 198; as a fact beyond dispute, 203; distinction of Darwinism from, 206; adverse criticisms of, 208; atheism gives welcome to, 210; sundry judgments on, 213; ignorance of terms in, 214; relation of agnosticism to, 254; the agnostic form unsound, 278; analogy of tree growth to, 283; as revealed in creation, 293; the Catholic idea of, 300; occasionalism excluded from, 301; anthropomorphism dispelled by, 302; no Divine interference in, 304; Dogma in relation to, 312; unaffected by notions on species,

318; man's creation viewed by, 350; how far Catholics may accept, 351; Gonzales on the Scripture and, 359; a point of harmony with Dogma, 364; story of creation viewed by, 367; as affected by teleology, 369; Asa Gray's summary of, 372; corroborated by teleology, 371; teleology ennobled by, 376; witnesses to the God of Scripture, 377; résumé of the history of, 378; its future standing, 386; not inimical to religion, 388; attitude of creationism toward, 398; insufficiency for moral man, 402; Scripture and theology reconcilable with, 414; Doctors of the Church on, 416; a theory not a doctrine, 417; viewed from many standpoints, 423; eminent Catholic adherents, 425; faith need fear nothing from, 428; the Creator a necessary postulate of, 432; an ennobling conception, 435; is a witness for the Deity, 437.

Evolutionists, several schools and classes of, 206; variety of theories among, 229.

Eye, cases of evolutionary development, 119.

Falloppio, amusing theory of fossils by, 33.

Father of Evolution, two Greek claimants as, 28.

Fathers of the Church, helped to build Evolution theory, 23; common belief in abiogenesis, 44; Evolution and the teachings of, 312.

Fish-Men, Anaximander's curious theory of, 26.

Fiske, Prof. John, converted by classification, 109; views on intermediary fossils, 174; theories resemble occasionalism, 301; on the origin of life, 327; on creation and Evolution, 390.

Florida, study of coral reefs in, 153.

Flourens, M. J., definition of species by, 95; views on Darwin and his work, 208.

Flowers, curious merging of species in, 188.

Fontenelle, eulogy of Bernard Palissy by, 34.

Fossils, early notions regarding, 31; Agricola and other ancients on, 32; Bernard Palissy's views on, 34; the Deluge supposed to explain, 35; fabled giants in relation to, 36; true significance apprehended, 37; world's age measured by, 38; Huxley on the evidence of, 128; generalized types among, 131; evidence on vegetable species in, 152; process of deposit, 165; Darwin on gradations of, 167; Romanes on fewness of, 170; low percentage of forms in, 171; types missing from, 172; intercalary forms in, 174; reviewing the arguments from, 420.

Fracostorio, teachings on fossils by, 32.

France, vast historic literature of, 19.

Francis of Assisi, St, friendship for the birds, 430.

French Academy, scientific controversy in, 39; Cuvier's classification announced to, 86.

Froschammer, on the origin of the soul, 347.

Fruits, identity of ancient with modern, 149.

Galen, species described by, 144.

Galileo, world's reception of discoveries by, 392.

Gastrula, place in the scale of life, 247.

Gaudry, Albert, studies in paleontology, 132; views on elastic types, 159; studies in fossil forms, 174; theory on missing types by, 175; as a Catholic evolutionist, 425.

Generation, the scholastic view of, 285.

Generationism, as a doctrine on the soul's origin, 347.

Generelli, right views on creation by, 35.

Genesis, account of man's creation in, 350; scientists on creation narrative, 365; lends itself to Evolution, 414; controversy on six days of, 419.

Genus, true relation of the term, 317.

Geography, physical, Evolution sustained by, 51; relation of to organic life, 123.

Geology, first regular investigations in, 39; Evolution theory aided by, 51; Agassiz' argument from, 80; relation of concordistic theory to, 93; distribution of species as witnessed by, 125; testimony as to permanence of species from, 154; comparative limit of researches in, 173; imperfection of record in, 176; Darwin on the value of research in, 181.

Germ theory, 326.

Giants, supposed relation of fossils to, 36.

Gladstone, W. E., on relations of science to Bible, 427, 429.

Gnostics, views on creation by, 217.

Goethe, Johann W., vast number of books written on, 19; anecdote regarding, 39; scientific rank of, 62.

Gonzales, Cardinal, on process of creation, 358.

Gore, Canon, on Romanes, 261.

Grand Eury, as an anti-evolutionist, 74.

Gray, Asa, views on defining species, 96; on species in British flora, 98; on triumph of teleology, 378; on Evolution and theism, 211.

Greece, science in, 14, 379.

Gregory of Nyssa, St., believer in one primordial element, 54; prophet of nebular hypothesis, 71; theistic Evolution of, 280.

Guillemet, Abbé, on theory of fixism, 417, 419; on common ancestral types, 135.

Güttler, Dr. C., views on Darwin by, 213.

Hæckel, as spokesman of atheistic Evolution, 83; on variability of species, 99; on perigenesis, 199; the five propositions of, 235; on soul and mind, 237; on abiogenesis, 329; on purpose in nature, 370; the monism of, 230; on origin of life, 246; cynicism of, 251; a type, 252; on missing link, 344; tribute to Mosaic cosmogony, 415.
Halloy, D'Omalius d', as Catholic and evolutionist, 425.
Hamard, Canon, on the Bible and transformism, 415.
Hamilton, Sir William, as precursor of Huxley, 256.
Harper, Father, explains the term generation, 285; on order of creation, 293; value of his work on scholasticism, 295.
Harvey, William, teaching foreshadowed by Aristotle, 27.
Hawkweed, the numerous species of, 98.
Hebraists, literary fiasco of, 405.
Heliopolis, a scientific priesthood at, 14.
Hellenists, absurd pretensions of, 405.
Helmont, J. B. van, amusing notions on abiogenesis, 45; a theory of life, 323.
Heraclitus, as precursor of Darwin, 379.
Herbert, Rev. W., on proofs from horticulture, 63.
Herculaneum, testimony from the ruins, 149.
Heredity, phenomena known to Aristotle, 27; principle discussed by Buffon, 60; as a factor of Evolution, 195.
Herschel, Sir W., theories forestalled by Kant, 57.
Hewit, Rev. A. F., anthority on Christian Agnosticism, 276.
Hieroglyphics, previous science disclosed by, 179.
Hildebrand, J. M., on floral species, 189.
Hindus, early science studies of, 14.
Hippocrates, on the vital processes, 324.
History, objections to Evolution from, 143.
Hobbes, Thomas, urges the principle of struggle, 71.
Holbach, P. H. d', Hæckel conforms with, 237.
Holmes, Oliver W., definition of life by, 324.
Homology, examples of in nature, 110, 114.
Horse, proofs of Evolution from the, 127.
Houdin, Robert, the secret of legerdemain, 245.
Hugo, Victor, agreement of Hæckel with, 238.
Huxley, Thomas H., review of Darwin's theory by, 66; on paleontology, 128; considers defects of classification, 133; on predictions in horse species, 137; on species variations, 161; on saltatory theory, 198; Evolution harmless to faith, 213; nature personified by, 226; coinage of term agnostic, 255; the Diety as conceived by, 277; confused ideas on creation, 307; on originating life artificially, 330; Evolution and teleology in harmony, 374; admits inadequacy of science, 407.
Hybrids, teachings from sterility of, 182.
Hylozoism, outgrowth of science speculations of, 15.

Infusoria, believers in spontaneous origin of, 48; scientists begin special study of, 49.
Inscriptions great students and interpreters of, 179.
Introduction the author's, XIII-XXX.
Ionians, science and teachings of, 14, 380; materialism of the, 216.

Jäger, notions on "soul stuff" by, 199.
Jussieu, A. L. de, definition of species by, 96.

Kant, Immanuel, many Evolution principles of, 57; a brilliant generalization by, 58; on the use of reason, 256.
Kelvin, Lord (Sir W. Thomson), on the origin of life, 325; on design in nature, 441.
Kepler, Johann, true basis of laws by, 25; reception of discoveries by, 393.
Kircher, Father A., curious recipe in abiogenesis, 45.
Kölliker, Rudolf A., an adherent of saltatory Evolution, 198.

Lamarck, J. B. de, scientific achievements of, 61; blunders in classification, 108; reply to anti-evolutionists, 158; Evolution factors held by, 193; reverent ideas of the Creator, 389.
Lanessan, estimate of Buffon's work by, 60.
Languages, pedigree of the Romance, 107; relations of certain groups, 108.
Law, Paley on true nature of, 376.
Layard, Sir Austin, evidence from Babylonian researches of, 148; value of Assyrian discoveries by, 179.
Le Conte, Joseph, views on Evolution, 214.
Leeuwenhoek, A. von, as student of infusoria, 49.
Legends, suggested by fossil remains, 36.
Leibnitz, G. W. von, Evolution ideas held by, 56; on origin of the soul, 347.
Lenormant, Charles, on the creation of man, 365.
Leo XIII, on scientific discussion, XVII; author's stand on teachings of, XXI.
Leroy, Père M. D., work on Evolution by, 212; his theory of creation, 363; on species and genus, 317.
Leuckart, Karl G., as authority on infusoria, 49.

GENERAL INDEX. 457

Leverrier, U. J., suggesting discovery of Neptune, 25.
Lewes, G. W., on special creation, 121.
Liebig, Baron, valuable studies of infusoria, 49.
Life, Greek ideas on origin of, 25; the antiquity of, 177; discussion of nature and origin, 320; various attempts to define, 324; on the germ of, 325; Darwin's idea of primordial, 326; science fails as to origin, 327; possible artificial production of, 330; the most science can say on, 333; Huxley's "physical basis" of, 334; a scientific origin found impossible, 336; collapse of mechanical theory, 337; Evolution fails to explain, 367.
Lilly, W. S., work on agnosticism by, 278.
Linnæus, Karl von, as a believing scientist, xxviii; views on special creation, 59; produced a reasonable classification, 86; ideas on species, 92; his binomial nomenclature, 94; on immutability of species, 142.
Littérateurs, careless use of term nature, 225.
Locke, John, views on continuity of species, 71.
Logan, Sir W., on the antiquity of life, 177.
Loligo, eye curiously developed of, 119.
Lucas, Dr. G. J., work on agnosticism by, 278.
Lucretius, statement on abiogenesis from, 43; on dabblers in science, 253.
Lyell, Sir Charles, biology brings conviction to, 54.

McCosh, Dr. James, on Evolution and Scripture, 212.
Maimonides, on creation of man, 365.
Maisonneuve, Dr., on rudimentary organs, 115.
Mammalia, type gradations in extinct, 130.
Man, embryonic development of, 116; Hæckel's genealogy of, 245; Wallace on origin of, 247; comparing attributes of, 305; question of simian origin, 340; Virchow on descent of, 341; Dogma and the animal origin of, 344; relation to apes not proven, 351; Mivart's speculations on, 352; modified theory of creation, 359; extravagant notions on origin, 365; question of pedigree reviewed, 430; headship in created universe, 435.
Mandeville, Sir John, as a tale-weaving traveler, 401.
Manicheans, views on creation by, 217; ideas on creation of soul, 346.
Mansel, Dean, an Anglican teacher of agnosticism, 258; a variety of atheism by, 259.
Maoris, curious proverb of the, 197.

Mariette, A. E., value of oriental researches by, 179.
Marsh, Prof. G. P. discovery of a missing type, 138; intermediate fossils found by, 174.
Marshall, A. M., on organic development, 119; on the ancestral equine forms, 128.
Marsupials, place of in Hæckel's life scale, 247.
Martineau, Rev. James, judgment on specialists, 209; on science and religion, 433.
Martins, Charles, views on Evolution, 214.
Maspero, G. C., value of oriental researches by, 179.
Mastiff, as depicted in Babylonian ruins, 148.
Materialism, product of science discussions, 15; Evolution hailed by its disciples, 209; in contrast with dualism, 215; as voiced by Hugo and others, 238; struggle of faith and science with, 427.
Materia Prima, the scholastic view of, 287.
Matter, the Ionians' view of, 216; ideas of the Schoolmen on, 286; fails at the brink of life, 338.
Mattioli, singular theory on fossils, 32.
Memphis, science of Egyptian priests at, 14.
Mercier, Mgr., in review of Balfour's work, 278.
Mesopotamia, exhumed records of, 13.
Metaphysics, question solvable only by, 308.
Microbes, multiplicity of species in, 99.
Microscopy, results of progress in, 52.
Middle Ages, Evolution in the Schools of, 23, 28.
Mill, J. Stuart, on God and matter, 217.
Milton, John, poetical record of species, 76; influence of his views, 318.
Mind, Darwin's bewilderment on, 310.
Mir, Padre, on problem of creation, 358.
Missing link, discussion of, 340; explorations in quest of, 351; a conceivable theory, 352.
Mivart, St. George, as disciple of Evolution, 68; on saltatory theory, 198; on our simian ancestry, 344; on genesis of man, 352; is severely criticised, 353; views not opposed to theology, 358; modified creation theory of, 359; on design in nature, 374; on the purpose in creation, 411.
Mollusca, development of the eye in, 119; curious pedigree of planorbis, 129.
Moneron, Hæckel's theory of the, 246.
Monism, as outcome of Evolution, 229, 230; formulated by Hæckel, 231; coinage of the term, 233; results of theory, 252; Agnosticism compared with, 254; abiogenesis necessary to, 329.
Monkeys, long identity of species, 144.
Monsabré, Father, on creationism, 363.
Monuments, evidence on species from, 147.

Sirens, position in life scale of, 247.
Sizzi, curious theory of planets by, 394.
Slime, theory of the primordial, 26.
Smith, George, valuable oriental studies by, 179.
Soul, as a corollary of monism, 237; theories on origin of, 345; various heretical views on, 346; St. Thomas on creation of, 356; Doctors and Schoolmen on same, 357. *See* Spirit.
Space, false philosophical notions of, 271.
Spalding, Bishop J. L., as writer on agnosticism, 278.
Spallanzani, Abbate, researches on the infusoria, 49.
Specialists, mental short comings of, 309, 311.
Species, ascertained vast numbers of, 51; believers in mutability of, 56; Buffon teaches mutation of, 60; difficulty of noting, 63; views of Naudin and D'Halloy on, 64; Darwin's great work on, 65; believers in continuity of, 71; evolutionary ideas on, 72, views of great thinkers on, 76, Miltonic hypothesis of, 77; Linnæus on, 78; Prof. Agassiz on, 79, 101; distribution of, 80; attempts to give definition of, 94; difficulties regarding, 97; the old doctrinaires of, 100; in the making, 102; cases showing mutation of, 103; geographical distribution of, 123; geological succession of, 125; Romanes on distribution, 127; revelations of the Tertiary on, 129; advocates of immutability in, 142; evidence from antiquity, 143; identity with antique forms, 145; what Egypt's vegetation tells of, 149; evidence from fossil flora, 152; Agassiz' strong argument on, 153; evidence from Silurian strata, 154; what the trilobite proves on, 155; conditions promoting permanence of, 158; elastic types of, 159; fewness of transitional forms, 162; an illustration from philology on, 163; cases of crowding out, 164; gradation of fossil forms of, 167; sterility of hybrids in, 182; morphology as test of, 185; the physiological test of, 187; relation of reproduction to, 190; Prof. Owen on integrity of, 191; curious experiments in Russia, 192; as a hopeless problem, 193; heredity and variation in, 197; saltatory theory regarding, 198; Nägeli on progress in, 199; Hæckel's chain of, 246; argument from analogy in, 249; scholastic doctrine of, 313; three aspects of the term, 315; term genus compared with, 317; Milton's doctrine of, 318; teleology as manifest in, 373.
Spectroscope, value of revelations by, 53.
Spencer, Herbert, defines Evolution, 18; not original with him, 23; antiquity of his pet idea, 26; as "philosopher" of Evolution, 67; Creator left out of creation by, 70; on structural homologies, 114; his term for natural selection, 195; as scientist of the "unknowable," 257; led by Anglican churchman, 258; on creation, 264; dicta on the unknowable, 267; notions of the Deity, 277; defines life, 324; confesses weakness of Evolution, 407.
Spirit, as understood in Hæckelism, 234; the unfathomable mystery, 272; Plato's ideas on, 323; positive claims for, 345. *See* Soul.
Sponges, Hæckel on the species of, 99; curious investigations in, 232.
Stalactites, ideas from the growth of, 33.
Stammbaum, classification on principle of, 88, 109.
Steinheim, discoveries in lake-bed at, 129.
Steno, Father Nicholas, true idea of fossils, 34.
Succession of types, Darwin's advocacy of, 126.
Sumer, sciences anciently studied in, 13.
Survival of fittest, germ of the theory ancient, 26; anticipated by Buffon, 60.
Swallow, extension of species in United States, 164.
Swammerdam, Prof., studies of infusoria by, 49.
Sycamore, specimens as old as Athens, 150.

Taxonomy, regarded as a science, 88.
Teleology, the old and new sciences of, 369; late developments of, 371; tributes of various scientists to, 373, 374; is ennobled by Evolution, 376; as held by Greek sages, 380.
Temple, Bishop F., on creation and Evolution, 436.
Tertullian, on origin of the soul, 346.
Thales, teachings on genesis of life, 25.
Theism, Pohle's views on, 212; as related to Evolution, 229; Evolution blended with, 297; Prof. Fiske's attempt to classify, 301.
Theology, Hæckel's defects as student of, 243; Mivart's relation to, 353; the "Great Architect" theory in, 361; how affected by man's derivative creation, 364; true and false science in relation to, 376; Evolution not in conflict with, 388.
Theophrastus, ideas on fossils by, 31.
Thomas Aquinas, St., a teacher of evolutionary ideas, 89; accepts contemporary views on abiogenesis, 44. Kant adopts opinions of, 57; as teacher of potential creation, 71; evolutionary views of creation, 284; on causality in creatures, 297; the doctrine of species, 314; species as defined by, 315; on the creation of Adam, 354.
Time, philosophic conceptions of, 270.

GENERAL INDEX. 461

Tournefort, J. P. de, pioneer in defining species, 94.
Traducianism, as outgrowth of science speculations, 15; its belief as to soul's creation, 346; famous modern adherents of, 347.
Trees, variability of species in, 99; studies of the oak, 103; organic life compared to, 326.
Treviranus, ranked among evolutionists, 62.
Trilobites, valuable facts on species from, 155.
Tycho Brahe, relation to Kepler's laws, 25.
Tyndall, Prof. John, views on design in nature, 373.

Unbelief, Jean Paul on the folly of, 435. *See* Atheism, etc.
Universe, questions of antiquity regarding the, 14.
Unknowable, The, philosophy and philosopher of, 257.
Urea, Wöhler's artificial production of, 333.
Urschleim, Oken's theory of anticipated, 26.
Urstoff, the supposed primitive element, 53.

Vallisneri, as student of infusoria, 49.
Variation, as a factor of Evolution, 196; Bateson's theory of discontinuous, 198.
Vatican Council, creation defined by, 221.
Vertebrates, transitional fossil forms of, 132.
Vinci, Leonardo da, discussion on fossils, 31.

Virchow, Prof. R., makes charges against Evolution, 210; his theory of life fails, 338; on the physical descent of man, 341; on origin of life, 342.
Virgil, instances of abiogenesis from, 320.
Vision, Evolution of the organ of, 119.
Vogt, Carl, of one mind with Hæckel, 238; a theory of life by, 341.

Wagner, Moritz, as adherent of Evolution, 68; theory of isolation by, 197.
Wallace, Dr. Alfred R., as co-discoverer with Darwin, 65; on the origin of man, 247; on design in nature, 373.
Watch, simile from the construction of, 298.
Weeds, studies of ancient Egyptian, 150.
Weismann, as disciple of the Evolution idea, 68; theory of heredity by, 199.
Whale, classification illustrated by the, 108; evidence from anatomy of, 111.
Whewell, Dr. William, on the fate of new discoveries, xxvii; on species and creation, 76.
Wiegand, on the movement of the age, 244.
Williamson, researches in vegetable fossils, 156.
Wöhler, F., artificial making of urea, by, 333.
Wolf, F. A., coinage of term monism by, 233.
Woods, identity of ancient and modern, 149.
Worms, order in the scale of life, 247.

Yung, a pioneer in defining species, 94.

Zoölogy, a result of recent progress in, 51; services of Linnæus to, 85.

www.ingramcontent.com/pod-product-compliance
Lightning Source LLC
Chambersburg PA
CBHW051721300426
44115CB00007B/415